Lecture Notes in Computer Science 1245

Edited by G. Goos, J. Hartmanis and J. van Leeuwen

Advisory Board: W. Brauer   D. Gries   J. Stoer

Springer
*Berlin
Heidelberg
New York
Barcelona
Budapest
Hong Kong
London
Milan
Paris
Santa Clara
Singapore
Tokyo*

Raymond Marie   Brigitte Plateau
Maria Calzarossa   Gerardo Rubino   (Eds.)

Computer Performance Evaluation

Modelling Techniques and Tools

9th International Conference
St. Malo, France, June 3-6, 1997
Proceedings

 Springer

Series Editors

Gerhard Goos, Karlsruhe University, Germany
Juris Hartmanis, Cornell University, NY, USA
Jan van Leeuwen, Utrecht University, The Netherlands

Volume Editors

Raymond Marie
IRISA/Université de Rennes 1
Campus de Beaulieu, F-35042 Rennes Cédex, France
E-mail: marie@irisa.fr

Brigitte Plateau
LMC, Institut Fourier
100, rue des Mathématiques, BP 53X, F-38041 Grenoble Cédex 9, France
E-mail: plateau@imag.fr

Maria Calzarossa
DIS, Università di Pavia
via Abbiategrasso 209, I-27100 Pavia, Italy
E-mail: mcc@alice.unipv.it

Gerardo Rubino
IRISA/ENSTB
IRISA, Campus de Beaulieu, F-35042 Rennes Cédex, France
E-mail: rubino@irisa.fr

Cataloging-in-Publication data applied for

Die Deutsche Bibliothek - CIP-Einheitsaufnahme

Computer performance evaluation : modelling techniques and tools
; ... international conference ... ; proceedings. - Berlin ; Heidelberg ;
New York ; Barcelona ; Budapest ; Hong Kong ; London ; Milan ;
Paris ; Santa Clara ; Singapore ; Tokyo : Springer

9. St. Malo, France, June 3 - 6, 1997. - 1997
(Lecture notes in computer science ; 1245)
ISBN 3-540-63101-1

CR Subject Classification (1991): C.4

ISSN 0302-9743
ISBN 3-540-63101-1 Springer-Verlag Berlin Heidelberg New York

Typesetting: Camera-ready by author
SPIN 10550332   06/3142 – 5 4 3 2 1 0   Printed on acid-free paper

Preface

Since the beginning of the series of International Conferences on Modeling Techniques and Tools for Computer Performance Evaluation, new challenges have arisen. Systems have evolved and we are faced with new problems due to, for example, fully distributed systems or statistical multiplexing of high speed networks. During the last decade, we have also noticed the implication of the concept of dependability on performance studies. On top of that, with the change in the systems came the change in the attitudes. An increasing number of system designers want to consider as a whole the qualitative and quantitative specifications of computing and communication systems. These designers believe increasingly that performance and dependability play a key role in the success of a new product. Moreover, they will trust the performance predictions more if these results are deduced directly from the original specifications.

However, real systems are so complex that often these requirements are not met. Automation of such performance evaluation processes needs the use of very powerful tools. Power here means that we should be able to use them for coping with a large variety of sophisticated systems. An evolution from specific approaches (with maybe more analytical results) to systematic solutions (using more hybrid techniques mixing numerical and simulation solutions) is thus emerging.

We believe that the 17 papers selected by the program committee, in addition to the 2 invited papers, are representative of the work done and the progress achieved in these directions. In addition a special focus was put on tool exhibitions: the tool fair includes 21 presentations. This ninth conference of the series comes after its predecessors:

1984 Paris	1991 Torino
1985 Sophia Antipolis	1992 Edinburgh
1987 Paris	1994 Wien
1989 Palma	1995 Heidelberg

We would like to express our thanks to all those persons and institutions which have contributed to this conference. In particular, we thank the program committee members for their work in refereeing and selecting the papers, the authors of the submitted papers, the invited speakers who accepted to share their experiences with us, the local organizing committee, and the sponsoring and supporting organizations.

Raymond Marie	Brigitte Plateau	Maria Calzarossa	Gerardo Rubino
General Chair	*General Vice-Chair*	*PC Chair*	*PC Chair*
IRISA Rennes	*IMAG-LGI Grenoble*	*University of Pavia*	*IRISA/ENSTB*
France	*France*	*Italy*	*France*

Program Committee

Gianfranco Balbo

Heinz Beilner

Onno Boxma

Maria Calzarossa (PC co-chair)

Adrian Conway

Larry Dowdy

Erol Gelenbe

Günter Haring

Peter Harrison

Gérard Hebuterne

Ulrich Herzog

Peter Hughes

Raj Jain

Hisashi Kobayashi

Pieter Kritzinger

Paul Kühn

Phillipe Mussi

Rob Pooley

Ramón Puigjaner

Guy Pujolle

Daniel A. Reed

Martin Reiser

Gerardo Rubino (PC co-chair)

William H. Sanders

Herb Schwetman

Giuseppe Serazzi

Connie Smith

Arne Solvberg

William Stewart

Hideaki Takagi

Satish K. Tripathi

Kishor S. Trivedi Allen Malony

Sponsored by

- Institut National de Recherche en Informatique et Automatique (INRIA)
- Région Bretagne
- Université de Rennes 1
- France Telecom

In cooperation with

- ACM Sigmetrics
- The IEEE Computer Society
- The IFIP W.G. 6.3 (Performance of Communication Systems)
- The IFIP W.G. 7.3 (Computer System Modelling)

Contents

Performance Prediction:
An Industry Perspective

(Extended Abstract)

Peter Utton & Brian Hill

BT Labs, Martlesham Heath, UK

1 Introduction – the role of software within BT

BT is a major IT user and software forms an integral part of both the systems that support our business and also of the services that form the heart of our business. Our use of software spans Operational Support Systems, Network Management, Telecommunication Services, and Service Creation Tools. We are a large business with large systems [1], [2]. Within BT we both develop our own systems, and procure systems and components from external suppliers.

2 Performance problems and issues

Poor performance is a major concern for software based systems within BT. It can:

- damage customer perceptions of the company;
- impact on users causing frustration, de-motivation and inefficiencies;
- incur high costs for correction (ie. retro-fitting performance); such rework could include software redesign, redevelopment, fixes and increased maintenance effort and
- lead to loss of revenue – for example inhibiting our ability to provide services to meet customer demand; preventing us from billing customers on time.

However, good performance engineering, apart from addressing the points above, can also provide:

- savings in the provision of equipment which can affect both capital costs and maintenance charges;
- new business opportunities. For example two recent bids for systems to be supplied externally were successful only because of modelling to demonstrate that the BT offered solutions would scale to meet customers requirements.

To summarise then, performance engineering has a direct impact on key business drivers such as:

- Cost – by assuring that system resources are adequately provided at minimum cost;

- Quality – because user perceptions are directly influenced by system performance;

As a consequence, we'd like to predict the performance of systems *before* we build and deploy them – ie. we don't like nasty surprises! We'd like BT development teams to be able to make informed design decisions and so deliver systems with adequate performance to improve customer satisfaction and control costs. We need to be able to model systems to predict their likely performance before major design decisions have been taken which 'lock' the system into a particular development route. In addition, scale is an important factor for BT. In terms such as numbers of users, workload and data volumes, our systems are amongst the largest in the world. Evaluating the impact of system scale on likely system behaviour is of paramount importance.

3 Current practice

Our current performance engineering practice ranges from the use of sophisticated predictive models to post development 'fire fighting' and performance tuning.

It is important to recognise that it's essential to have performance *requirements* defined for a system and that performance engineering should be on a 'fitness for purpose' basis – there's no business benefit in over engineered solutions. With these ground rules established, simple (analytical) models, potentially complex simulation models (usually built by experts), functional prototypes and performance testing and monitoring all have their place in the battle to combat inadequate performance.

However, currently performance modelling is a specialism and there are insufficient specialists to go round. We need to make performance prediction and modelling accessible to the typical systems and software engineer.

We need to get performance issues considered earlier in the systems development lifecycle and treated as an integral part of the development process. We'd like designers to be able to readily explore 'what-if' scenarios, assessing the implications of changing application logic, the system's execution environment (ie. the processing platforms, network technology and network topology) and user behaviour (workload) – factors which all impact on a system's performance – in order to be able to make informed decisions within the design process. We want to be able to build simple models early in the lifecycle which can provide useful insights into likely behaviour but which can be refined and expanded as a designer's understanding of the eventual system becomes more complete to give increasingly accurate predictions.

4 Integrating performance analysis within the systems development process

To this end, we have recently undertaken a case study to investigate integrating performance analysis within the systems development process.

By integration we mean that performance analysis is:

- based on notations designers are familiar with and which are in regular use;
- treated as part of the overall systems design method;
- not considered as an afterthought;

Eventually we would hope that such practice becomes a natural process that's regarded as 'business as usual' and one where essentially, the performance results 'fall out for free'.

In current practice performance issues are often not addressed until late in development (often during test and integration), and performance models are constructed with no direct relationship to the application design. The case study attempted to demonstrate how performance analysis might be carried out on systems as part of the development process, throughout the lifecycle, with attention to varying levels of detail at different stages.

BT (for historical and continuing business reasons) operates within a diverse range of software environments, development methods and tools. However steps are being taken to rationalise this diversity [3]. For object oriented analysis and design, BT follows an approach based heavily on the Booch method [4] including the idea of Booch 'macro' and 'micro' process, within which system performance may be evaluated as part of the micro process.

5 Case study experiences

The project selected for the case study was concerned with the development of a major BT system for the analysis of network faults. The project in question had followed the BT OO method and application design models had been produced using the Rational Rose CASE tool.

For the case study, the software execution threads for a given system usage were represented using object-oriented constructs. The approach was based on:

- use cases [5] and scenarios
- interacting objects (sequence of method calls)

The full paper will expand on these ideas.

The case study demonstrated the value of use cases in linking a workload model to the application model. A use case specifies part of the user interaction with the system, and is a suitable hook for hanging workload details.

However, one clear conclusion from the case study is that transformation of models is a complex process and it is not possible to simply take an existing system design and 'crunch' it into a performance model.

Several conclusions can be drawn:

- If performance evaluation is to be included as part of a system's design, as we believe it must, then the performance engineering activity must be included as an integral part of the design process to enable access to design rationale and to ensure that the design provides a basis for performance modelling. Currently design documentation does not generally contain all the necessary information for an outsider to produce a performance model, however expert they may be. Clearly designers are the best people to construct these models and the availability of performance results directly based on their designs should motivate them to provide additional input data where it's needed.

- However at this stage the automatic generation of performance models from design information is far from a simple *handle-turning* exercise – there are significant modelling and notational issues to be overcome (mapping to resources, representation of a performance model, integrating diverse models, the informal nature of design notation).
- Tools to support development methods are essential; limitations of the toolset used can be a constraint on the ability to implement performance analysis in design. The Rose tool is currently limited in its ability to model system behaviour – however this seems to be more a problem of implementation rather than of the Booch method itself.
- There is a cost to performance modelling (as there is to VV&T activities), which needs to be recognised up front. However we believe that in the majority of cases this will more than pay for itself over the lifetime of the system.
- However these points notwithstanding, the fundamental approach of embedding performance analysis within the OO design method appears feasible and desirable.

The case study illustrated the weakness of current methods and tools in representing system behaviour. The techniques considered in the study provided a promising framework for encouraging designers to define system behaviour throughout the lifecycle.

For the future, the Unified Modelling Language (UML) specification [6] includes features that could overcome some of the difficulties we experienced using Rose V3 and Booch notation.

6 Our vision/requirements for the future

Remembering that our key objectives are to address performance issues earlier in the lifecycle and treat them as an integral part of the development process, the full paper will step outside the constraints of the case study and walkthrough a fictitious example, applying performance analysis within an iterative systems design process, to illustrate how we'd like to be able to operate in the future.

However the world is getting a more complex place and in the future, performance of software systems will become more critical as systems increase in complexity, interconnectivity and scale.

ATM is a new networking technology that finally promises to realise the long predicted convergence of communications and computing. It is likely to be a key enabling technology for the future. Its arrival is likely to herald a step change in the design and capability of computer systems, the significance of which could well rival the impact of the microprocessor itself. By the year 2000, ATM technology operating at 600+ Mbps will be available. This speed is comparable with leading internal bus speeds a few years ago. As CPU power doubles every 18 months (and is expected to continue to do so for the next 25 years), the arrival of high speed ATM to the desktop means that in 5 years time, a group of networked PCs could be regarded as a single massively parallel virtual computer. Another way of looking at it is that computing power will be 'on tap' and available to desktop clients seamlessly across a virtual network. By either network or computer oriented view, ATM is set to revolutionise computer systems and therefore the way we think about software applications.

Meanwhile, advances in Internet technology, steady decreases in the cost of high-end servers and steady increases in (or at least increasing awareness of) the total cost of ownership of PCs have already prompted a recent trend towards adopting a Network Centric model of computing. Certainly the promise of server controlled software updates/downloads and reduced management overheads for application delivery are attractive. But performance is increasingly being recognised as a major concern in such systems. Questions upper-most in designers minds are: where to locate the application and data servers to optimise performance; what capacity network links do we need?

ATM also enables multiple streams of information (such as audio, video and data), each of which has very different characteristics, to be simultaneously carried over the same network infrastructure. ATM provides opportunities for high and variable bit rates and dynamic (negotiated) variations in quality of service thus increasing the need for, and the benefits to be gained from, tools that evaluate the performance implications of application design choices. Furthermore, ATM is likely to involve sophisticated tariffing arrangements which will also influence application design decisions.

With these developments in mind, our eventual goal is to be able to adequately model the performance of applications operating in a future broadband distributed computing environment and incorporating support for multimedia.

References

1. N. Furley, The BT operational support systems architecture, BT Technology Journal, Vol 15, No. 1, Jan 1997.
2. P. F. Harrison, Customer Service System – past, present and future, BT Technology Journal, Vol 15, No. 1, Jan 1997.
3. S Valiant, Review of software tools and methods used in operational support systems development, BT Technology Journal, Vol 15, No. 1, Jan 1997.
4. Grady Booch, Object-Oriented Analysis and Design with Applications. 2nd Edition. Benjamin Cummings, 1994.
5. Ivar Jacobson, Object-Oriented Software Engineering – A Use Case Driven Approach. 4th Edition. Addison-Wesley, 1994.
6. Booch G., Jacobson I. and Rumbaugh J. "The Unified Modeling Language for Object-Oriented Development," Document Set Version 1.0, January 1997, Rational Software Corporation, http://www.rational.com/uml/

TANGRAM-II: A Performability Modeling Environment Tool *

Rosa M. L. R. Carmo[1], Luiz R. de Carvalho[1], Edmundo de Souza e Silva[1],
Morganna C. Diniz[1] and Richard R. R. Muntz[2]

[1] Federal University of Rio de Janeiro
Computer Science Department, NCE, Coppe/Sistemas
Cx.P. 2324, Rio de Janeiro, RJ 20001-970, Brazil
[2] University of California at Los Angeles, Computer Science Department
Los Angeles, CA 90024, USA

Abstract. TANGRAM-II is a modeling environment tool developed for
research and educational purposes that provides a flexible user interface
to describe computer and communication system models. It has a sophisticated graphic interface based on the public domain software package TGIF (Tangram Graphic Interface Facility) and an object oriented
description language. The tool is a second and significantly more sophisticated version than the original prototype developed during the TAN-
GRAM project. The current version is implemented in C++ and C and
has several solvers for transient and steady state analysis of performance
and availability metrics.

1 Introduction

In the past 20 years, many modeling tools have been developed to aid the modeler
in the design process of computer and communication systems. Many tools were
tailored to specific application domains, such as queueing network models (e.g.
[22, 25], see also [1] for a survey of many tools developed prior to 1988) and
availability modeling (e.g. [2, 13]). Others allow the specification of a general
class of models, such as the Petri net based tools, e.g. [8, 21, 7, 16], those based
on formal description languages, e.g. [4, 18, 17], and those which adopted a user
interface description language specially developed for the tool, e.g. [23, 5, 3].
The tools also vary in terms of the flexibility of the user interface, the measures
that can be obtained, and the sophistication of the analytic and/or simulation
techniques provided to the modeler.

Many issues must be addressed during the development of a modeling tool.
For instance, the user interface should be tailored to the application domain with
which the user is concerned. In other words, if the user is developing an availability model, then the tool should allow her to specify system components that
can fail, interactions between components, repair policies, operational criteria,
etc. Such an interface is provided by the SAVE package [13]. On the other hand,

* The work of R.M.L.R. Carmo, L.R. de Carvalho, E. de Souza e Silva and M.C. Diniz
is partially supported by grants and fellowships from CNPq(Brazil).

it is desirable that many modeling paradigms can be supported by the tool, or the interface should allow the description of general classes of models.

Petri net interfaces are particular suited for describing general models but the price paid for this flexibility is that the specifications do not resemble the way the modeler thinks about her system. Several tools have been proposed based on this formalism as cited above or have constructs closely related to those of Petri-nets, such as UltraSAN [21] where models are specified using the so called stochastic activity networks.

There are tools based on other general settings such as the concept of balls and buckets employed by MARCA [23]. In that tool, the user describes the number of buckets in the system and a list of inter-bucket transitions that represent the movement of a ball from one bucket to another. The claim is that models from different application domains can be easily described in terms of balls and buckets. METFAC [5] is another example of a tool that allows the specification of a general class of models. METFAC uses production rules operating on the global system state variables to describe system behavior. Others have proposed the adoption of formal high level specification languages such as Estelle [4, 18] and LOTOS [17].

Aiming to provide a general user interface, and yet supporting the development of different application domains, by constructing specialized objects for each domain of interest, Berson *et al* developed an object oriented paradigm [3] which allows the specification of Markovian models in a symbolic high-level language. A prototype was developed in Prolog that facilitates the implementation of the user interface language, as well as the description of complex component behavior in symbolic form. Although the use of Prolog has many advantages as described in [3], portability is a problem, as well as storage requirements for large systems.

Another important issue that must be dealt with when implementing a modeling tool is the large space cardinalities of most real system models. This problem influences not only the generation phase of the state transition matrix for the solvers, but also their implementation.

The identification of special structures in the model is also a desirable feature that affects the choice of the proper solution technique. Yet another issue is related to the interaction between the interface and the solvers. Several measures require special information to be provided by the user. For instance, in availability modeling, the user must specify the conditions in which the system is considered operational. In performability modeling, reward rates must be specified for the states. If the model to be solved is non-markovian, then the interface has to provide more information than that required to solve Markovian models, as will be exemplified later.

The software package we describe deals with several of the issues mentioned above, and is based on the object oriented paradigm of [3]. The research is a continuation of the work done at UCLA and UFRJ. The tool is developed for research and educational purposes and combines a sophisticated user interface and new solution techniques for performance and availability analysis. In section

2 we present the basic architecture of the tool. Section 3 briefly describes the solution techniques currently available. Section 4 presents an example to illustrate the main features of the tool, and in section 5 we present our conclusions.

2 Architecture

The tool contains three main modules : the *User Interface* , the *Mathematical Model Generation* and the *Solvers* modules. The *User Interface* module is based on the public domain TANGRAM Graphic Interface Facility TGIF [6], developed at UCLA. This interface is used to construct a system model from objects and their behavior as specified by the user. After the model is built, the *Mathematical Model Generation* module will generate a Markov chain and related data to solve it, if the model is Markovian, or the structures necessary to solve a class of non-Markovian models. Then, the user will be able to call the *Solvers* module and choose one of the options to obtain the steady state and/or transient measures of interest. The *User Interface* and the *Mathematical Model Generation* modules are organized in layers as proposed in [3].

The modeling paradigm we use was proposed in [3]. In this paradigm, the system being modeled is represented by a collection of objects which interact by sending and receiving messages. We choose to represent the internal state of each object by a set of *buckets* and the number of balls contained in each one, as in the MARCA tool.

Objects evolve with time and their state can be modified by an action that is taken either after an event is executed or after receiving a message from another object. Events are generated spontaneously by an object, provided that the conditions specified when the object was instantiated are satisfied. These conditions are expressions evaluated using the current state of the object. Each event has a rate associated with it, which can presently be exponential or deterministic. Messages are just an abstraction used to represent the interaction among objects, and are delivered (and reacted to) in zero time.

An action is taken when an event is executed or when a message is received. As a consequence of an action, the object's state may change and messages may be sent to other objects in the model. The user can also associate a probability to each action that can be executed when an event occurs.

The state of the model is given by the states of each object and the set of "undelivered" messages. A *vanishing* state is the one in which one or more undelivered messages are present. States with no messages undelivered are the *tangible* states, and only those are used in the computation of the measures of interest. The transition rate between a pair of tangible states can be easily determined from the event rates and from the probabilities associated with the sequences of vanishing states which start and end in tangibles states. The model description language is illustrated by means of an example in section 4.

The *Mathematical Model Generator* explores all possible states in the model and calculates the transition rates between any two states. When a state is generated, the generator must determine if this state was previously explored, or if it is a new state. One way to perform this task is to store the full state descriptor for each state (the vector of buckets.) However, this may be impractical for very large models due to the large storage requirements necessary for this process. Another possibility is to use some form of hashing technique to map state descriptors into identifiers. At issue is to choose a proper hashing function that uniquely maps each state descriptor vector into identifier, different from any other state identifier. We adopted the hash function used in SAVE (not published) for generating the transition rate matrix. Roughly, the technique employed identifies a lexicographic order for the state vectors according to the number of consecutive empty buckets from the rightmost element in the vector. The state space is divided into sets according to this ordering. Then, a table that stores the number of states in each set is built. From that table, one can uniquely map the state vectors into identifiers with little cost. The details are omitted for conciseness.

From an initial state given by the user for each object, the generator finds a list of all the events that can execute in that state. One event is then chosen to fire and all messages that can be sent after an action is executed for that event are found. We recall that all states with messages pending (yet to be delivered) are *vanishing* and are not part of the final state space of the model. The algorithm recursively finds all states (vanishing or tangible) reachable from the current state being explored, and the new tangible states found are inserted in the list of non-explored states (depth first search).

The data structures generated for the class of non-Markovian models that can be solved by the tool are more complex than those needed for Markovian models, since many chains must be identified and generated as required by the solution method employed. Roughly, the generator needs to find all tangible states assuming that all transitions in the model are exponential. Then, for each special (e.g. deterministic) event defined by the user, the generator finds one or more Markov chains associated with the mini-interval of time in which the event is enabled.

3   Solution Methods

The tool described in this work provides a number of solution techniques for obtaining steady state as well as transient measures. Our main goal is to use the tool for educational and research purposes, and so we implement some traditional methods and algorithms recently developed, which are used for our own research work. Below, we briefly describe the solution methods which are currently implemented in the tool.

It is well known that we can divide the techniques used to obtain the steady state solutions into direct and iterative methods. In general, direct methods are appropriate when the state space of the model is not very large and when the state transition matrix of the model is not sparse. Iterative methods, on the other hand, are appropriate when the state transition matrix is large and sparse, since they preserve the sparseness of the matrix.

In our tool the GTH algorithm [15] is the steady state solution method of choice. Basically the algorithm works by eliminating one state at a time from the set of states in the model. The block version of the algorithm [14] is also implemented. Recently, a new algorithm was developed which has lower computational requirements than existing methods when used to solve common communication system models [19]. This algorithm is specially attractive for block Hessenberg matrices (say upper Hessenberg matrices) when the lower diagonal blocks are easy to invert, and it is is currently been implemented as part of the steady state solvers.

The iterative methods implemented in the tool are those based on a regular splitting of the transition probability matrix. The user can select one of the following methods: Jacobi, Gauss-Seidel, Successive Over Relaxation (SOR), and Power [24]. For these methods, the user can specify the desired tolerance of the solution as well as the maximum number of iterations allowed.

Transient analysis has been used not only to obtain measures of interest over a finite interval, but also as an intermediate step in the calculation of steady state measures for some non-Markovian systems. Among the available methods for transient analysis, the Uniformization technique has proven to be very efficient and the algorithms we implemented are based on this method.

Our tool is particularly rich concerning the type of transient measures it can calculate, and it implements several algorithms as detailed below. The simplest measure calculated is the point probability, i.e. the state probabilities at time t. It is implemented using the basic equation of the Uniformization method, with special care to avoid underflow for large Λt values.

Expected performability measures can also be obtained from the Markov models. If we associate reward rates with each state in the model, the expected total accumulated reward is one example of this type of measure. A related measure is the expected total time above a given reward level. Other measures include the expected lifetime during an observation period and the mean time to failure.

Transient distributions are also available to the user. One of the measures of interest is the distribution of cumulative time the model spends in a subset of states during the observation interval. The algorithm of [9] is used in this case, with the approach developed in [20] to improve storage requirements for availability modeling with large Λt values. The reliability and the operational time density function during the interval $(0, t)$ of the system can also be evaluated from a given model.

Also implemented is an algorithm recently developed to obtain the distribution of cumulative reward over a finite interval. In this case, the user can specify both reward rates to states and impulse rewards to transitions. In order to calculate this distribution, the algorithm developed in [10] is used (see also [12]), which is shown to have lower computational requirements than other algorithms to calculate this kind of measure and, in addition, can handle both rate and impulse rewards.

The tool allows the specification of non-exponential events, in particular deterministic events. The class of models that can be solved allows at most one of these events to be enabled at a time. Each of these events can execute when the associated firing time expires but also may be disabled when other events in the system are executed.

The solution method used is given in [11]. In this method, an embedded Markov chain is constructed at time points in which a deterministic event is disabled, or is enabled when no other of these events is enabled. Mini-intervals between embedded points are identified and a Markov chain that governs the model behavior in each mini-interval is isolated. From their transient analysis, the transition probabilities for the embedded Markov chain is obtained.

For many models, the Markov chain associated with each mini-interval can be decomposed into independent chains, i.e. chains that evolve independently during the mini-interval. The solution technique takes advantage of this decomposition to reduce the computational requirements for obtaining the transition probabilities of the embedded chain.

4 Example

In this section we present an example to illustrate the use of TANGRAM II. It models a jitter control mechanism for an ATM network.

Consider a real-time voice traffic passing through an ATM network. In this example, cells are generated at rate $1/T$ during emission periods, and no cell is generated during silence periods. Note that the arrival of cells at the network output is not periodic as they are when generated during the emission period. This is mainly due to cell queueing time in the ATM nodes, and it is possible to have short periods with many cell arrivals, and long periods with no cell arrivals. The name *jitter* is used to identify the random variable defined as the interval between arrivals of consecutive cells at network output minus T.

Large absolute jitter values in a voice connection can have a drastic negative effect on the receiver ability to recreate the voice. A proposal to eliminate the jitter at network output is to buffer the cells of the connection at the destination host and to deliver them to the end user at the same transmission rate $1/T$. However, buffering cells and delivering them with rate $1/T$ only guarantees that the negative jitter is eliminated. To reduce the positive jitter, it is necessary to store a number of cells before starting delivering them to the application.

Let N_{min} be the number of cells stored at the beginning of a emission period. When either a silence period occurs or there are more than N_{min} cells at the queue, then the cell delivery process is initiated. If the queue is emptied during an emission period, the cell delivery is re-initiated with the next cell arrival. In the following, we use the tool to analyze this jitter control mechanism. To model the jitter control mechanism, we define two objects. The first object models the arrival process and the second models the special queueing mechanism at the destination.

First we describe the object used to model the queue of cells at the destination: the *jitter_control_queue*. Figure 1 corresponds to the *jitter_control_queue*

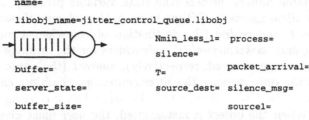

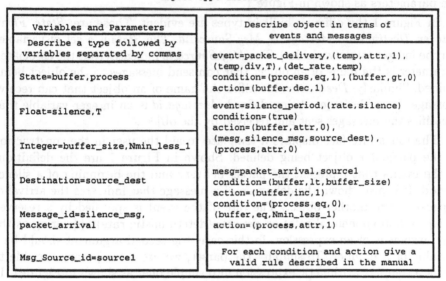

Fig. 1. Jitter control queue.

object. The state of this object is represented by two state variables: the *buffer* (number of cells in the queue) and the *process* (which is a condition to start the delivery process). The number of cells in the queue can vary from zero to *buffer_size*. The state variable *process* can be zero or one.

Two events are associated with this object. The event *silence_period* is enabled when a silence period is detected. When this event is executed all packets in the queue are flushed and the state variable *process* is set to zero. After that, packets will be accumulated in the buffer until the N_{min} value is reached (the state variable *process* is set to one). This condition will enable the event *packet_delivery*. The delivery time of a packet is deterministic and equal to T.

The *jitter_control_queue* object may be retrieved from a library of object types or may be built from scratch by the user. In the later case the user must follow a set of steps to define its behavior as detailed below.

A set of parameters must be defined for the object. The user defines the parameters as in any computer language, giving the parameter's name and type. This is shown in Figure 1 where the user specifies ten parameters: *buffer* (the state variable *buffer*), *process* (the state variable process), *silence* (the rate of the event *silence_period*), *T* (time between the delivery of two cells), *buffer_size*, *Nmin_less_1*, *source_dest* (the destination object when a message is sent), *silence_msg* and *packet_arrival* (the identifiers for the message sent by the object and the message received, respectively), *source1* (the name of the object that can send the only message the *jitter_control_queue* object can receive). All parameters will be later referenced by the user when specifying the *conditions* and *actions*. When the object is instantiated, the user must give specific values to the parameters as shown in Figure 1.

In Figure 1 the different built in types are evident. Those are: *State, Float, Integer, Destination, Message_id, Msg_Source_id*. The *State* is a set of variables of type integer (state variables). The *Msg_Source_id* indicates that the associated parameter is the name of an object that can send messages to the object being defined. Similarly, *Destination* identifies the name of an object that can receive messages from the object being defined. *Message_id* is an integer variable that identifies the messages sent and received by the object.

The tool's interface displays a template to aid the user in the construction of the particular object being defined. Shown in Figure 1 are the definitions of the events that represent the packet delivery and the beginning of a silence period. It is also shown the definition of a message that indicates the arrival of a packet from another object. The rate of the event is specified by a reserved string: *rate* (exponential rate) or *det_rate* (deterministic rate) appearing as the first argument of an expression. In this case, the second argument should be a variable or a number. To simplify the parser, we use a temporary variable to break a complex arithmetic expression into simple ones as shown in Figure 1. In a new version of the tool, a more sophisticated parser will be provided.

Each condition for the event to occur is specified as shown by the set of parenthesized logic and relational expressions after the condition. The expression is a three-tuple (*v, op, value*) where *v* is a variable, *op* is a boolean or relational operator and *value* is an integer, a float or a variable. (Currently the tool allows only the concatenation, denoting a logical conjunction of conditions, of simple expressions, but general expressions will be allowed in the future.) Each condition is followed by an action taken when the event occurs under the specified condition.

An action is given by a set of expressions which are three-tuples, similar to conditions, consisting of a variable, an arithmetic operator and a variable or a number. We can associate a probability of occurrence with each action. This probability is specified by using a reserved key word *prob* followed by a variable or a number. In Figure 1, when the event *packet_delivery* occurs, the number of cells in the buffer is decremented by one.

The messages an object can receive and the actions that can take place when a message arrives are described similarly to the event specification. Each message has a name associated with it. The message body contains the sender identification and a list of variables that are passed from the sender to all recipients. In the example, the *jitter_control_queue* receives a message *packet_arrival* from *source1* and takes the following actions. If the buffer is not full, the cell is stored in the queue. If the state variable *process* is equal to zero and the buffer is equal to $N_{min} - 1$ then the state variable *process* is set to one. This action will enable the event *packet_delivery*.

In order to study the behavior of the jitter control mechanism under different traffic characteristics, two source models are specified: a two-state Markov Modulated Poisson Process (MMPP) and a r-stage Erlangian process. In the MMPP case, one state has exponential arrival rate less than or equal to the source rate $(1/T)$, while the other one has arrival rate greater than the source rate. In the Erlangian case, we have r states, where every state has rate $1/(rT)$ and a cell arrival occurs only after r transitions. Note that it is possible to model traffic with large variance values for the cell interarrival times (in comparison with exponential interarrival times) with the MMPP model, and low variance values with the Erlangian model.

Objects corresponding to one of the source models described above are available in the tool library: the *MMPP_source* and *erlangian_source*.

Figure 2 shows the *MMPP_source* object. This object has only one state variable which indicates the source state. When the source is in state zero, packets are generated with rate λ_0 (event *packet_generation0*) and it remains in the same state with probability $(1 - p)$. The source state changes to state one with probability p. When the source is in state one, packets are generated with rate λ_1 (event *packet_generation1*). The source state changes to state zero with probability q.

The *erlangian_source* object is presented in the Figure 3. The state of the object is represented by only one state variable that varies from one to *max_stages*. Initially, it is one, and it is incremented by one at rate *stage_rate*. The source generates a packet only when the state variable reaches the *max_stages* value. After the generation of a packet or after a silence period has been detected, the state variable is set to one again.

It is important to note that this model is not Markovian since there is one deterministic event corresponding to the time (T) between the delivery of two cells. When the *Mathematical Model Generation* module generates the global states and their transitions, it includes a flag in every global state description: a flag zero indicates that there are only exponential events enabled, while a flag one indicates that there is a non-exponential event enabled. Normally, the next step is the generation of independent chains. However, for this example, there are no independent chains.

The module *Solvers* can be called and the option *Non-markovian Models* will be selected. In order to solve the model, an embedded Markov chain is identified using the global state description, as briefly described in section 3. The transitions between two consecutive embedded points are obtained from Markov chains that are generated, and associated with the mini-intervals. In the following, we present some results obtained for the model above using our tool.

Consider a source generating cells with constant rate 1/20 time units. The cells are sent through an ATM network to their destination. We assume a cell

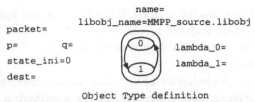

Object Type definition

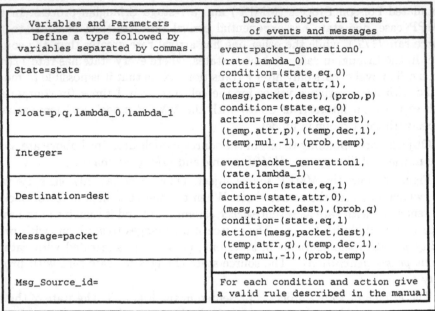

Fig. 2. MMPP source.

loss probability equal to zero, and the buffer size equal to 30. Figure 4(a) shows the jitter distribution at the network output (J_s) using a standard deviation (σ) equal to 8.9, obtained when the arrival process is modeled by a 5-stage Erlangian process. The figure also shows the jitter distribution obtained after the control queue when we set $N_{min} = 1$, and $N_{min} = 5$.

Figure 4(b) displays the jitter distribution using a standard deviation of 30 at the network output, obtained when the arrival process is modeled as an MMPP with the parameters: $\lambda_0 = 0.1$, $\lambda_1 = 0.022222$, $p = 0.00004$, and $q = 0.0001$. The values used for N_{min} are 1, 10, and 20. For both examples we assume that the interval of time between silence periods is exponentially distributed with rate 0.001.

5 Conclusions

We have briefly described the TANGRAM II tool. The interface is evolving to provide several object types to the user and incorporate other facilities. One of

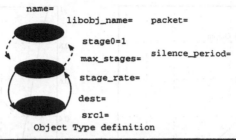

```
              name=
                    libobj_name=     packet=
                      stage0=1
                      max_stages=    silence_period=
                      stage_rate=
                      dest=
                      src1=
                Object Type definition
```

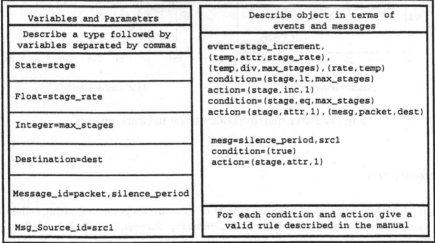

Variables and Parameters	Describe object in terms of events and messages
Describe a type followed by variables separated by commas	event=stage_increment, (temp,attr,stage_rate), (temp,div,max_stages),(rate,temp) condition=(stage,lt,max_stages) action=(stage,inc,1) condition=(stage,eq,max_stages) action=(stage,attr,1),(mesg,packet,dest)
State=stage	
Float=stage_rate	
Integer=max_stages	
Destination=dest	mesg=silence_period,src1 condition=(true) action=(stage,attr,1)
Message_id=packet,silence_period	
Msg_Source_id=src1	For each condition and action give a valid rule described in the manual

Fig. 3. Erlangian source.

these is the addition of a more sophisticated parser than currently provided to allow the specification of complex arithmetic expression. Another module being added to the interface will allow the user to display the transition probability matrix generated, in such a way that will facilitate the identification of special structures in the model. A white board is also in the final stages of implementation. It will allow users at different sites to jointly design a single model by sharing the same distributed board. Furthermore, more solution techniques are being added. Presently, the tool is been incorporated in an environment specialized for the analysis of communication systems.

Acknowledgments

We would like to thank J.C. Guedes and Y. Wu who contributed to the current version of the tool. We also thank W. Chen, designer of TGIF, for all his help.

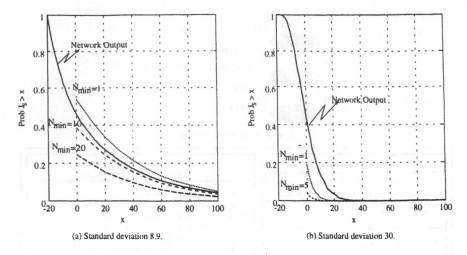

(a) Standard deviation 8.9.

(b) Standard deviation 30.

Fig. 4. Jitter distributions at the network output.

References

1. Jr. A.M.Johnson and M. Malek. Survey of software tools for evaluating reliability, availability and serviceability. *ACM Computing Surveys*, 20:227–271, 1988.
2. C. Béounes, M. Aguéra, J. Arlat, S. Bachmann, C. Bourdeau, J.-E. Doucet, K. Kanoun, J.-C. Laprie, S. Metge, J. M. de Souza, D. Powell, and P. Spiesser. SURF-2: A program for dependability evaluation of complex hardware and software systems. In *Proceedings of the Twenty-Third International Symposium on Fault-Tolerant Computing*, pages 668–673, june 1993.
3. S. Berson, E. de Souza e Silva, and R.R. Muntz. An object oriented methodology for the specification of Markov models. In *Numerical Solution of Markov Chains*, pages 11–36. Marcel Dekker, Inc., 1991.
4. G.V. Bochmann and J. Vaucher. Adding performance aspects to specification languages. In S. Aggarwal and K. Sabnani, editors, *Proceedings of Protocol Specification, Testing and Verification VIII - IFIP*, pages 19–31. North-Holland, 1988.
5. J.A. Carrasco and J. Figueras. METFAC: Design and implementation of a software tool for modeling and evaluation of complex fault-tolerant computing systems. In *FTCS-16*, pages 424–429, 1986.
6. W. Chia-Whei Cheng. *The TANGRAM graphical interface facility (TGIF) manual*. TGIF WWW at http://bourbon.cs.ucla.edu:8801/tgif/.
7. G. Chiola. A software package for analysis of generalized stochastic Petri net models. In *Proceedings of the International Workshop on Timed Petri Net Models*, pages 136–143, Torino,Italy, july 1985.
8. G. Ciardo, J. Muppala, and K.S. Trivedi. SPNP: stochastic Petri net package. In *Proceedings of the Third International Workshop on Petri-nets and Performance Models*, pages 142–151, 1989.
9. E. de Souza e Silva and H.R. Gail. Calculating cumulative operational time distributions of repairable computer systems. *IEEE Trans. on Computers*, C-35(4):322–332, 1986.

10. E. de Souza e Silva and H.R. Gail. An algorithm to calculate transient distributions of cumulative rate and impulse based reward. Technical report, UCLA Technical Report CSD-940021, May 1994.

11. E. de Souza e Silva, H.R. Gail, and R.R. Muntz. Efficient solutions for a class of non-Markovian models. In *Computations with Markov Chains*, pages 483–506. Kluwer Academic Publishers, 1995.

12. E. de Souza e Silva, H.R. Gail, and R. Vallejos Campos. Calculating transient distributions of cumulative reward. In *Proc. Performance '95 and 1995 ACM SIGMETRICS Conf.*, pages 231–240, 1995.

13. A. Goyal, W.C. Carter, E. de Souza e Silva, S.S. Lavenberg, and K.S. Trivedi. The system availability estimator. *FTCS-16*, pages 84–89, 1986.

14. W.K. Grassmann and D.P. Heyman. Equilibrium distribution of block-structured markov chains with repeating rows. *J. App. Prob.*, 27:557–576, 1990.

15. W.K. Grassmann, M.I. Taksar, and D.P. Heyman. Regenerative analysis and steady state distributions for Markov chains. *Operations Research*, 33(5):1107–1116, 85.

16. C. Lindemann. DSPNexpress: A software package for the efficient solution of deterministic and stochastic Petri nets. In *Proceedings of the Sixth International Conference on Modelling Techniques and Tools for Computer Systems Performance Evaluation*, pages 15–29, Edinburgh, Great Britain, 1992.

17. M. A. Marsan, A. Bianco, L. Ciminiera, R.Sisto, and A. Valenzano. Integrating Performance Analysis in the context of LOTOS-Based Design. In *Proceedings of the 2nd MASCOTS*, Durham, North Carolina, USA, january 1994.

18. P. Mejia Ochoa, E. de Souza e Silva, and Aloysio Pedrosa. Peformance evaluation of distributed systems specified in Estelle (in portuguese). In $10^{\underline{o}}$ *Brazilian Simposium on Computer Networks*, 1992.

19. M. Meo, E. de Souza e Silva, and M. Ajmone-Marsan. Efficient solution for a class of Markov chain models of telecommunication systems. In *Proc. Performance '96*, volume 27&28, pages 603–625, 1996.

20. G. Rubino and B. Sericola. Interval availability distribution computation. In *FTCS-23*, pages 48–55, 1993.

21. W.H. Sanders, W.D. Obal II, M.A. Qureshi, and F.K. Widjanarko. The UltraSAN modeling environment. *Performance Evaluation*, October/November 1995.

22. C.M. Sauer, E.A. MacNair, and J.F. Kurose. Queueing network simulations of computer communication. *IEEE Journal on Selected Areas in Communications*, SAC-2:203–220, 1984.

23. W.J. Stewart. MARCA Markov chain analyzer, a software package for Markov chains. In *Numerical Solution of Markov Chains*, pages 37–61. Marcel Dekker, Inc., 1991.

24. W.J. Stewart. *Introduction to the Numerical Solution of Markov Chains*. Princeton University Press, 1994.

25. M. Veran and D. Potier. QNAP2: A portable environment for queueing systems modeling. *Intl. Conf. Modeling Technique and Tools for Perf. Eval.*, 1984.

PENELOPE
dependability evaluation and the optimization of performability

Hermann de Meer and Hana Ševčíková

Department of Computer Science, TKRN, University of Hamburg
Vogt-Kölln-Str. 30, 22527 Hamburg, Germany
email: {demeer@,sevcikov@ro2.}informatik.uni-hamburg.de

Abstract

A new performance and performability modeling tool is introduced in this paper. PENE-LOPE is the first tool which incorporates evaluation and optimization algorithms. It is the result of a combination between the performability modeling concept and Markov decision theory. Different algorithms are adopted and included in the tool under the unifying paradigm of reconfigurability as the basis for adaptation and optimization. In addition to transient and steady-state performability measures, also transient and stationary control functions can be computed and graphically presented. Model specification and specification of transient or stationary control functions can be separately performed and deliberately combined with each other. Besides providing a new modeling paradigm, the tool supports model creation, experimentation, storage and presentation of results by means of an easily usable interface and an integrated model data base system.

1   Introduction

During the last decade there has been an increasing interest in performability modeling [14]. The development of software tools supporting performability modeling and analysis has been an active area of research.

Metaphor [4], developed 1984, was the first tool for performability modeling. It addressed only a limited set of Markov models; input and output were textual. The tool SPNP [2] is a stochastic Petri nets package, which supports specification, generation, and solution of continuous time Markov chains (CTMCs). Steady-state, transient, and cumulative performability measures, defined by Markov reward models (MRMs), can be computed. The model description is done via C. The tool UltraSAN [3] is based on stochastic activity networks. In addition to numerical algorithms, UltraSAN provides also simulation methods. Surf-2 [1] has been developed for dependability and performability evaluation. Models can either be MRMs or generalized stochastic Petri nets. SPNP, Ultra-SAN and Surf-2 provide an output in tabular form. Additionally, Surf-2 allows a graphical representation of the results. Deterministic and general type time distributions are complementing exponential distribution in DSPNexpress [7] and in other work. Many more tools do exist, most of them being covered in the overview paper by Haverkort and Niemegeers [5].

This paper describes the new software package PENELOPE [10]. PENE-LOPE is the first tool which incorporates *evaluation* and *optimization* algorithms. It can be applied for the integrated computation of performance/performability functions and of optimal control strategies. It constitutes the implementation of the concept of a combination between performability modeling and Markov decision theory [13].

In addition to transient and steady-state *performability measures*, also transient and steady-state *control functions* can be computed and graphically presented. Model specification and specification of transient or steady-state control structure can also be separately performed and deliberately combined with each other. This allows the immediate comparison of the impact of various control strategies for a given model on the resulting performance measures.

The specification of control strategies is built on the paradigm of reconfigurability [8, 9]. The intuition behind is, decisions must be made to reconfigure or not to reconfigure a system from one state to another in order to optimize a given performance/performability measure. The mapping of the reconfiguration options on internal model representations suitable for the optimization algorithms and the application of appropriate algorithms is hidden from the user.

PENELOPE provides a friendly usable interface for model generation and experimentation. In particular, the creation of model variations is supported as well as the execution of series of experiments and the integrated presentation of the results of those experiments. This includes the presentation of performability functions and, in particular, the presentation of control strategies. No interference of the user is necessary to prepare the graphical presentation of control strategies and performability functions. The control functions are automatically related to the original specification of reconfigurability options and series of experiments. Thus, the execution of an optimization study can be considered as a meta-experiment that comprises many single experiments which are related to each other.

This paper is organized as follows. Section 2 contains a description of the general functionality of PENELOPE. Section 3 illustrates by means of a simple example important features of the tool, such as model generation, experiment set-up and execution, or presentation of results. Section 4 concludes the paper.

2 Description of PENELOPE

PENELOPE is based on the theory of *extended Markov reward models* (EMRMs) [8, 9]. It offers a modeling methodology that combines MRMs and Markov decision processes [13].

PENELOPE allows to create parameterized models of arbitrary finite size and to provide automatically the models with concrete values. To each parameter an arbitrary set of concrete values can be allocated. For each possible combination of parameter values, PENELOPE performs an experiment. Whole series of experiment can thus be easily specified and executed.

Additionally, PENELOPE offers the following functionalities: automated checking of model consistency, mechanism for hierarchical and iterative modeling, graphical preparation of experimental results, interactive preparation of computed strategies, printing of models and results for documentation purposes.

The mathematical background of EMRMs will be briefly presented in this section as far as it is necessary to introduce the analysis techniques of our tool. Let $Z = \{Z(t), t \geq 0\}$ denote a CTMC with finite state space $\mathbf{C}$. To each state $s \in \mathbf{C}$ a real-valued *reward rate* $r(s)$, $r : \mathbf{C} \to \mathbb{R}$, is assigned, such that if the CTMC is in state $Z(t) \in \mathbf{C}$ at time t, then the *instantaneous reward rate* of the CTMC at time t is defined as $X(t) = r_{Z(t)}$. In the time horizon $[0, t)$ the *total reward* $Y(t) = \int_0^t X(\tau)d\tau$ is accumulated. Note that $X(t)$ and $Y(t)$ depend on $Z(t)$ and on an initial state. The distribution function $\Psi(y, t) = P(Y(t) \leq y)$ is called the *performability*. For ergodic models the instantaneous reward rate and the time averaged total reward converge in the limit to the same overall reward rate $\lim_{t \to \infty} E[X(t)] = \lim_{t \to \infty} \frac{1}{t} E[Y(t)] = E[X]$.

EMRMs provide a framework for the combined evaluation and optimization of reconfigurable systems by introducing some new features for MRMs. A *reconfiguration* arc, which can be placed between an arbitrary Markov state and any other state in a model, specifies an optional, instantaneous state transition that can be *controlled for optimization*. Zero, one, or more reconfiguration arcs may originate from any Markov state. The resulting strategy provides optimal reconfiguration decisions for each option in the model. At every point of time a different decision is possible for each reconfiguration arc. A strategy $\mathbf{S}(t)$ comprises a tuple of decisions for all options in the model at a particular point of time t, $0 \leq t \leq T$. Strategies can be time dependent, $\mathbf{S}(t)$, or time independent, $\mathbf{S} = \mathbf{S}(t)$.

The so-called *branching* states provide another feature of EMRMs. No time is spent in such states, but a pulse reward may be associated with them. The introduction of branching states has motivation similar to the introduction of immediate transitions to stochastic Petri nets [2].

Two types of methods are offered for computation of optimal strategies and performance functions:

- **Transient Optimization**, where the expected accumulated reward $E[Y_i(t)]$ is used as an optimization criterion. The algorithm which has been introduced in earlier work [8, 9] is applied for an analysis within a finite period of time $[0, t)$. Transient optimization for acyclic CTMC was introduced and its correctness proved by Lee & Shin [6]. The algorithm was adopted by de Meer [8] and extended to general CTMC. Additionally, the correctness of EMRM aproach in terms of Markov decision processes was proved. The algorithm is based on Taylor series[1].

- **Stationary Optimization**, which is performed for an infinite time horizon $[0, \infty)$. As optimization criteria, we distinguish between *time averaged mean total reward in steady-state*, $E[X] = E[X_i] = \lim_{t \to \infty} \frac{1}{t} E[Y_i(t)]$ for all i, where $E[X_i]$ is independent of initial state i for a particular strategy, and the *conditional accumulated reward until absorption*, $E[Y_i(\infty)] = \lim_{t \to \infty} E[Y_i(t)]$, which is computed for non-ergodic models containing absorbing and transient states. $E[Y_i(\infty)]$ is dependent on initial

---

[1] Taylor series for transient analysis (without optimization) has also later been discussed by Stewart [12].

state i. The optimization itself is performed by deployment of variants of *value iteration* or *strategy iteration* type methods [8], relying on numerical algorithms such as Gaussian elimination, Gauss-Seidel iteration, successive over-relaxation (SOR), and the power method. All these methods are implemented in the tool and can be deliberately chosen for a computation.

With $X^{\mathbf{S}}$, $Y_i^{\mathbf{S}}(\infty)$, $Y_i^{\mathbf{S}(t)}(t)$ denoting performability measures gained *under strategy* $\mathbf{S}$ *or* $\mathbf{S}(t)$ respectively, a strategy $\hat{\mathbf{S}}(t)$ is optimal, iff

$$
\begin{aligned}
E[Y_i^{\hat{\mathbf{S}}(t)}(t)] &\geq E[Y_i^{\mathbf{S}(t)}(t)] \; \forall \mathbf{S}(t) \; \forall i && \text{transient optimization,} \\
E[X^{\hat{\mathbf{S}}}] &\geq E[X^{\mathbf{S}}] \; \forall \mathbf{S} && \text{stationary optimization (ergodic),} \\
E[Y_i^{\hat{\mathbf{S}}}(\infty)] &\geq E[Y_i^{\mathbf{S}}(\infty)] \; \forall \mathbf{S} \; \forall i && \text{stationary optimization (nonergodic).}
\end{aligned}
$$

In addition to optimization, PENELOPE offers procedures for computations of performability measures under fixed deliberately eligible strategies:

- **Simulation**, where model evaluations can be simulated under fixed strategies.
- **Transient analysis**, where transient numerical evaluations can be carried out under fixed transient or stationary strategies.
- **Stationary analysis**, where stationary numerical evaluations can be carried out under fixed stationary strategies.

3 A Simple Example

3.1 Description

The features of PENELOPE will be demonstrated by means of a simple example. In packet-switched networks there exists the special case that applications, generating mixed traffic (data, video, voice etc.) with different quality-of-service requirements, are communicating via a single switching node. This is a typical situation in particular in a local-area environment, where the switch may be used as a PBX(Private Branch Exchange). One of the most important problems to be solved with respect to traffic management is related to congestion control. Congestion control for real-time traffic by selectively discarding packets has been investigated by Schulzrinne et al. [11]. We adopt a similar scenario in a simplified setting as depicted in Fig. 1(left). n classes of packet streams are distinguished, where the classes differ from each other with respect to response time limits and loss thresholds. Packets are continuously fed into the system according to independent Poisson processes with arrival rates $\lambda_1, ..., \lambda_n$. The packets are processed with rate μ using the service strategy *first come first served*. The problem of congestion control through discarding of last arriving packets will be investigated.

Keeping it as simple as possible, a system with $n = 2$ arrival streams will be considered. The different response time limits[2] of both classes are assumed to be

---

[2] We define response time as waiting time plus service time.

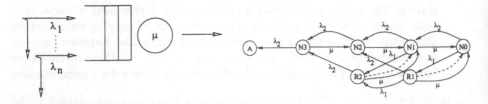

Figure 1: A queueing system with n classes of arriving packets (left) and the baseline model as an EMRM (right).

proportional to the mean service time $\frac{1}{\mu}$ with different factors. The first class is *loss-tolerant* but more delay-sensitive. While having no limit for losses, the mean response time limit of these packets is assumed to be $\frac{2}{\mu}$ time units. There is no use in keeping class one packets if their expected response time is larger than that, that is, if there are already at least two packets in queue upon their arrival. The second class is highly loss-sensitive, no packet of this class may get lost. The less restrictive mean response time limit, on the other hand, is assumed to be $\frac{3}{\mu}$ units of time. Packets of the second class can be accepted as long as there are at most two packets in the queue ahead of them. Since loss of class two packets cannot be tolerated, service is assumed to be immediately stopped if such an event occurs. The admission policies, optimizing different reward functions, will be studied in this simple example for purpose of demonstrating the features of the tool.

The baseline model is depicted as an EMRM in Fig. 1(right). In states N_j, $j \in \{0, 1, 2, 3\}$, j packets are in the system. In states R_i, $i \in \{1, 2\}$, i packets are in the system and the last arriving packet is a packet of the first class. Whenever the system is in state R_i, a decision has to be made whether the last arriving packet should be dropped or not. In case of a positive decision the system is reconfigured to the corresponding state N_{i-1}. The reconfiguration options are graphically indicated by dashed lines in the EMRM of Fig. 1(right). If loss of a second class packet occurs, then the absorbing state A is reached and all further arriving packets, regardless of their class, are considered to be lost. First, we will investigate the strategy, which maximizes the mean throughput in terms of the number of packets served in finite time or before service interruption occurs. Then, the strategy which minimizes the expected number of lost packets and differences in the strategies will be discussed.

In PENELOPE the resulting model can be easily created with the help of the graphical model editor as illustrated by Fig. 2, which is provided as part of the user interface.

$E[Y_i(t)]$, as a measure of accomplishment, is used as a criterion of optimization. Series of experiments for different reward structures will be investigated. It is interesting to compare the impact of various control strategies on the resulting performance measures. As it will turn out, transient strategies yield better performance results than stationary strategies do. In addition, the difference will be investigated between using the mean accumulated reward in finite

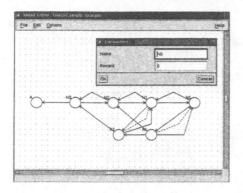

state	reward rate
N_0	0
N_i	μ
R_j	μ
A	0

$$i \in \{1, 2, 3\}, j \in \{1, 2\}$$

Figure 2: Model editor of PENELOPE.

time as an optimization criterion and applying the mean accumulated reward until absorption as a criterion.

3.2 Experiments

3.2.1 Maximization of Throughput

To specify the throughput per unit of time, the reward rate is defined as the service rate *times* the number of active processors in each state. The resulting reward structure is attached to Fig. 2. The set of parameters is summarized in Tab. 1. Users can define parameter values either directly in the model editor or in the parameter set editor, which allows one to explicitly specify an arbitrary set of concrete values to be substituted for formal parameters. One can equivalently specify parameter value-ranges and step widths, where for each of the resulting values a computation will automatically be executed. Usage of the parameter set editor is exemplified by Fig. 3(left).

parameter	value	meaning
λ_1	0.02	arrival rate of the class 1
λ_2	0.02	arrival rate of the class 2
μ	$[0.01, ..., 0.13]$	service rate

Table 1: Set of parameters.

Using the experiment editor, which is shown in Fig. 3(right), complete series of experiments can be specified and executed.

Transient Optimization In our example transient optimization is performed in the time horizon $[0, 6000)$. Assuming one unit of time corresponding to 10 msec, the total arrival rate $\lambda_1 + \lambda_2$ results in 1 packet/250 msec$= 4$/sec. The time horizon would cover 1 min. The resulting dynamic control strategy, which maximizes the throughput, is depicted in Fig. 4(left). With respect to

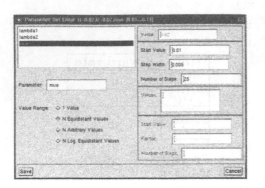

Figure 3: Parameter set editor (left) and experiment editor (right).

state R_2, the two-dimensional decision space, given by the covered set of parameter values of μ and the considered time interval, is partitioned into two regions, which are divided by the curve with the label $'R_2 \to N_1'$ attached to it. In the region *above* the curve the indicated strategy applies: A message of class one should be discarded in favor of potentially arriving class two messages. If, however, conditions are given such that the current situation is classified to be in the region *underneath* the curve, the alternative strategy should be applied in state R_2 and class one message should not be discarded in order to maximize the overall throughput. The region is indicated by label $'R_2 \to R_2'$.

With respect to state R_1, the two-dimensional decision space comprises a single region. Neither time nor service rate affect the curve labeled $'R_1 \to R_1'$. This means that the strategy *'do not discard the last arriving packet in state R_1'* is applied in the whole decision space.

The curves, also referred to as switching curves, represent for each state the instants of time where the strategy switches with respect to the remaining time. For example, if the service rate is $\mu = 0.08$, that is, 1 packet/125 msec, and if the time to go is 500 units, that is, 5 sec, an arriving packet of the first class should be accepted. The point $(0.08, 500)$ is located in the region $R_2 \to N_1$ and $R_1 \to R_1$. The throughput would decrease by dropping a packet in such a situation. The strategy reveals the following monotony: the smaller the service rate, the less packets of the first class are accepted. Of course, the loss risk of a second class message is higher with a decreasing service rate.

In Fig. 5, the throughput for the initial states N_0, N_1, N_2, and N_3 is depicted as a function of the service rate. The reward functions are computed assuming the optimal strategy. The throughput behaves in a way which might be anticipated: the higher the service rate, the higher the throughput. In the right part of Fig. 5, it is to be seen that the system reaches the highest throughput with the initial state N_1. Note that in PENELOPE one can arbitrarily select strategy/performance curves to be graphically presented. In Fig. 5, four curves were selected.

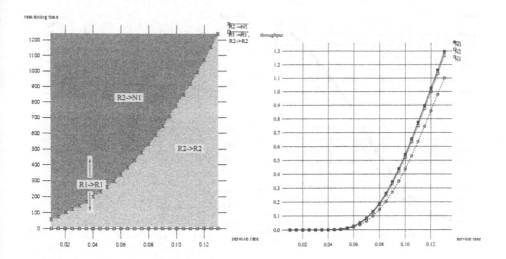

Figure 4: Transient strategies for maximizing the throughput (left) and difference graph of throughput computed under different strategies (right).

In what follows, the impact of arrival rates λ_1 and λ_2 on the optimal control strategy will be investigated, while $\mu = 0.04$ will be kept fixed. For the computations relating to the left part of Fig. 6, the arrival rate λ_1 of class one messages is varied, while $\lambda_2 = 0.02$ is kept fixed. In the right part, the arrival rate λ_2 of the second class messages is varied, while $\lambda_1 = 0.02$ is kept fixed. It is interesting to note that the strategy switching curves decrease with increasing arrival rates in both cases. But the strategy as a function of λ_2 is much more sensitive to an increase of the parameter value than in the first case. If λ_2 is significantly larger than λ_1 the option to discard class one message in state R_2 is "nearly always" selected. Note that in state R_1 a message should never be discarded.

Stationary Optimization The stationary optimization is performed for the same parameter set as in Tab. 1. The strategy iteration with Gauss-Seidel

service rate	strategy
$[0.01, ..., 0.13]$	$R_1 \rightarrow R_1$
	$R_2 \rightarrow N_1$

Table.2: Optimal stationary strategy.

computation method is chosen due to the small size of the model. $E[Y_i(\infty)]$ is used as a criterion of optimization. The resulting strategy is summarized in Tab. 2. It applies for the whole interval of considered service rates. If one compares the stationary strategies in Tab. 2 with the transient strategies in Fig. 4(left), it can be seen how they relate to each other. In the long run

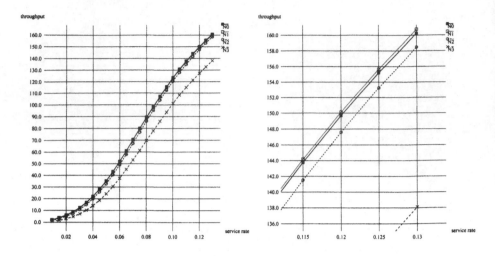

Figure 5: Throughput as a function of the service rate.

messages should always be discarded in state R_2 and never in state R_1. But in state R_2 the optimal strategy is strongly time-dependent for shorter periods of time.

Transient Analysis PENELOPE allows to save and modify computed strategies, or to create arbitrary new strategies, and to apply them in computations. Using this feature, it is possible to execute series of experiments under different strategies and to compare their impact on performance. To compare, for example, the impact of optimal transient strategies (OTS) and optimal stationary strategies (OSS) on the performance in our scenario, a transient analysis under the OSS from Tab. 2 is performed.

For easy comparison of the results, we use another feature of PENELOPE: the provisioning of difference graphs, which can be derived by combining arbitrary experiments. In Fig. 4(right), a difference graph for states N_0, N_2, and N_3 is depicted. Each point of this graph is a result of a subtraction $a - b$, where a is the throughput computed under the OTS (Fig. 4 left), and b is the throughput computed under the OSS (Tab. 2) for corresponding service rates. As is to be seen from Fig. 4(right), no difference in performance can be observed for service rates $\mu < 0.04$, that is, if $\frac{\lambda_1 + \lambda_2}{\mu} > 1$. The relative high load causes the system to reach the absorbing state quickly, regardless of the type of optimization being applied. Therefore, the mean accumulated throughput of the system in the time horizon $[0, 6000)$ is equal to the mean throughput until absorption in both cases. If the service rate becomes sufficiently large, $\mu \geq 0.04$, the difference strongly increases. In other words, the higher the service rate, the better the resulting performance becomes when adopting the OTS as opposed to the OSS.

Simulation PENELOPE also provides simulation as a method of evaluation. Under fixed deliberately eligible strategies the behavior of the system can be sim-

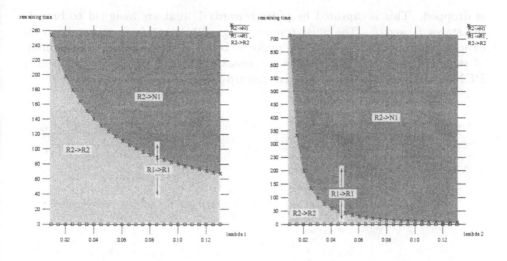

Figure 6: Dynamic control strategies as a function of time and of arrival rates.

ulated for a fixed time horizon. The simulation component enhances flexibility of the modeling tool and provides means for verification of the numerical results.

3.2.2 Minimization of Losses

The optimal strategy, which minimizes the mean number of lost class one packets, will be investigated. In order to do that, we have to modify the model from Fig. 1(right) slightly. In Fig. 7 *branching states* I_0, I_1, and I_2 were added. The new resulting reward structure is summarized in table which is attached to Fig. 7. We assign the reward (cost) rate λ_1 to states in which arriving class one packets get lost, that is, if there are at least two messages ahead, or if the absorbing state has already been reached. Furthermore, if a reconfiguration is

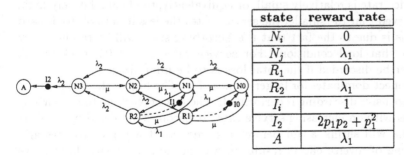

state	reward rate
N_i	0
N_j	λ_1
R_1	0
R_2	λ_1
I_i	1
I_2	$2p_1p_2 + p_1^2$
A	λ_1

$$i \in \{0,1\}, j \in \{2,3\},$$
$$p_1 = \frac{\lambda_1}{\lambda_1+\lambda_2}, p_2 = 1 - p_1 = \frac{\lambda_2}{\lambda_1+\lambda_2}$$

Figure 7: The modified EMRM model.

executed from state R_i to state I_{i-1}, $i \in \{1,2\}$, one packet of the first class is dropped. This is captured by pulse rewards 1, that are assigned to branching states I_0 and I_1. The pulse reward assigned to state I_2 corresponds to the expected number of lost class one packets, being in the system at the moment of service disruption. Note that a minimization of $E[Y_i(t)]$ can be realized in PENELOPE by specifying negative reward rates.

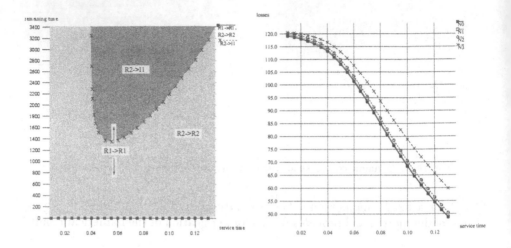

Figure 8: OTS for minimization of lost packets (left) and mean total loss under this OTS (right).

The OTS is depicted in the left part of Fig. 8. If the system is in the state R_1 then the strategy is the same as the one of the throughput model: Packets of class one are accepted for the whole time horizon and for all values of the considered service rate parameter interval. If the system is in the state R_2, however, two overlapping effects are observed.

If the service rate is relatively small, or equivalently, the load relatively high, it can be observed that the smaller the service rates the less it pays off to discard a packet. This is due to the fact that the absorbing state will be reached very quickly under that load condition. For service rates $\mu < 0.04$, packets will therefore never be discarded if the total loss is to be minimized.

A reverse effect dominates for larger values of μ: The higher the service rate, the less the expensive discarding is performed. The risk of reaching the absorbing state decreases with an increasing service rate. It becomes more and more likely that the queue will shrink again before next arrival of a class two message. The overlapping of reverse effects results in a minimum of the switching curve $R_2 \rightarrow I_1$, which partitions the decision space into regions, where alternative strategies apply, at $\mu \approx 0.055$.

The right part of Fig. 8 shows the total loss in time horizon $[0, 6000)$ as a function of the service rate for the initial states N_0, N_1, N_2, and N_3. With increasing service rate the $E[Y_i(t)]$ decreases. It is also evident, that the less packets are initially in the queue, the less packets get lost.

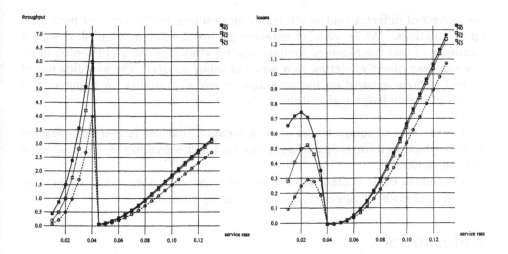

Figure 9: Difference graph of throughput and losses computed under different strategies.

It is also interesting to investigate the impact of the OTS, minimizing the total loss, on the performance in terms of mean accumulated throughput. We refer back to the parameter set summarized in Tab. 1 and select again the time horizon $[0, 6000)$ for transient analysis. With the throughput model (Fig. 1 right) and the attached reward structure from Fig. 2, a transient analysis under the strategy from Fig. 8(left), which minimizes losses, is performed. Since this strategy is not optimal for the throughput model, the resulting performance is poorer than the one in Fig. 5, gained under the optimal strategy. The difference graph is depicted in the left part of Fig. 9. Each point is a result of a subtraction $a - b$, where a is the throughput computed under the transient strategy, which is optimal for the throughput model (Fig. 4 left), and b is the throughput computed under the transient strategy, which is optimal for the loss model (Fig. 8 left).

The right part of Fig. 9 shows results from a reverse experiment. The baseline model is the model from Fig. 7, with the attached reward structure. a is the mean accumulated loss computed under the transient strategy, which is optimal for the loss model (Fig. 8 left), and b is the mean accumulated loss computed under the transient strategy optimal for the throughput model (Fig. 4 left).

4 Conclusions

We have presented a new modeling tool which can be used for the combined optimization and evaluation of reconfigurable systems. The important features of PENELOPE have been introduced by means of example. In particular, it was demonstrated how transient optimization techniques and optimization until absorption can be applied for congestion control problems by providing selective packet discarding strategies. It was shown how model structures and optimization strategies could be easily combined with each other in order to compare the impact of different control strategies on resulting performance or performability functions. While series of experiments are flexibly accomplished with a minimum of user interference, complex control strategies can be presented in an abstract way directly relating to a series of input models. The specification of control options is based on the paradigm of reconfigurability. A knowledge of details of the underlying algorithms is therefore not necessary in order to apply optimization techniques.

For the sake of completeness we may mention that the largest optimization models which were investigated with our tool had a size in the order of some $100,000$ states.

Continuing effort is made to improve the interface further and to extend the class of implemented numerical optimization algorithms.

References

[1] Béounes, C., Aguéra, M., Arlat, J., Bachmann, S., Bourdeau, C., Doucet, J.-E., Kanoun, K., Laprie, J.-C., Metge, S., Moreira de Souza, J., Powell, D., Spiesser, P.: "Surf-2: A program for dependability evaluation of complex hardware and software systems"; *Proc. FTCS 23, IEEE Computer Soc. Press.*, 1993, pp. 668-673.

[2] Ciardo, G., Muppala, J., Trivedi, K.S.: "SPNP: Stochastic Petri net package"; *Proc. PNPM'89, IEEE Computer Soc. Press*, 1989, pp. 142-151.

[3] Couvillion, J.A., Freire, R., Johnson, R., Obal II, W.D., Qureshi, A., Rai, M., Sanders, W.H., Tvedt, J.E.: "Performability modelling with UltraSAN"; *IEEE Software*, September 1991, 69-80.

[4] Furchtgott, D.G., Meyer, J.F.: "A performability solution method for degradable non-repairable systems"; *IEEE Trans. Comput.* 33(6), 1984, 550-554.

[5] Haverkort, B.R., Niemegeers, I.G.: "Performability Modelling Tools and Techniques"; *Performance Evaluation*, Vol. 25, No. 1, March 1996.

[6] Lee, Y.H., Shin, K.G.: "Optimal Reconfiguration Strategy for a Degradable Multimodule Computing System", *Journal of the ACM*, Vol. 34, No. 2, 1987.

[7] Lindemann, C., German, R.: "DSPNexpress: A software package for efficiently solving deterministic and stochastic Petri nets"; *Performance Tools 1992*, Edinburgh University Press, Edinburgh 1993.

[8] de Meer, H.: "Transiente Leistungsbewertung und Optimierung rekonfigurierbarer fehlertoleranter Rechensysteme"; *Arbeitsberichte des IMMD der Universität Erlangen-Nürnberg*, Vol. 25, No. 10, October 1992.

[9] de Meer, H., Trivedi, K.S., Mario Dal Cin: "Guarded Repair of Dependable Systems"; *Theoretical Computer Science, Special Issue on Dependable Parallel Computing*, Vol. 129, July 1994.

[10] de Meer, H., Ševčíková, H.: "XPenelope User Guide, Version 3.1"; Technical Report, FBI-HH-M-265/96, University of Hamburg, November 1996.

[11] Schulzrinne, H., Kurose, J.F., Towsley, D.: "Congestion Control for Real-Time Traffic in High-Speed Networks"; *IEEE INFOCOM'90*, 1990.

[12] Stewart, W.J.: *Introduction to the Numerical Solution of Markov Chains*, Princeton University Press, 1994.

[13] Tijms, Henk C.: *Stochastic modelling and analysis : a computational approach*; John Wiley, 1986.

[14] "Special Issue on Performability"; *Performance Evaluation*, February 1992.

Porting SHARPE on the WEB:
Design and Implementation of a
Network Computing Platform Using JAVA

Antonio Puliafito[1], Orazio Tomarchio[1], Lorenzo Vita[2]

[1] Istituto di Informatica, Università di Catania
Viale A. Doria 6, 95025 Catania - Italy
E-mail:{ap,otomarch}@iit.unict.it

[2] Dipartimento di Matematica, Università di Messina
C.da Papardo - Salita Sperone
98166 Messina - Italy
E-mail:vita@mat520.unime.it

Abstract. Although on the one hand the Web has made a large amount of information easy to access for a great number of users, on the other it does not offer any simple mechanisms to facilitate the use of a calculation application on the Internet. Recently, however, Java has been developed, a new language defined by Sun whose features make it ideal for the development of network applications. In this paper we show how it is possible to use this technology to create a network computing platform for the Web sharing of applications which were not specifically devised for network use. The platform developed is also equipped with adequate security mechanisms which provide authentication services and, if required encryption. The approach proposed has been applied to porting the Sharpe tool (Symbolic Hierarchical Automated Reliability/Performance Evaluator) onto the Web.

Keywords: Network Computing, Java, Web, Security, Sharpe

1 Introduction

The increasing development of distributed computing, along with the growing calculating power of desktop systems, has led to the adoption of distributed computing models based on a number of computers interconnected in a network. Consequently the client/server model has become widespread: powerful servers, when applied to by clients with limited calculating power, carry out complex processing operations.

The recent development of the Internet has partly altered this calculation model, not least due to the relative simplicity with which connections can be set up with remote geographical locations to access data and information in any part of the world [10]. In the last few years there has been a real boom in the Internet phenomenon: its rapid spread has provided a large number of users, many of whom are not exactly experts in using new computing tools, with access to this worldwide communications network (commonly known as the *Web*). The Web makes it possible to organize a series of multimedia documents connected by hypertextual links which allow the user to go from one document to another by simply clicking on appropriate portions of highlighted text (*links*), irrespective of the physical location of the documents in question [2]. Another factor contributing to the success of the Web is that the format of *html* documents does not depend on any particular hardware platform, and there are Web browsers for all the hw/sw architectures on the market.

If on the one hand the Web has made a large amount of information easy to access for a great number of users, on the other it does not offer any simple mechanisms to facilitate the use of a calculation application on the Internet. Currently, in fact, either remote connections are used (telnet), which require character interfaces as well as the need for access to the server, or there are proprietary solutions which, although efficient, preclude the use of heterogeneous architectures, thus wasting previous economic investments. Users, however, want to be able to exploit to the full the services offered by communication networks. Besides the immediate wish to communicate with each other, they want to access the data they need wherever it is and whatever format it is in. Also increasingly evident is the need for simple, safe use of the applications present on the Internet without having to possess specific hardware and software architectures.

The recent development of Java, however, has allowed great steps forward to be made in this direction. Java is an object-oriented, portable, interpreted, multithreaded programming language developed by Sun [1, 3, 4]. It was devised for the development of safe, robust applications in heterogeneous network environments. With Java it is possible to write applications (*applets*) which, once directly inserted onto Web pages, can be sent to the user's browser simply by a click of the mouse and then executed using local calculation resources. This specific feature of Java has not only made it possible to create Web pages containing animation and sound and other features which were previously impossible, thus making the world of the Web more pleasant; its potential goes far beyond such simple use.

In this paper, in fact, we will show how it is possible to use this technology to create a network computing platform for the Web sharing of applications which were not specifically devised for network use. The aim is to allow access to an application from any node connected with the Internet as long as it possesses a Java-enabled Web browser. To regulate the use of applications inserted into the network, making them available only to authorized users, the platform is also equipped with adequate seciurity mechanisms based on public and private key algorithms, which provide authentication services and, if required, encryption. In this way only users with regular licences can access the applications.

As a specific case, the approach proposed was used to port the Sharpe tool (Symbolic Hierarchical Automated Reliability/Performance Evaluator) onto the Web [8]. Sharpe is a well-known tool for the specification and evaluation of models of dependability, performance and performability originally endowed with a purely textual interface and devised for use on stand-alone machines. Using the mechanisms provided by the platform developed, it has been possible to make Sharpe accessible on the Internet by means of a Java-enabled Web browser. In addition, exploiting Java's powerful graphic libraries, a new graphic interface has been developed which considerably simplifies the model specification phase. The new application, called *GISharpe* (*Graphical Interface Sharpe*) is quite independent of the user platform, which can be Unix or Windows95 or Mac: the only requirement is a Web browser which can execute code written in Java, such as Netscape 3.0. GISharpe also provides authentication services made available by the network computing platform, in order to allow only authorized users to use the tool.

The rest of the paper is organized as follows: in Section 2 we will describe how the proposed architecture works, including the security mechanisms; we will also list a series of possible applications in which the platform would be particularly useful. In Section 3 we will show application of the approach to porting Sharpe onto the Web, describing in detail the graphic interface of GISharpe. The fourth and final section presents our conclusions.

2 Description of the Network Computing Platform

The network computing platform developed is based on the following points:

- granting a generic user access to possibly complex calculation applications through the Web;
- making applications not originally devised for network use easy to use in a distributed environment, and endowing them with a simple graphic interface;
- regulating access to the applications by appropriate security mechanisms.

The range of applications to which the technique can be applied is very vast; the greatest advantages, as far as performance is concerned, are, however, obtained with applications in which interaction is for a limited, concentrated period of time. In such applications (without user-friendly interfaces) it is often necessary to prepare a script with the operations to be performed which are then sent in batch to the application. Currently to use an application of this kind on a network it is necessary to start up an interactive session (telnet), which frequently causes a slowing-down due to network congestion, and of course the user has to possess a login to access the remote machine. With the approach proposed here it is possible to detach the work performed on the client from the calculations made by the server. In this way the network will have no problems as long as the user executes operations on the graphic interface, which is executed locally on the client. And all this is possible by moving around a Web page which is easy to use and does not require an interactive session to be held for any length of time.

Fig. 1 illustrates the software modules needed on the client and server for the network computing platform proposed to function correctly. As can be seen,

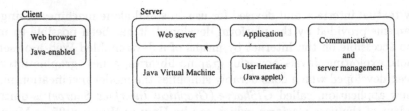

Fig. 1. Software modules needed on the client and server

the only requirement for the client is a Java-enabled Web browser. The server, on the other hand, needs the following software modules:

- Web server;
- Java Virtual Machine;
- Application to be made available on the network;
- Java applet of the user interface;
- Software module to run the communication session with the client.

The last module, entirely developed in Java, in reality comprises two submodules. One of these in particular is transferred onto the client when the latter forwards a request for access to the server and provides the client with the mechanisms needed to run the communication sessions just started. The second submodule, on the other hand, is always in execution on the server and deals with accepting requests from various clients, robustly managing the various connections with clients, and sending clients the results put out by the server. It also keeps a memory of the correspondence between clients and the applications they use.

To describe the functioning of the technique proposed in greater detail, we refer to Fig. 2, which is a scheme of the various phases of interaction between client and server.

Through his Web browser, with a simple click of the mouse, the client sends a request in http format to the server, who transmits the html page in question. On this page there will be a link providing access to the application which allows a Java applet to be loaded, containing the graphic interface developed for the software involved. At this point the first phase of the client-server interaction ends. The client now has the software to view and run the graphic interface with which to formulate the request to be sent to the server. The user can thus specify his request using his own calculation resources. When this phase ends the request is transmitted to the server, possibly after conversion into a format accepted by the specific software, which is then executed on the data provided by the user. The whole calculation request is now shifted to the server, while the client waits for the processing results. At the end of this phase the server sends the client the processed data.

The presence of security mechanisms, if any, involves an extension of the first phase of the communication protocol to check the real identity of the user. Fur-

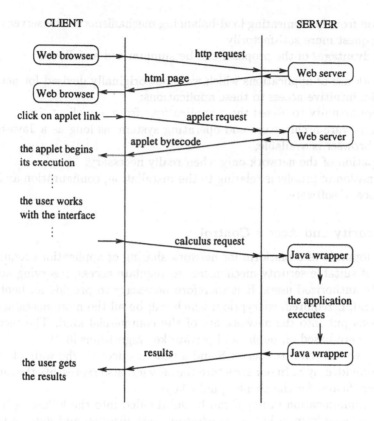

Fig. 2. Interaction between client and server

ther details of how to implement a security service will be given in the following section.

At this point we should point out some differences between the technique described above and normal use of Java applets. In our architecture the classical approach of Java applets is in a sense turned upside down. An applet is, in fact, an application written in Java which can be executed through Web locally on a client. Once it is transferred to a client, applet execution is entirely local without any interaction with the server. In our case, instead, the applet is only the interface with a much more complex and computationally onerous application which is executed on a remote machine. In addition, this application is not written in Java (in most general cases); on the contrary, to offer better performance it often greatly depends on the machine on which it is executed. The end user therefore does not have any problems of managing and optimizing the software involved. He may not be aware, and probably does not need to be, of whether the machine with the role of server is a pool of processors or several machines connected together to make the service more reliable. These problems are taken into consideration and solved by the Java application on the server which converses with the applet on the client; there is nothing, therefore, to prevent the application from implementing load-balancing mechanisms on the server to meet clients' request more satisfactorily.

The advantages of the proposal can be summarized as follows:

- network use of applications which were not originally devised for networks;
- simple, intuitive access to these applications;
- the opportunity to access these applications from any client, irrespective of the hardware architecture and operating system, as long as a Java-enabled Web browser is available;
- occupation of the network only when really necessary;
- elimination of problems relating to the installation, configuration and maintenance of software.

2.1 Security and Access Control

The development of a platform for network sharing of applications requires the creation of suitable security mechanisms to regulate access, reserving access to previously authorized users. It is therefore necessary to provide authentication services and, if required, encryption, which will be all the more necessary if the applications put into the network are of the commercial kind. The techniques we will use are based on public and private key algorithms [6, 9].

Below we will refer to a server S and a generic client C who wants to use the services provided by S. In our structure the server S also represents the authority issuing certificates for the clients' public keys.

The communication protocol can be subdivided into the following 3 stages, shown in scheme form in Fig. 3: *registration, initialization* and *data transfer*.

Registration Stage: In this stage of the security protocol C and S agree on the type of services offered/required and the access modes. C then generates two keys, a private one and a public one, giving the latter to S through a safe channel (typically not through the same communication channel that subsequent connections will use) and keeping the private one safely (the key is often encrypted with an alphanumerical password and then memorized). To S, receipt of C's public key represents a request for registration. S then creates a certificate for C's public key, signing it with its own private key, after which it delivers its own public key to C (again on a safe channel) along with the certificate for C's key. It should be pointed out that this stage is only carried out once in the validity period of the registered key.

Initialization Stage: This stage starts when C decides to link up with S to use a certain application. Neglecting the loading of the applet through Web, as any security mechanisms are incorporated in the Web browser, this stage can be schematically represented as follows:

- C send S a connection request;
- S sends a signed message indicating that the request has been received;
- C replies sending a signed message containing the security services required (confidentiality and authentication or authentication alone), and a code identifying its public key

– S checks C's signature on the message received and if it is recognized sends C a signed acknowledgement and starts to transfer the data; if the authentication stage fails the connection is immediately interrupted.

Data Transfer Stage: during this stage each message sent is treated according to the security services requested. If confidentiality and authentication have been requested the message will be composed of two fields, one in which the data is encrypted and another containing the sender's signature.

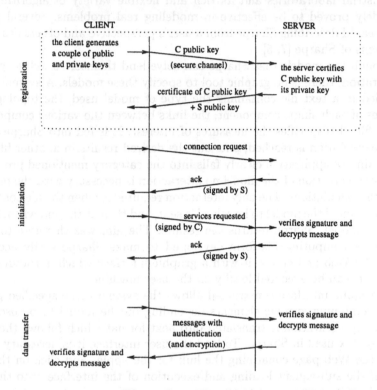

Fig. 3. Security protocol

3   An Example of Application: GISharpe

The technique proposed has been applied to port Sharpe (Symbolic Hierarchical Automated Reliability/Performance Evaluator), a tool for the modelling and analytical evaluation of systems, onto the Web [8].

The Sharpe package provides a specification language and a wide variety of efficient algorithms for analyzing various kinds of dependability, performance and performability models. Sharpe is a modeler's design aid in that it provides alternative tunable algorithms and a flexible mechanism for combining different modeling techniques. Using Sharpe, one can specify and analyze the following model types separately or in combination: fault trees, reliability block diagrams, reliability graphs, product-form queueing networks, series-parallel acyclic directed graphs, Markov and semi-Markov chains and generalized stochastic Petri nets. Users are allowed to deal with the problems caused by large and/or ill-conditioned models by choosing the best solution algorithm and by combining possibly heterogeneous models.

The Sharpe package has been in use at over 120 sites, including universities and industrial laboratories and its rich and flexible variety of algorithms has been widely proved to be effective in modeling real problems. Several papers have appeared describing Sharpe from a user's perspective and others describing applications of Sharpe [7, 5].

Although the models that Sharpe can solve lend themselves well to graphic representation, there is no graphic tool to specify these models. A system model is specified in a text file containing the type of model used, the topology, the properties of each single component, the links between the various components, etc. The file also specifies the measures of interest. It is fed into Sharpe which, when the resolution is reached, puts out the desired results in another file.

This kind of application clearly falls into the category mentioned previously, as during the creation of the model no interaction is necessary with the program making the calculations. The only interaction required is when the file containing the description of the model to be solved is sent, and then at the end when, having solved the model, Sharpe returns the results. The aim was therefore to adopt the network computing platform developed to make Sharpe easily accessible through the Web and endow it with a graphic interface which, structured as a Java applet, can be executed locally on the user machine.

The graphic interface constructed allows the system to be specified graphically by combining graphic elements depending on the model to be used, and then this representation is translated into aext format which follows the specification syntax used in Sharpe. To load the user interface it is necessary to link up with the Web page conatining the link for the applet and click on the relative icon: the subsequent loading and execution of the interface onto the local machine is quite transparent to the user.

The main GISharpe display, shown in Fig. 4, has the following four zones:

- a Menu panel;
- a control panel;
- a design area;
- a status panel.

The Menu offers the usual choices - besides the submenus *File* and *Edit* there is also *Models*, through which the user chooses the type of model he is interested in. Once the model has been selected a further menu is displayed with items which allow the user to select the graphic elements to be used in the specification phase. More immediate use of the graphic functions is provided by a series of push buttons on the left hand side of the display which summarize the main graphic functions on the menu.

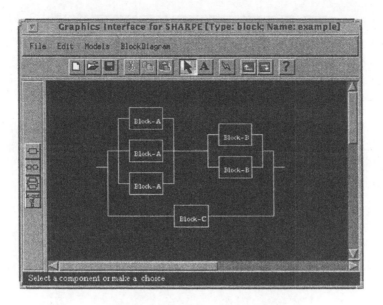

Fig. 4. Main display of GISharpe

The Control panel can be used to activate a series of functions to create, load and save a model; there are also the classical cut, copy and paste functions and others to activate resolution of the model and manage hierarchical models.

The design area is where the user provides a description of the model in graphic terms and connecting links between them. Significant graphic symbols and the associated dialogue boxes are enabled for each model.

Finally, the status panel gives run-time indications regarding the status of the interface, signalling the occurrence of any event that may be of interest to the user.

By way of example, let us now analyze one of the models that can be solved with Sharpe: series-parallel block diagrams (see Fig. 4). The graphic elements the user is provided are activated by clicking on:

- *block:* to add an elementary block;
- *block series:* to insert or connect several blocks in a series;
- *block parallel:* to insert or connect several blocks in parallel;
- *k-out-of-n:* to insert a block k-out-of-n

With a double click on a generic block one gains access to a dialogue box like the one in Fig. 5, with which it is possible to specify the properties of the block. In the case of block diagrams a name can be assigned to a component and the distribution function of the failure time associated with it can be selected. The possible choices (exp, general, polynomial, ...) are obviously those supported by Sharpe. More specifically, by selecting the *cdf* button it is possible to associate a block with a distribution function obtained from the solution to another model. following a hierarchical approach.

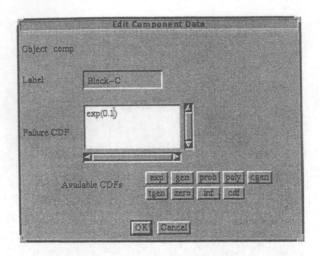

Fig. 5. Specifying the properties of a block

Once the model specification stage is completed, the user passes to the analysis stage simply by pressing the *Analyze* key which opens a dialogue box in which the user specifies the evaluation indices he wants. Fig. 6 shows the dialogue box for block diagrams where, besides the name and type of model, it is possible to choose between evaluation:

- of the cumulative distribution function (*cdf*);
- of a generic function for varying time parameters (*eval*);
- of a generic expression (*expr*).

Pressing the *Ok* button the graphic representation is converted into text format using the Sharpe specification syntax. The ASCII file thus created is then transferred onto the server where the management module supplied by the platform begins execution of a new Sharpe instance.

Once the processing is completed the results are transmitted to the client and displayed in a dialogue box like the one shown in Fig. 7.

This is the end of a typical session using the tool; having viewed the results, the user can decide to continue to analyze the system by modifying certain parameters or redefining the model.

The user can also decide to save the model in a directory for future use. This function can only be offered if the applet was loaded by means of the *appletviewer* supplied by Sun together with the Java Development Kit (JDK). Applets generally, in fact, have great limitations on access to the local file system: using Netscape as a browser, for instance, it is not possible to read or write files locally. With the appletviewer, on the other hand, system variables can be set in such a way as to remove these limitations. These variables are *acl.read* and *acl.write* and have to be set with the path of the directory in which the user wants to read or write. For example, if the client is using a SUN machine, the variables are to be found in the file ∼/.hotjava/properties.

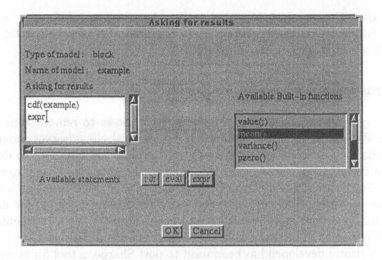

Fig. 6. Specification of the evaluation indices

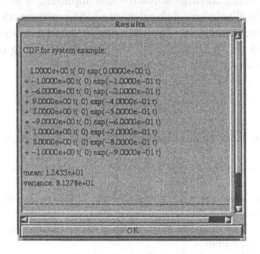

Fig. 7. Results presentation

Another possibility offered by GISharpe is saving the graphic description of a model in the *Xfig* format. Xfig is a public domain tool for vector graphics on Unix, frequently used in academic circles. By exporting the design in this format it can be edited exploiting all the features provided by Xfig, besides being converted into one of the many graphic formats provided (e.g. PostScript).

Finally, the user interface developed incorporates a whole system of hypertext help. There is both a general help function, accessed by choosing Help from the menu, and a contextual one which gives information on a specific element selected. The general help is in the hypertext format, i.e. the user passes from one topic to another using hypertextual links which facilitate and speed up consultation. Contextual help, on the other hand, gives information about a specific GISharpe element, whether it is a graphic element belonging to the model or one belonging to the interface.

4 Conclusions

In this paper we have presented a technique for access to remote applications through Web-based interfaces, adapting the classical client/server model to a heterogeneous geographical network environment like the Internet. To do so we used the development environment supplied by Java, the new language developed by Sun, with which a network computing platform has been implemented to enable use of applications which were not necessarily designed for use in a distributed environment. Great care has been taken to define authentication mechanisms, so as to reserve use of the applications to authorized users.

The platform developed has been used to port Sharpe, a tool for system performance modelling and analysis, onto the Web. The implementation has shown the advantages of using Java in software development. The use of an object-oriented language facilitated modular design of the program and allowed parallel development of several modules. The libraries supplied for network communications also simplified the development of the modules relating to management of the connections between client and server.

References

1. The Java Virtual Machine Specification. Technical report, Sun Microsystems, October 1995.
2. T. Berners Lee et al. The World Wide Web. *Communications of the ACM*, 37(8), August 1994.
3. J. Gosling. The Java Language Environment: a White Paper. Technical report, Sun Microsystems, May 1995.
4. M. A. Hamilton. Java and the shift to Net-centric Computing. *IEEE Computer*, 29(8):31–39, August 1996.
5. D. Heimann, N. Mittal, and K. S. Trivedi. Availability and reliability modeling of computer systems. In M.Yovitss, editor, *Advances in Computers*, volume 31, Academic Press, Orlando, 1991.
6. L. Hughes. *Actually Useful Internet Security Techniques*. New Riders Publishing, 1995.
7. R. Sahner and K. S. Trivedi. Reliability modeling using SHARPE. *IEEE Transaction on Reliability*, 36(2):186–193, June 1987.
8. R. A. Sahner, K. S. Trivedi, and A. Puliafito. *Performance and Reliability Analysis of Computer Systems*. Kluwer Academic Publishers, November 1995.
9. W. Stalling. *Network and Internetwork Security Principles and Practice*. Prentice Hall, 1995.
10. E. Yourdon. Java, the Web, and Software Development. *IEEE Computer*, 29(8):25–30, August 1996.

Storage Alternatives for Large Structured State Spaces[*]

Gianfranco Ciardo and Andrew S. Miner

College of William and Mary, Williamsburg VA 23187-8795, USA

Abstract

We consider the problem of storing and searching a large state space obtained from a high-level model such as a queueing network or a Petri net. After reviewing the traditional technique based on a single search tree, we demonstrate how an approach based on multiple levels of search trees offers advantages in both memory and execution complexity. Further execution time improvements are obtained by exploiting the concept of "event locality". We apply our technique to three large parametric models, and give detailed experimental results.

1 Introduction

Extremely complex systems are increasingly common. Various types of high-level models are used to describe them, study them, and forecast the effect of possible modifications. Unfortunately, the logical and dynamic analysis of these models is often hampered by the combinatorial explosion of their state spaces, a problem inherent with discrete-state systems.

It is quite common to use exact methods in the early stages of a system's design, when studying rough models over a wide range of parameter combinations, then focus on more detailed models using approximate methods or simulation. Indeed, many approximate decomposition approaches use exact methods at the submodel level, thus introducing errors only when exchanging or combining (exact) results from different submodels. Then, the ability of applying exact methods to larger models will normally result in better approximations: it is likely that the study of a large model decomposed into four medium-size submodels, each solved with exact methods, will be more accurate than that of the same model decomposed into ten small-size submodels.

The first problem when applying exact methods is the generation and storage of the state space. After that, if the goal of the study is performance or reliability, the model is then used to generate a stochastic process, often a continuous-time Markov chain (CTMC), which is solved numerically for steady-state or transient measures. The state space can be of interest in itself, though, since it can be used to answer questions such as existence of deadlocks and livelocks or liveness.

* This research was partially supported by the National Aeronautics and Space Administration under NASA Contract No. NAS1-19480 and by the Center for Advanced Computing and Communication under Contract 96-SC-NSF-1011

In this paper, we focus on techniques to store and search the state space. However, while we do not discuss the solution of the stochastic process explicitly, our results apply not only to the "logical" analysis of the model, but even more so to its "stochastic analysis" (indeed, this was our initial motivation). This is particularly true given the recent developments on the solution of complex Markov models using Kronecker operators [2] which do not require to store the infinitesimal generator of the CTMC explicitly. In this case, the storage bottleneck is indeed due to the state space and the probability vectors allocated when computing the numerical solution.

Sections 2 and 3 define the type of high-level formalisms we consider and discuss the reachability set and its storage, respectively. Our main contributions are in Sections 4 and 5, where we introduce a multilevel data structure and show how it can be used to save both memory and execution time when building the reachability set. Finally, Section 6 contains our final remarks.

2 High-Level Model Description

We implemented our techniques in the generalized stochastic Petri net (GSPN) formalism. However, these techniques can be applied to any model expressed in a "high-level formalism" that defines:

- The "potential set", $\hat{\mathcal{R}}$. This is a discrete set, assumed finite, to which the states of the model must belong[2].
- A finite set of possible events, $\mathcal{E}$.
- An initial state, $\mathbf{i}^0 \in \hat{\mathcal{R}}$.
- A boolean function defining whether an event is active (can occur) in a state, $Active : \mathcal{E} \times \hat{\mathcal{R}} \to \{True, False\}$.
- A function defining the effect of the occurrence of an active event on a state: $New : \mathcal{E} \times \hat{\mathcal{R}} \to \hat{\mathcal{R}}$.

Fig. 1 and 2 show the two GSPNs used throughout this paper to illustrate the effect of our techniques (ignore for the moment the dashed boxes). The first GSPN models a kanban system, from [2]. It is composed of four instances of essentially the same sub-GSPN. The synchronizing transitions t_{synch_1} and t_{synch_2} can be either both timed or both immediate, we indicate the two resulting models as kanban-timed and kanban-immediate. The second GSPN models a flexible manufacturing system, from [3], except that the cardinality of all arcs is constant, unlike the original model (this does not affect the number of reachable markings). We indicate this model as FMS. We do not describe these models in more detail, the interested reader is referred to the original publications where they appeared. In all cases, their initial marking is a function of a parameter N.

---

[2] A point about notation: we denote sets by upper case calligraphic letters. Lower and upper case bold letters denote vector and matrices, respectively. $\eta(\mathbf{A})$ is the number of nonzero entries in a matrix $\mathbf{A}$; $\mathbf{A}_{i,j}$ is the entry in row i and column j of $\mathbf{A}$; $\mathbf{A}_{\mathcal{X},\mathcal{Y}}$ is the submatrix of $\mathbf{A}$ corresponding to the set of rows $\mathcal{X}$ and the set of columns $\mathcal{Y}$.

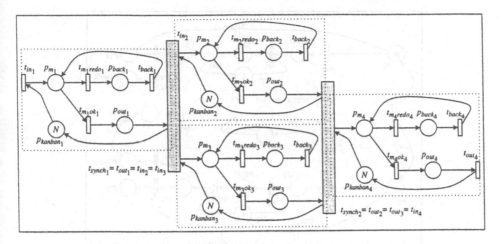

Fig. 1. The GSPN of a Kanban system.

3 The Reachability Set

From the high-level description, we can build the "reachability set", $\mathcal{R} \subseteq \hat{\mathcal{R}}$. This is the set of states that can be reached from i^0 through the occurrence of any sequence of enabled events. Formally, $\mathcal{R}$ is the smallest subset of $\hat{\mathcal{R}}$ satisfying:

1. $i^0 \in \mathcal{R}$, and
2. $i \in \mathcal{R} \wedge \exists e \in \mathcal{E}, Active(e, i) = True \wedge i' = New(e, i) \Rightarrow i' \in \mathcal{R}$.

While a high-level model usually specifies other information as well (the stochastic timing of the events, the measures that should be computed when solving the model, etc.), the above description is sufficient for now, and it is not tied to any particular formalism.

$\mathcal{R}$ can be generated using the state-space exploration procedure *BuildRS* shown in Fig. 3, which terminates if $\mathcal{R}$ is finite. This is a search of the graph implicitly defined by the model. Function *ChooseRemove* chooses an element from its argument (a set of states), removes it, and returns it. Procedure *SearchInsert* searches the first argument (a state) in the second argument (a set of states) and, if not found, it inserts the state in its third argument (also a set of states).

The "reachability graph" $(\mathcal{R}, \mathcal{A})$ has as nodes the reachable states, and an arc from i to j iff there is an event e such that $Active(e, i) = True$ and $New(e, i) = j$. Depending on the type of analysis, the arc might be labeled with e; this might result in a multigraph, if multiple events can cause the same change of state. While we focus on $\mathcal{R}$ alone, the size of $\mathcal{A}$ affects the complexity of *BuildRS*.

A total order can be defined over the elements of $\hat{\mathcal{R}}$: $i < j$ iff i precedes j in lexical order. We can then define a function *Compare* : $(\hat{\mathcal{R}} \times \hat{\mathcal{R}}) \rightarrow \{-1, 0, 1\}$ returning -1 if the first argument precedes the second one, 1 if it follows it, and 0 if the two arguments are identical. This order allows the efficient search

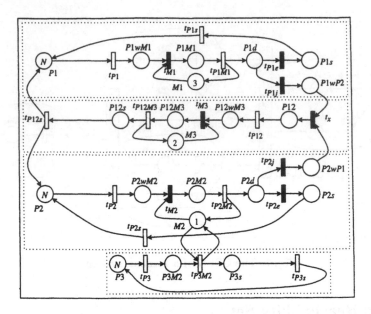

Fig. 2. The GSPN of a FMS system.

```
BuildRS(in: Events, Active, New; out: R);
1.  R ← ∅; /* R: states explored so far */
2.  U ← {s⁰}; /* U: states found but not yet explored */
3.  while U ≠ ∅ do
4.      i ← ChooseRemove(U);
5.      R ← R ∪ {s};
6.      for each e ∈ ℰ s.t. Active(e, i) = True do
7.          j ← New(e, i);
8.          SearchInsert(j, R ∪ U, U);
```

Fig. 3. Procedure *BuildRS*

and insertion of a state during *BuildRS*. Once $\mathcal{R}$ has been built, we can define a bijection $\Psi : \mathcal{R} \rightarrow \{0, \ldots, |\mathcal{R}| - 1\}$, such that $\Psi(i) < \Psi(j)$ iff $i < j$.

Common techniques to store and search the sets $\mathcal{R}$ and $\mathcal{U}$ include hashing and search trees. Hashing would work reasonably well if we had a good bound on the final size of the reachability set $\mathcal{R}$, but this is not usually the case. We prefer search trees: when kept balanced, they have more predictable behavior than hashing.

We consider two alternatives, both based on binary search trees: splay trees [4] and AVL trees [5]. The execution complexity[3] of *BuildRS* when using either

---
[3] We leave known constants inside the big-Oh notation to stress that they do make a difference in practice, even if they are formally redundant.

method is

$$O\left(|\mathcal{R}| \cdot |\mathcal{E}| \cdot C_{Active} + |\mathcal{A}| \cdot (C_{New} + \log|\mathcal{R}| \cdot C_{Compare})\right),$$

where C_x is the (average) cost to a call to procedure x. For AVL trees, the storage complexity, expressed in bits, is

$$O\left(|\mathcal{R}| \cdot (B_{state} + 2B_{pointer} + 2)\right),$$

where B_{state} is the (average) number of bits to store a state, $B_{pointer}$ is the number of bits for a pointer. The additional two bits are used to store the node balance information. For splay trees, the complexity is the same, except for the two-bit balance, which is not required.

Regarding the use of binary search trees in *BuildRS*, we have another choice to make. We can use a single tree to store $\mathcal{R} \cup \mathcal{U}$ in *BuildRS* as shown in Fig. 4(a,b,c), or two separate trees, as in Fig. 4(d). Using a single tree has some advantages:

- No deletion, possibly requiring a rebalancing, is needed when moving a state from $\mathcal{U}$ to $\mathcal{R}$.
- Procedure *SearchInsert* performs a single search requiring $O(\log|\mathcal{R} \cup \mathcal{U}|)$ comparisons, instead of two searches in the two trees for $\mathcal{R}$ and $\mathcal{U}$, which overall require more comparisons (up to twice as many), since

$$\log|\mathcal{R}| + \log|\mathcal{U}| = \log(|\mathcal{R}| \cdot |\mathcal{U}|) > \log(|\mathcal{R}| + |\mathcal{U}|) = \log(|\mathcal{R} \cup \mathcal{U}|)$$

(of course, we mean "the current $\mathcal{R}$ and $\mathcal{U}$" in the above expressions).

However, it also has disadvantages. As explored and unexplored states are stored together in a single tree, there must be a way to identify and access the nodes of $\mathcal{U}$. We can accomplish this by:

1. Maintaining a separate linked list pointing to the unexplored states. This requires an additional $O(2|\mathcal{U}| \cdot B_{pointer})$ bits, as shown in Fig. 4(a).
2. Storing an additional pointer in each tree node, pointing to the next unexplored state. This requires an additional $O(|\mathcal{R}| \cdot B_{pointer})$ bits, as shown in Fig. 4(b).
3. Storing the markings in a dynamic array structure. In this case, the nodes of the tree contain indices to the array of markings, instead of the markings themselves. If markings are added to the array in the order they are discovered, $\mathcal{R}$ occupies the beginning of the array, while $\mathcal{U}$ occupies the end. This requires an additional $O(|\mathcal{R}| \cdot B_{index})$ bits, where B_{index} is the number of bits required to index the array of markings, as shown in Fig. 4(c)

The size of $\mathcal{R}$ for our three models is shown in Table 1, as a function of N. Since the models are GSPNs, they give rise to "vanishing markings", that is, markings enabling only immediate transitions, in which the sojourn time is zero. In all our experiments, these markings are eliminated "on the fly" so that all our figures regarding $\mathcal{R}$ reflect only the "tangible" reachable markings.

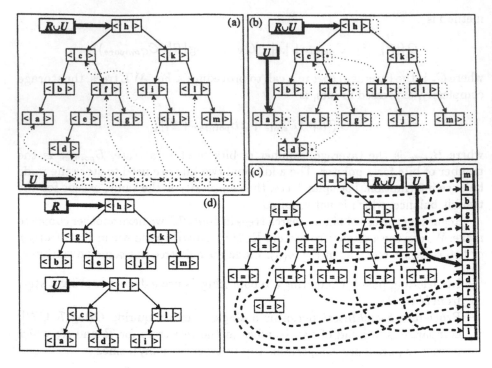

Fig. 4. Four simple storage schemes for $\mathcal{R}$ and $\mathcal{U}$.

N	$\|\mathcal{R}\|$ for kanban-timed	$\|\mathcal{R}\|$ for kanban-immediate	$\|\mathcal{R}\|$ for FMS
1	160	152	54
2	4,600	3,816	810
3	58,400	41,000	6,520
4	454,475	268,475	35,910
5	2,546,432	1,270,962	152,712
6	11,261,376	4,785,536	537,768
7	—	—	1,639,440

Table 1. Reachability set size for the three models, as a function of N.

4   A Multilevel Search Tree to Store $\mathcal{R}$

We now assume that $\hat{\mathcal{R}}$ can be expressed as the Cartesian product of K "local" state spaces: $\hat{\mathcal{R}} = \mathcal{R}^0 \times \cdots \times \mathcal{R}^{K-1}$, and that $\mathcal{R}^k$ is simply $\{0, \ldots n_k - 1\}$, although n_k might not be known in advance. Hence, a (global) state is a vector $\mathbf{i} \in \{0, \ldots n_0 - 1\} \times \cdots \times \{0, \ldots n_{K-1} - 1\}$. For example, if the high-level model is a single-class queuing network, $\mathbf{i}_k$ could be the number of customers in queue k. However, a realistic model can easily have dozens of queues; so it might be more efficient to partition the queues into K sets, and let $\mathbf{i}_k$ be the number of

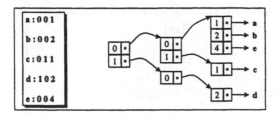

Fig. 5. Chiola's storage scheme to store the reachability set of a SPN.

possible combinations of customers into the queues of partition k. An analogous discussion applies to stochastic Petri nets (SPNs), and even to more complex models, as long as they have a finite state space.

Our lexical order can be applied just as well to $\hat{\mathcal{R}}$, hence we can define a bijection $\hat{\Psi} : \hat{\mathcal{R}} \rightarrow \{0, \ldots, |\hat{\mathcal{R}}| - 1\}$, analogous to Ψ. Indeed, $\hat{\Psi}$ has a fundamental advantage over Ψ: its value equals its argument interpreted as a mixed base integer,

$$\hat{\Psi}(\mathbf{i}) = (\ldots((\mathbf{i}_0)n_1 + \mathbf{i}_1)n_2 \cdots)n_{K-1} + \mathbf{i}_{K-1} = \sum_{k=0}^{K-1} \mathbf{i}_k \cdot n_{k+1}^{K-1},$$

where $n_i^j = \prod_{k=i}^{j} n_k$. The reachability set $\mathcal{R}$ may coincide with $\hat{\mathcal{R}}$, but it is more likely to be much smaller, since many combinations of local states might not occur.

We extend work by Chiola, who defined a multilevel technique to store the reachable markings of a SPN [1]. Since the state, or marking, of a SPN with K places can be represented as a fixed-size vector $\mathbf{i} = (\mathbf{i}_0, \mathbf{i}_1, \ldots, \mathbf{i}_{K-1})$, he proposed the strategy illustrated in Fig. 5, copied from [1]. In the figure, it is assumed that the SPN has three places, and that there are five reachable markings, a through e. A three-level tree is then used. The first level discriminates markings on their first component (either 0 or 1); the second level discriminates on their second component (also either 0 or 1) within a given first component; finally, the third level fully determines the marking using the third component (1, 2, or 4).

We instead use a multilevel approach with K levels, one for each submodel (a sub-GSPN), as shown in Fig. 6. Before explaining this data structure, we need to define two classes of sets.

- The set of reachable substates up to k:

$$\mathcal{R}_0^k = \{(\mathbf{i}_0, \ldots, \mathbf{i}_k) \in \mathcal{R}^0 \times \cdots \times \mathcal{R}^k :$$
$$\exists (\mathbf{i}_{k+1}, \ldots, \mathbf{i}_{K-1}) \in \mathcal{R}^{k+1} \times \cdots \times \mathcal{R}^{K-1}, (\mathbf{i}_0, \ldots \mathbf{i}_{K-1}) \in \mathcal{R}\}.$$

Clearly, $\mathcal{R}_0^{K-1}$ coincides with $\mathcal{R}$ itself, while $\mathcal{R}_0^0$ coincides with $\mathcal{R}^0$ iff every element of the local state space 0 can actually occur in some global state, and so on.

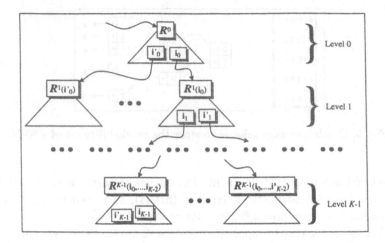

Fig. 6. A multilevel storage scheme for $\mathcal{R}$.

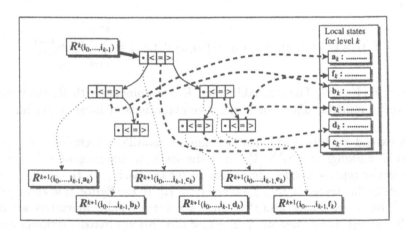

Fig. 7. A tree at level $k < K - 1$, pointing to trees at level $k + 1$.

– The set of reachable local states in $\mathcal{R}^k$ conditioned on a reachable substate $(\mathbf{i}_0, \ldots, \mathbf{i}_{k-1}) \in \mathcal{R}_0^{k-1}$:

$$\mathcal{R}^k(\mathbf{i}_0, \ldots, \mathbf{i}_{k-1}) = \{\mathbf{i}_k \in \mathcal{R}^k : (\mathbf{i}_0, \ldots, \mathbf{i}_k) \in \mathcal{R}_0^k\}.$$

Clearly, this set, when defined (i.e., when indeed $(\mathbf{i}_0, \ldots, \mathbf{i}_{k-1}) \in \mathcal{R}_0^{k-1}$), is never empty.

In Fig. 6, level $k \in \{0, \ldots, K - 1\}$ contains $|\mathcal{R}_0^{k-1}|$ search trees, each one storing $\mathcal{R}^k(\mathbf{i}_0, \ldots, \mathbf{i}_{k-1})$, for a different reachable substate $(\mathbf{i}_0, \ldots, \mathbf{i}_{k-1}) \in \mathcal{R}_0^{k-1}$. Thus, a generic tree at level $k < K - 1$ has the structure shown in Fig. 7. In each one of its nodes, the "•" pointer points to a tree at level $k + 1$. In the drawing, the local states for level k are stored in an unsorted dynamically extensible array, in the order in which they are found, and pointed by the "=" pointer in each node. Alternatively, it is possible to store a local state directly in the node. If the submodel is quite complex, this second alternative might be not as memory effective, since a local state can require several bytes for its encoding, which are then repeated in each node, instead of just a pointer. Furthermore, if we can assume an upper bound on the number of local states for a given submodel (e.g., 2^{16}), we can use an index (16 bits) into the local state array, instead of a pointer (usually 32 bits).

The total number of nodes used for trees at level k equals the number of reachable substates up to that level, $|\mathcal{R}_0^k|$, hence the total number of tree nodes for our multilevel data structure is

$$\sum_{k=0}^{K-1} |\mathcal{R}_0^k| > |\mathcal{R}_0^{K-1}| = |\mathcal{R}|$$

where the last expression is the number of nodes required in the standard single-level approach of Fig. 4. Two observations are in order.

First, the total number of nodes at levels 0 through $K-2$ is a small fraction of the nodes at level $K-1$, that is, of $|\mathcal{R}|$, provided the trees at the last level, $K-1$, are not "too small". This is ensured by an appropriate partitioning of a large model into submodels. In other words, only the memory used by the nodes of the trees at the last level really matters.

Second, the nodes of the trees at the last level do not require a pointer to a tree at a lower level, hence each node requires only three pointers (96 bits). Again, if we can assume a bound on the number of local states for the last submodel, $|\mathcal{R}^{K-1}| \leq 2^b$, we can in principle implement dynamic data structures that require only $3b$ bits per node, plus some overhead to implement dynamic arrays. Given a model, there is usually some freedom in choosing the number of submodels, that is, the number of levels K. We might then be able to define the last submodel in such a way that is has at most 2^8 local states, resulting in only slightly more than $3|\mathcal{R}|$ bytes to store the entire reachability set. When this is not the case, the next easily implementable step, 2^{16}, is normally more than enough. Even in this case, the total memory requirements are still much better than with a single-level implementation.

We stress that, while this discussion about using 8 or 16 bit indices seems to be excessively implementation-dependent, it is not. Only through the multilevel approach it is possible to exploit the small size of each local space. In the single-level approach, instead, the total number of states that can be indexed (pointed by a pointer) is $|\mathcal{R}|$, a number which can be easily be 10^7, and possibly more. In this case, we are forced to use 32-bit pointers, and we can even foresee a point in the not-so-distant future where even these pointers will be insufficient, while the multilevel approach can be implemented using 8 or 16 bit indices at the last level regardless of the size of the reachability set, if $\mathcal{R}^{K-1}$ is not too large.

Just as with a single search tree, we can implement our multilevel scheme using splay or AVL trees. However, the choice between storing $\mathcal{R}$ and $\mathcal{U}$ sep-

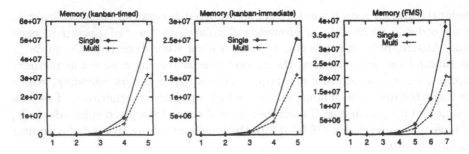

Fig. 8. Memory usage (bytes) for single vs. multilevel approach, as a function of N.

arately or as a single set has subtler implications. If we choose to store them as a single set, distinguishing between explored and unexplored states or, more precisely, being able to access the unexplored states only, still requires one of the approaches discussed for the single-level case (Fig. 4). Since only local states are stored for each level, without repetition, we can no longer use the state array approach of Fig. 4(c). The other two methods, which involve maintaining a list of unexplored states, would only allow us to access nodes in trees at level $K - 1$, which are meaningless if we do not know the entire path from level 0. In other words, we would only know the last component of each unexplored state, but not the first $K - 1$ components. To obtain all the components, we must add a backward pointer from each node (conceptually, from each tree, since all the nodes in a given tree have the same previous components) to a node in the previous level, and so on. This additional memory overhead could be substantial.

With the single-level approach, then, we store $\mathcal{R} \cup \mathcal{U}$ in a single tree, using the state array described in Fig. 4(c). With the multilevel approach, instead, we store $\mathcal{R}$ and $\mathcal{U}$ separately. In this second case, states are truly deleted from $\mathcal{U}$. However, we are free to remove states in any order we choose. With AVL trees, we can always use the balance information to choose, at each level, a state in a leaf of the tree in such a way that no rebalancing is ever required.

Fig. 8 shows the number of bytes used to store $\mathcal{R}$ and $\mathcal{U}$ for our three models, using the single vs. the multilevel approach. The dashed boxes in Fig. 1 and 2 indicate the decomposition into submodels, in all cases $K = 4$.

The multilevel approach is clearly preferable, especially for large models. Indeed, we could not generate the state space using the single-level approach for $N = 6$ for the kanban-timed model, while we could using the multilevel approach (all our experiments where run on a Sun-clone with a 55 MhZ HyperSparc processor and 128 Mbyte of RAM, without making use of virtual memory).

5   Execution Time

Several factors need to be considered when studying the impact of our approach on the execution time. First, we explored possible differences due to using splay

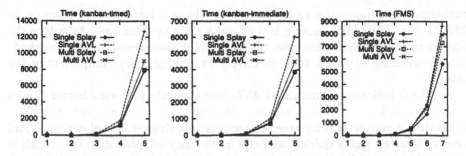

Fig. 9. Execution times (seconds) for splay vs. AVL trees, as a function of N.

trees vs. AVL trees. Fig. 9 shows that splay trees typically perform better than AVL trees. This is most likely due to the property of splay trees that recently inserted items are close to the root of the tree. In the case of multilevel trees, the difference between splay and AVL is not as great, since the trees at each level are relatively small. The effect of the peculiar splay tree behavior is further addressed in Section 5.1.

Next, we compare the differences due to using single-level vs. multilevel trees. The multilevel approach has many advantages.

Consider first the case when *BuildRS* searches for a state i not yet in the current $\mathcal{R}$ (the same discussion holds for $\mathcal{U}$). With a single-level tree, the search will stop only after reaching a leaf, hence $O(\log|\mathcal{R}|)$ comparisons are always performed. In the multilevel approach, instead, the search stops as soon as the substate $(i_1, \ldots, i_k)$ is not reachable, for some $k \leq K - 1$. If all the trees at a given level are of similar size, this will require at most $O(\log|\mathcal{R}_0^k|)$ comparisons. In practice, the situation is even more favorable, because, for any level $l < k$, the tree searched, which stores $\mathcal{R}^l(i_1, \ldots, i_{l-1})$, contains the substate i_l we are looking for, so the jump from level l to level $l + 1$ might occur before reaching a leaf.

If i is already in $\mathcal{R}$, instead, the search on the single-level tree will sometimes find i before reaching a leaf, but this is true also at each level of the multilevel approach, just as, in the previous case, for the levels $l < k$.

Perhaps even more important, though, regardless of whether i is already in the tree or not, is the complexity of each comparison. With the multilevel approach, only substates are compared, and these are normally small data structures. For GSPNs, this could be an array of 8 or 16 bit integers, one for each place in the sub-GSPN (memory usage is not an issue, since each local state for level k is stored only once). On the other hand, with the single-level approach, entire states are compared. If the states are stored as arrays, the comparison can stop as soon as one component differs in the two arrays. However, as the search progresses down the tree, we compare states that are increasingly close in lexical order, hence likely to have the same first few components; this implies that comparisons further away from the root tend to be more expensive.

Furthermore, storing states as full arrays is seldom advisable. For example, in SMART, a sophisticated packing is used, on a state-by-state base, to reduce the memory requirements. In this case, the state in the node needs to be "unpacked" before comparing it with i, thus effectively examining every component of the state.

As Fig. 9 indicates, a multilevel AVL tree typically performs better than a single-level AVL tree; while a single-level splay tree performs just as well or better than a multilevel splay tree. The ability of a single-level splay tree to find recently inserted states quickly and the inefficiency of splay deletion, which is required for the multilevel approach, are possible explanations for this difference.

5.1 Exploiting event locality

Our multilevel search tree has an additional advantage which can be exploited to further speed up execution. To illustrate the idea, we define two functions:

- $LocalSet(k, I_{k-1})$, which, given a submodel index k, $0 \le k < K$, and a pointer I_{k-1} to a reachable substate $(i_0, \ldots, i_{k-1}) \in \mathcal{R}_0^{k-1}$, returns a pointer to the tree containing the set $\mathcal{R}^k(i_0, \ldots, i_{k-1})$.
- $LocalIndex(k, I_{k-1}, i_k)$, which, given a submodel index k, $0 \le k < K$, a pointer I_{k-1} to a a reachable substate $(i_0, \ldots, i_{k-1}) \in \mathcal{R}_0^{k-1}$, and a local state index $i_k \in \mathcal{R}^k$, returns the pointer I_k to substate $(i_0, \ldots, i_k)$, if reachable, null otherwise.

Given our data structure, "a pointer I_k to a reachable substate $(i_0, \ldots, i_k) \in \mathcal{R}_0^k$" points to the node corresponding to the local state i_k in the tree containing the set $\mathcal{R}^k(i_0, \ldots, i_{k-1})$.

To find whether state i is in (the current) $\mathcal{R}$, we can then use a sequence of K function calls

$$LocalIndex(K-1, \underbrace{LocalIndex(K-2, \ldots LocalIndex(0, \text{null}, i_0), \ldots i_{K-2})}_{I_{K-2}}, i_{K-1}).$$

The overall cost of these K calls is exactly what we just discussed when comparing the single and multilevel approaches. However, if i is reachable and we now wanted to find the index of a state i' differing from i only in its last position, we could do so with a single call $LocalIndex(K-1, I_{K-2}, i'_{K-1})$, provided we saved the value I_{K-2}, the index of the reachable substate $(i_0, \ldots, i_{K-2})$. A similar argument applies to other values of k. Only for $k = 0$ do we need to perform an entirely new search.

We can then exploit this "locality" by considering the possible effects of the events on the state. Given $\hat{\mathcal{R}} = \mathcal{R}^0 \times \cdots \mathcal{R}^{K-1}$, we can partition $\mathcal{E}$ into $\mathcal{E}^0, \ldots, \mathcal{E}^{K-1}$, such that

$$e \in \mathcal{E}^k \Leftrightarrow \left(\forall i \in \hat{\mathcal{R}}, Active(e, i) = True \wedge j = New(e, i) \Rightarrow \forall l, 0 \le l < k, i_l = j_l \right),$$

that is, events in $\mathcal{E}^k$ can only change local states k or higher. For example, for GSPNs, this is achieved by assigning to $\mathcal{E}^k$ all the transitions whose enabling and firing effect on the state depends only on places in sub-GSPN k, and possibly in sub-GSPNs $k + 1$ through $K - 1$, but not in sub-GSPNs 1 through $k - 1$. This can be easily accomplished through an automatic inspection even in the presence of guards and inhibitor and variable cardinality arcs (although in this case the partition might be overly conservative, that is, it might assign a transition to a level k when it could have been assigned to a level greater than k).

When exploring state i in procedure *BuildRS*, we remove i from $\mathcal{U}$, we insert it into $\mathcal{R}$, and we record the sequence of pointers $I_{-1} = $ null, $I_0, \ldots, I_{K-2}$, to the reachable substates $(i_0), \ldots, (i_0, \ldots, i_{K-2})$. Then, we can examine the events in $\mathcal{E}$ in any order. As soon as we find an enabled event $e \in \mathcal{E}^k$, we generate $i' = New(e, i)$, and we are guaranteed that its components 0 through $k - 1$ are identical to those of i. Hence, we can search for it starting at I_{k-1}, that is, we only need to perform the $K - k$ calls

$$LocalIndex(K - 1, \ldots LocalIndex(k + 1, LocalIndex(k, I_{k-1}, i_k), i_{k+1}), \ldots, i_{K-1}).$$

The savings due to these accelerated searches depend on the particular model and the partition chosen for it. We show the results for our three models in Fig. 10. In the case of AVL trees, execution time savings of 20% are achieved, while the reduction is more modest, from 5 to 10%, for splay trees. Only in the FMS model does the single level approach (with splay trees) perform better that the multilevel approach with the exploitation of locality.

The comparatively good performance of the single level approach with splay trees can be attributed to our implementation choice of storing $\mathcal{R}$ and $\mathcal{U}$ separately in the multilevel approach, resulting in the lowest storage requirements, but higher overhead. We also observe that it is exactly the inherent properties of splay trees that make them perform well: after searching for a state i, searches for states lexicographically close to it will result in few comparisons. This achieves an effect similar to that obtained by locality, but only if the order of the events explored from state i is "lucky": if i reaches both i' and i'', and $i > i' > i''$, it is best if i' is searched before i''. We verified this intuition by generating random orderings in which the transitions in our three models are considered for exploration. In the case of the single level approach with splay trees, runtime variations were as high as 12%, while much smaller effects were observed in the other cases.

6 Conclusion

We have presented a detailed analysis of a multilevel data structure for storing and searching the large set of states reachable in some high-level model. Memory usage, which is normally the main concern, is greatly reduced. In some cases, this reduction is achieved not at the expense of, but in conjunction with, execution efficiency. A further technique based on event locality achieves an additional reduction in the execution time, at absolutely no cost in terms of memory. The results substantially increase the size of the reachability sets that can be managed.

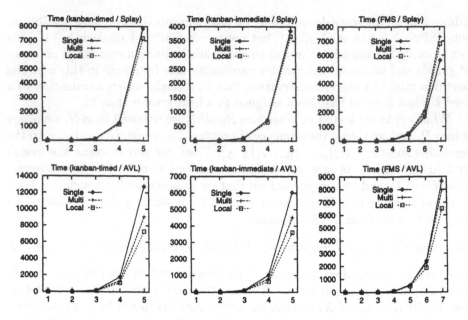

Fig. 10. Execution times (seconds) using splay or AVL trees, as a function of N.

In the future, we will investigate how to use our approach in a distributed fashion, where N cooperating processes explore different portions of the reachability set. In particular, we plan to apply the data structure we presented and to explore ways to balance the load among the cooperating processes automatically.

References

1. G. Chiola. Compiling techniques for the analysis of stochastic Petri nets. In *Proc. 4th Int. Conf. on Modelling Techniques and Tools for Performance Evaluation*, pages 13–27, 1989.
2. G. Ciardo and M. Tilgner. On the use of Kronecker operators for the solution of generalized stochastic Petri nets. ICASE Report 96-35, Institute for Computer Applications in Science and Engineering, Hampton, VA, 1996.
3. G. Ciardo and K. S. Trivedi. A decomposition approach for stochastic reward net models. *Perf. Eval.*, 18(1):37–59, 1993.
4. T. H. Cormen, C. E. Leiserson, and R. L. Rivest. *Introduction to algorithms*. The MIT Press, Cambridge, MA, 1990.
5. D. E. Knuth. *Sorting and Searching*. Addison-Wesley, Reading, MA, 1973.

An Efficient Disk-Based Tool for Solving Very Large Markov Models

Daniel D. Deavours and William H. Sanders*

Center for Reliable and High-Performance Computing
Coordinated Science Laboratory
University of Illinois at Urbana-Champaign
{deavours,whs}@crhc.uiuc.edu

Abstract. Very large Markov models often result when modeling realistic computer systems and networks. We describe a new tool for solving large Markov models on a typical engineering workstation. This tool does not require any special properties or a particular structure in the model, and it requires only slightly more memory than what is necessary to hold the solution vector itself. It uses a disk to hold the state-transition-rate matrix, a variant of block Gauss-Seidel as the iterative solution method, and an innovative implementation that involves two parallel processes: the first process retrieves portions of the iteration matrix from disk, and the second process does repeated computation on small portions of the matrix. We demonstrate its use on two realistic models: a Kanban manufacturing system and the Courier protocol stack, which have up to 10 million states and about 100 million nonzero entries. The tool can solve the models efficiently on a workstation with 128 Mbytes of memory and 4 Gbytes of disk.

1 Introduction

A wide variety of high-level specification techniques now exist for Markov models. These include, among others, stochastic Petri nets, stochastic process algebras, various types of block diagrams, and non-product form queuing networks. In most cases, very large Markov models result when one tries to model realistic systems using these specification techniques. The Markov models are typically quite sparse (adjacent to few nodes), but contain a large number of states. This problem is known as the "largeness problem." Techniques that researchers have developed to deal with the largeness problem fall into two general categories: those that avoid the large state space (for example, by lumping,) and those that tolerate the large state space (for example, by recognizing that the model has a special structure and storing it in a compact form). While many largeness avoidance and tolerance techniques exist, few are applicable to models without special structure. Methods are sorely needed that permit the solution of very large Markov models without requiring them to have special properties or a particular structure.

* This work was supported, in part, by NASA Grant NAG 1-1782.

In this paper, we describe a new tool for solving Markov models with very large state spaces on a typical engineering workstation. The tool makes no assumptions about the underlying structure of the Markov process, and requires little more memory than that necessary to hold the solution vector itself. It uses a disk to hold the state-transition-rate matrix, a variant of block Gauss-Seidel as the iterative solution method, and an innovative two-process implementation that effectively overlaps retrieval of blocks of the state-transition-rate matrix from disk and computation on the retrieved blocks. The tool can solve models with ten million states and about 100 million transitions on a machine with 128 Mbytes of main memory. The state-transition-rate matrix is stored on disk in a clever manner, minimizing overhead in retrieving it from disk. In addition, the tool employs a dynamic scheme for determining the number of iterations to perform on a block before beginning on the next, which we show empirically to provide a near optimum time to convergence. Solution time is typically quick even for very large models, with only about 20% of the CPU time spent retrieving blocks from disk and 80% of the CPU resources available to perform the required computation.

In addition to describing the architecture and implementation of the tool itself, we illustrate its use on two realistic models: one of a Kanban manufacturing system [2], and another of the Courier protocol stack executing on a VME bus-based multiprocessor [14]. Both models have appeared before in the literature, and are excellent examples of models that have very large state spaces for realistic system parameter values. In particular, both models have been used to illustrate the use of recently developed Kronecker-based methods [2, 7], and the Courier protocol has been used to illustrate an approximate method based on lumping [14]. Both numerical results and solution times are presented for each model and, when possible, compared to previously obtained values and solution times. In each case we can obtain an exact solution (to the desired precision) in significantly less time than previously reported using Kronecker-based methods. It is thus our belief that if sufficient disk space is available to hold the state-transition-rate matrix, our approach is the method of choice for exact solutions.

The remainder of the paper is organized as follows. First, in Section 2, we address issues in the choice of a solution method for very large Markov models, comparing three alternatives: Kronecker-based methods (e.g., [7, 2]), "on-the-fly" methods [3], and the disk-based method that we ultimately choose. This section presents clear arguments for the desirability of disk-based methods if sufficient disk space is available. Section 3 then describes the architecture and implementation of the tool, describing solutions to issues we faced in building a practical implementation. Finally, Section 4 presents the results of the use of the tool on the two models described earlier.

2   The Case for Disk-Based Methods

For our tool implementation, we considered three numerical solution techniques for tolerating large state spaces: Kronecker-based techniques, "on-the-fly" tech-

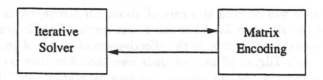

Fig. 1. Solution paradigm.

niques, and disk-based techniques. To evaluate each method, we introduce a paradigm based on Figure 1. Here, we divide the numerical solution process into the iterative solver and the matrix encoding. The key to solving large matrices is to encode the matrix so that it takes little main memory (RAM), but still allows quick access to matrix elements. The iterative solver is thus a data consumer, and the matrix encoder is a data producer. We would like for both to be as fast as possible to obtain a solution quickly. An additional important factor is how effectively a particular iterative method uses the data it consumes. For example, certain iterative methods, such as Gauss-Seidel [12] and adaptive Gauss-Seidel [5], typically do more effective work with the same number of accesses to the matrix as Jacobi or the Power method, and hence do not require as high a data production rate to efficiently obtain a solution. We want to find a fast but general matrix encoding scheme and an effective iterative method with a low data consumption rate.

The first class of encoding schemes we consider are those of Kronecker-based methods. These methods require and make use of the fact that in certain models, particular parts of the model (called submodels) interact with one another in a limited way. One way to insure a model has this structure is to construct it according to a prescribed set of rules from smaller models, as is done, for example, in the case of stochastic automata networks [12]. If one follows these rules, one may easily express the transition rate matrix for the entire model as a function of Kronecker operators on the transition rate matrices of the submodels.

More recently there has been work on a type of model decomposition called superposed generalized stochastic Petri nets (SGSPNS) [1, 2, 4, 6, 7]. SGSPNs are essentially independent models that may be joined by synchronization of a transition. We believe [2] to be the state of the art in Kronecker operator methods, and although the more recent techniques can solve a much larger class of models than originally proposed in [4], they are still restrictive in the models that they can effectively solve.

To evaluate the speed of the Kronecker operator methods, we observe rates in which the iterative solver and matrix encoding operate. We have observed that on our computer (120 MHz Hewlett-Packard Model C110), the SOR iterative solver can consume data at a rate of about 50 Mbyte/second. From numbers published by Kemper [7], we estimate that his implementation of the Kronecker-based method can produce data at a rate of 700 Kbyte/second on an 85 MHz Sparc 4, and we extrapolate that the rate would be about 2 Mbyte/second on our HP C110. Since both the data production and consumption require the CPU, the whole process will proceed at a rate of about 1.9 Mbyte/second. Kemper's method is also restricted to Jacobi or the Power method, which usually exhibit poor convergence characteristics, so the effectiveness of its use of generated data is low. Ciardo and Tilgner [2] present their own tool, but they do not present data in such a way that we can analyze the data generation rate. We can compare actual times to solution for their benchmark model, however, and do so in Section 4. Ciardo gives algorithms to perform Gauss-Seidel on a Kronecker representation in [1], but has not yet built a tool with which we can compare our approach.

The second class of encoding schemes we considered for implementation in this tool are "on-the-fly" methods introduced in [3]. On-the-fly methods have none of the structural restrictions of Kronecker-based methods, and they can operate on nets with general enabling predicate and state change functions, such as are present in stochastic activity networks [9, 10]. In addition, they can obtain a solution with little additional memory, or perhaps even less memory than needed by SGSPN solvers, while at the same time using Gauss-Seidel or variants. However, the prototype implementation described in [3] generates data at about 440 Kbyte/second on a HP C110. Although [3] introduces iterative methods that are usually more effective than Jacobi or the Power method in their use of data, the overall solution speed for these methods will be somewhat slower than for Kronecker-based methods, but still reasonable, given that they can be used without restrictions on the structure of a model.

The final class we considered was that of disk-based methods, where the workstation disk holds an encoding of the state-transition matrix. If we can find an iterative method that accesses data from the state-transition-rate matrix in a regular way and use a clever encoding, disks can deliver data to an iterative algorithm at a high rate (5 Mbyte/second or higher) with low CPU overhead. Furthermore, high performance disks are inexpensive relative to the cost of RAM, so we would like to find a way to utilize disks effectively. Experimental results show that if we can do both disk I/O and computation in parallel, we can perform Gauss-Seidel at a rate of 5 Mbyte/second while using the CPU only 30% of the time. Thus disk-based methods have the potential to greatly outperform Kronecker and on-the-fly methods, at the cost of providing a disk that is large enough to hold the state-transition-rate matrix of the Markov model being solved. The challenge is to find a more effective solution method that has a data consumption rate of about 5 Mbytes/second at 80% CPU utilization.

Clearly, the method of choice depends on the nature of the model being solved, and the hardware available for the solution. If the state-transition-rate matrix is too large to fit on available disk space and the model meets the requirements of Kronecker-based methods, then they should be used. If the model does not fit on disk and does not meet the requirements of Kronecker-based methods, on-the-fly methods should be used. However, SCSI disks are inexpensive relative to RAM (in September 1996, approximately $1400 for 4 Gbyte fast wide SCSI), so space may inexpensively be made available to store the state-transition-rate matrix. Since a single disk can provide the high data production rate only for sequential disk access, the efficiency of disk-based methods will depend on whether we can find a solution algorithm that can make effective use of the data in the sequential manner. We discuss how to do this in the following sections.

3 Tool Architecture and Implementation

In this section, we discuss the architecture of our tool and its implementation on an HP workstation. In particular, we discuss the basic block Gauss-Seidel (BGS) algorithm and how it maps onto a program or set of programs that run on a workstation. An important issue we solve is how to effectively do computation and disk I/O in parallel. We develop a flexible implementation with many tunable parameters that can vary widely on different hardware platforms and models.

The mathematics of BGS is generally well known (see [12], for example). We wish to solve for the steady state probability vector π given by $\pi Q = 0$. To review BGS briefly, partition the state-transition-rate matrix Q into $N \times N$ submatrices of (roughly) the same size, labeled Q_{ij}. BGS then solves

$$\Pi_i^{(k+1)} Q_{ii} = - \left(\sum_{j=1}^{i-1} \Pi_j^{(k+1)} Q_{ji} + \sum_{j=i+1}^{N} \Pi_j^{(k)} Q_{ji} \right) \tag{1}$$

for Π_i for i ranging from 1 to N, where Π_i is the corresponding subvector of π. This is called the k-th BGS *iteration*. Solving for Π_i can be done by any method; our tool uses (point) Gauss-Seidel. One Gauss-Seidel iteration to solve (1) is called an *inner* iteration, and solving (1) for $1 \le i \le n$ is an *outer* iteration.

The sequential algorithm for a single BGS iteration follows directly. In particular, let $r \in \mathcal{R}^n$ be an auxiliary variable.

$$
\begin{aligned}
&\text{for } i = 1 \text{ to } N \\
&\quad r = 0 \\
&\quad \text{for } j = 1 \text{ to } N | j \ne i \\
&\quad\quad r = r - \Pi_j Q_{ji} \\
&\quad \text{Solve } \Pi_i Q_{ii} = r \text{ for } \Pi_i
\end{aligned}
$$

One can easily see that the access to Q is very predictable, so we may have blocks of Q ordered on disk in the same way that the program accesses them. This way the program accesses the file representing Q sequentially entirely throughout an iteration. One could then easily write an implementation of BGS and a utility to write Q appropriately to a file. What is not trivial is to build a tool that overlaps computation (the solution of $\Pi_i Q_{ii} = r$) and reading from disk in a flexible, efficient way.

Tool Architecture Our solution to this is to have two cooperating processes, one of which schedules disk I/O, and the other of which does computation. Obviously, they must communicate and synchronize activity. We use System V interprocess communication mechanisms since they are widely available and simple to use.

For synchronization, we use semaphores, and for passing messages, such as a block of Q, we use shared memory. We call the process that schedules I/O the *I/O process*, and we call the process that solves $\Pi_i Q_{ii} = r$ the *compute process*. To minimize memory usage, we want to have as few blocks of Q in memory at one time as possible, so we must be careful how we compute the step $r = r - \Pi_j Q_{ji}$, $\forall j \neq i$. For simplicity, we assign the task of computing r to the I/O process.

We first looked at several large matrices that were generated by GSPN models. (We looked at GSPNs because they can easily create large transition rate matrices, not because our solution technique is limited to them.) We noticed that the matrix is usually very banded; that is, for reasonable choices for N, the number of non-zero elements in the blocks $Q_{i,j} : |i - j| > 1$ is small, if not zero. By lumping all the blocks in a column into a smaller number (three) of larger blocks, we can eliminate the overhead of reading small or empty blocks. For the i-th column, we call $Q_{i,i}$ the *diagonal* block; $Q_{i-1,i}$ is the *conflict* block; all other blocks are lumped into a single block that we call the *off* block. We use the term *off block* because it includes all the off diagonal blocks except the conflict block. Let D represent the diagonal block, C the conflict block, and O the off block. The following represents a matrix where $N = 4$.

$$\begin{pmatrix} \begin{array}{c|c|c} D & O & C \\ \hline C & D & O \\ \hline O & C & D & O \\ \hline & O & C & D \end{array} \end{pmatrix}^T$$

The reason we have a conflict block will be apparent soon.

Lumping several blocks into the off block complicates 1), but does not require any extra computation. The actual mechanics of the computation of $\Pi Q_{\text{off},i}$ are no different than for the computation of $\Pi_j Q_{ji}$. For the formula $r = \Pi Q_{\text{off},i}$, we compute $r = \sum_{k \neq i, i-1} \Pi_k Q_{ki}$. We may now compute r the following way:

$$r = -\Pi Q_{\text{off},i}$$
$$r = r - \Pi_{i-1} Q_{\text{conflict},i}$$

Let us denote $r_i = \Pi_i Q_{ii}$ to distinguish between different r vectors. In order to make the computation and disk I/O in parallel, the program must solve $\Pi_i Q_{ii} = r_i$ while at the same time compute r_{i+1}. Therefore, while the compute process is solving $\Pi_i Q_{ii} = r_i$, the I/O process is prefetching $Q_{i+1,i+1}$, and reading $Q_{\text{off},i+1}$ and $Q_{\text{conflict},i+1}$ to compute r_{i+1}. Notice that when computing r_{i+1}, we need the most recent value of Π_i to multiply by $Q_{\text{conflict},i}$, which introduces a data dependency. Thus, we can not completely compute r_{i+1} while in parallel computing Π_i. (We could also use a less recent value of Π_i, but that would reduce the effectiveness of BGS.)

Finally, we add synchronization to ensure that the I/O process has the most recent version of Π_i to compute r_{i+1}. The full algorithm we use is presented in Figure 2. We used a large, shared memory array to represent the steady state probability vector Π, two shared diagonal block buffers Q_{diag0} and Q_{diag1}, and

Shared variables: Π, Q_{diag0}, Q_{diag1}, r_0, r_1
Semaphores: S_1 locked, S_2 unlocked

Compute Process	*I/O Process*
Local variable (unshared): t	Local variable (unshared): t, Q_{tmp}
$t = 0$	$t = 0$
while not converged	do forever
for $i = 1$ to N	for $i = 1$ to N
Lock(S_1)	$Q_{\text{diag}t} = $ disk read(Q_{ii})
for $j = 1$ to *MinIter*	$Q_{\text{tmp}} = $ disk read($Q_{\text{off},i}$)
Do GS iteration: $\Pi_i Q_{\text{diag}t} = r_t$	$r_t = -\Pi Q_{\text{tmp}}$
$j = MinIter + 1$	$Q_{\text{tmp}} = $ disk read($Q_{\text{conflict},i}$)
while $j \leq MaxIter$ and	Lock(S_2)
I/O process not blocked on S_2	$r_t = r_t - \Pi_{i-1} Q_{\text{tmp}}$
Do GS iteration: $\Pi_i Q_{\text{diag}t} = r_t$	Unlock(S_1)
$j = j + 1$	$t = \bar{t}$
Unlock(S_2)	
$t = \bar{t}$	

Fig. 2. Compute and I/O processes for BGS algorithm.

two r vectors r_0 and r_1. The processes share two diagonal block and r variables so that one can be used to compute (1) while the other one is being prepared for the next computation. The processes also share two locking variables, S_1 and S_2, which they use to communicate and control the relative progress of the other process.

Compute Process We first explain the compute process. A local variable t alternates between 0 and 1, which indicates which of the two shared block and r variables the process should use. After each step, t is alternated between 0 and 1, which we denote $t = \bar{t}$. The function Lock(S_1) will lock S_1 if S_1 is unlocked. If S_1 is already locked, it will block until S_1 is unlocked (by the I/O process); then it will lock S_1 and proceed. While the compute process is blocked on S_1, it uses no CPU resources.

The compute process has two parameters, *MinIter* and *MaxIter*. The compute process is guaranteed to do at least *MinIter* Gauss-Seidel inner iterations to approximately solve (1). Then the compute process will proceed to do up to *MaxIter* iterations or until the I/O process is complete with the current file I/O and is waiting for the compute process to unlock S_2, whichever comes first. This allows the compute process to do a dynamic number of Gauss-Seidel iterations, depending on how long the I/O process takes to do file I/O. We ignore the boundary conditions in the figures for simplicity. If $i - 1 = 0$, for example, then we use N for $i - 1$ instead.

The convergence criterion we use in this tool is a modification to the $||\pi^{(k+1)} - \pi^{(k)}||_\infty$ criterion. In particular, we compute $||\Pi_i^{(k+1)} - \Pi_i^{(k)}||_\infty$ for the *first* inner iteration and take the $\max_i ||\Pi_i^{(k+1)} - \Pi_i^{(k)}||_\infty$ to be the number we use to test for convergence. We use this for two reasons: the first inner iteration usually results in the greatest change of Π_i, so computing the norm for all inner iterations is usually wasteful, and the computation of the norm takes a significant amount of time. We have observed experimentally that this measured norm is at least as good as the the $||\pi^{(k+1)} - \pi^{(k)}||_\infty$ criterion.

The dynamic nature of the iteration count is an interesting feature of this tool. If the system on which the program is running is doing other file I/O and slowing the I/O process down, the compute process may continue to proceed to do useful work. At some point, however, additional Gauss-Seidel iterations may not be useful at all, presumably after *MaxIter* inner iterations, so the process will stop doing work and block waiting for S_1 to become unlocked. Choosing a good *MinIter* and *MaxIter* is difficult and requires some knowledge about the characteristics of the transition rate matrix. If we allow the compute process to be completely dynamic, some blocks may consistently get fewer inner iterations and converge more slowly than other blocks, causing the whole system to converge slowly. In Section 4, we show some experimental results of varying these parameters.

Input/Output Process The I/O process is straightforward. The greatest complexity comes in managing the semaphores properly. This is a case of the classical producer-consumer or bounded buffer problem, and we defer the reader to [13] or a similar text on operating systems to show the motivation and correctness of this technique. The primary purpose of the I/O process is to schedule disk reads and compute r_t. It does this by issuing a C function to read portions of the file directly into the shared block variable or the temporary block variable. Because the I/O process may execute in parallel with the compute process, the I/O process may issue read requests concurrently with the computation, and since file I/O uses little CPU (under 20%), we can effectively parallelize computation and file I/O on a modern, single-processor workstation.

This implementation of BGS uses relatively little memory. The size of the steady state probability vector Π is proportional to the number of states, which is unavoidable using BGS or any other exact method. Other iteration methods, such as Jacobi, require additional vectors of the same size as Π, which our program avoids. Two diagonal blocks, Q_{diag0} and Q_{diag1}, are necessary; the compute process requires one block to do the inner iteration, and the I/O process reads the next diagonal block at the same time. Two r variables are also required for the same reason. Finally, the I/O process requires a temporary variable Q_{tmp} to hold Q_{off} and Q_{conflict}. We could eliminate Q_{tmp} by instead using Q_{diagt}, but doing so would require us to reverse the order in which we read the blocks, causing us to read Q_{diagt} last. This would reduce the amount of time we could overlap computation and file I/O. We chose to maximize parallelization of computation at the expense of a modest amount of memory.

N	States	NZ Entries	Size (MB)	e_1	e_2	e_3	e_4	τ
1	160	616	0.008	0.90742	0.67136	0.67136	0.35538	0.09258
2	4,600	28,128	0.34	1.81006	1.32851	1.32851	0.76426	0.17387
3	58,400	446,400	5.3	2.72211	1.94348	1.94348	1.52460	0.23307
4	454,475	3,979,850	47	3.64641	2.51298	2.51298	1.50325	0.27589
5	2,546,432	24,460,416	290	4.58301	3.03523	3.03523	1.81096	0.30712
6	11,261,376	115,708,992	1,367	5.53098	3.50975	3.50975	2.07460	0.33010

Table 1. Characteristics and reward variables for the Kanban model.

4 Results

To better understand the algorithms presented in the previous section, we implemented them and tested the resulting tool on several large models presented in the literature. We present the models here and discuss the performance measures we took in order to better understand the issues in building and using a tool to solve large matrices, so we are not so interested here in the results of the models as much as using the models to understand the characteristics of our solver. All the solutions we present here, with the exception of one, can be solved on our HP workstation with 128 Mbyte of RAM (without using virtual memory) and 4 Gbyte of fast disk memory.

Kanban Model The Kanban model we present was previously used by Ciardo and Tilgner [1, 2] to illustrate a Kronecker-based approach. They chose this model because it has many of the characteristics that are ideal for superposed GSPN solution techniques, and it also does not require any mapping from the product space to the tangible reachable states. We refer to [2] for a description of the model and specification of the rates in the model. Briefly, the model is composed of four subnets. At each subnet, a token enters, spends some time, and exits or restarts with certain probabilities. Once the token leaves the first subnet, it may enter the second or third subnet, and to leave the system, the token must go through the fourth subnet. We chose to solve the model where the synchronizing transitions are timed transitions.

Table 1 shows some information about the model and the corresponding transition rate matrix. Here, N represents the maximum number of tokens that may be in a subnet at one time. There are two important variables that we may vary, the number of blocks and the number of inner iterations, that greatly affect performance. We present two experiments. First, we vary the number of blocks while keeping the number of inner iterations fixed, and second, we vary the number of inner iterations while keeping the number of blocks fixed.

For the first experiment, we use the Kanban model where $N = 5$. We divide the transition rate matrix into 32×3 blocks, and perform a constant number of inner iterations. We vary the number of inner iterations from 1 to 20. The results of the solution execution time and the number of BGS iterations are shown in the top two graphs in Figure 3. All the timing measurements that we present in this paper are "wall clock" times. The plots show the time to achieve three levels of accuracy based on the modified $||\Pi^{(k+1)} - \Pi^{(k)}||_\infty < \{10^{-6}, 10^{-9}, 10^{-12}\}$ convergence criterion explained in Section 3.

Figure 3 shows how doing an increased number of inner iterations yields diminishing returns, so that doing more than about 7 inner iterations does not significantly help reduce the number of BGS iterations. For this model, setting *MaxIter* to 6 or 7 makes sense. It also shows that the optimal number of inner iterations with respect to execution time is 4. For fewer than four inner iterations, the compute process spends time idle and waiting for the I/O process. This leads us to choose *MinIter* to be 3 or 4.

It is interesting to note that solving this model with a dynamic number of inner iterations takes 10,436 seconds, which is more time than is required if we fix the number of inner iterations to be 3, 4, or 5 (10269, 10044, and 10252 seconds respectively). We observed that some blocks always receive 4 or fewer inner iterations, while others always receive 7 or more. This shows us several important things. First, some blocks always receive more iterations than others, and we know that the solution vector will converge only as fast as its slowest converging component. Second, we argued above that doing more than 7 inner iterations is wasteful, so allowing the number of inner iterations to be fully dynamic is wasteful since the I/O process does not read data quickly enough to keep the compute node doing useful work. Finally, if the compute process is always doing inner iterations, it checks to see if the I/O process is blocked on S_2 only after completing an inner iteration. This requires the I/O process to always block on S_2 and wait for the compute process to complete its inner iteration, which is wasteful since the I/O process is the slower of the two processes.

For the next experiment, we set the number of inner iterations to be 5, vary the number of blocks, and observe convergence rate, execution time, and memory usage. The bottom two plots of Figure 3 range the number of blocks from 8 to 64 and plot execution time and number of iterations respectively for the convergence criteria $||\Pi^{(k+1)} - \Pi^{(k)}||_\infty < \{10^{-6}, 10^{-9}, 10^{-12}\}$. Table 2 shows how memory usage varies with the number of blocks. Notice that between 8 and 64 blocks, the execution time is nearly double while the memory usage is about one third. We see that there is clearly a memory/speed tradeoff. Note that the solution vector for a 2.5 million state model alone takes about 20 Megabytes of memory.

Finally, as a basis for comparison, we present results given in [2] in Table 3 and compare the solution times to those of our tool. The column titled 'Case 1' represents the tool in [2] with mapping from the product space to tangible reachable states enabled, while 'Case 2' is with no mapping (an idealized case). Cases 1 and 2 are performed on a Sony NWS-5000 workstation with 90 MB of memory. We present no results for $N = 1, 2, 3$ because the matrix was so small that the operating systems buffered the entire file in memory. In addition to computing the reward variables (see Table 1) for the Kanban model to greater accuracy than [2], we were also able to solve for the case where $N = 6$.

Courier Protocol Model The second model we examine is a model of the Courier protocol given in [8, 14]. This is a model of an existing software network protocol stack that has been implemented on a Sun workstation and on a VME bus-

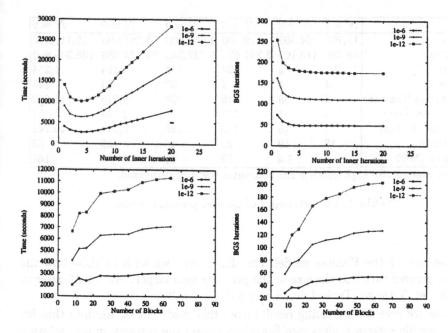

Fig. 3. Performance graphs of Kanban model ($N = 5$).

N	Memory (MB)
8	95
12	71
16	59
24	48
32	40
40	37
48	35
56	33
64	32

Table 2. Number of blocks versus memory.

N	Case 1	Case 2	BGS time	No. Blocks	Memory
1	1 s	1s	-	-	-
2	13 s	2 s	-	-	-
3	310 s	2 s	-	-	-
4	4,721 s	856 s	225 s	4	28 MB
5	22,215 s	6,055 s	2,342 s	16	59 MB
6	-	-	18,563 s	128	111 MB

Table 3. Comparison of performance.

based multiprocessor. The model is well specified in [8, 14]. The GSPN models only a one-way data flow through the network. For our experiment, we are only interested in varying the window size N. The transport space and fragmentation ratio is kept at one. Varying N corresponds to initially placing N tokens in a place, and it has a substantial impact on the state space size!

Table 4 shows the characteristics of the model. The column 'Matrix Size' contains the size of the matrix in megabytes if the matrix were to be kept entirely in memory. One can see that this transition-rate matrix is less dense

	$N = 1$	$N = 2$	$N = 3$	$N = 4$	$N = 5$	$N = 6$
States	11,700	84,600	419,400	1,632,600	5,358,600	15,410,250
Nonzero	48,330	410,160	2,281,620	9,732,330	34,424,280	105,345,900
Matrix	0.6	5	28	118	414	1,264
Blocks	4	4	4	32	64	128
Generation Time (s)	5	38	218	938	3,716	11,600
Conversion Time (s)	3	24	136	581	2,076	*14,482
Solution Time (s)	2	16	143	1,138	6,040	20,742
Iterations	18	19	23	49	69	85
Memory (MB)	0.4	3.4	18	21	57	144

(*) Time abnormally high because the computer was not dedicated.

Table 4. Characteristics of Courier protocol model.

than the one for the Kanban model. For this model, we wish to show how the solution process varies as the size of the problem gets larger. We set *MaxIter* to be 6 and let N range. Table 4 summarizes these results.

There are several interesting results from this study. First, we note that for $N < 3$, the file system buffers significantly decrease the conversion and solution times, so they should not be considered as part of a trend. More traditional techniques would probably do as well or better for such small models. For $N \geq 3$, the model becomes interesting. We wrote our own GSPN state generator for these models, and it was optimized for memory (so we could generate large models), not for speed. It was also designed to be compatible with the *UltraSAN* solvers and reward variable specification. The conversion time is the time it took to convert the Q-matrix in *UltraSAN*'s format to one used by the tool, which involves taking the transpose of Q and converting from an ASCII to binary floating point representation. The conversion time shown for $N = 6$ is the wall clock time, but it is abnormally large since it was not run in a dedicated environment. We estimate from the user time that the conversion process would take about 7,000 seconds on a dedicated system.

The data gives us a rough idea about the relative performance of each step in the solution process. The conversion process takes between half and two thirds the generation time. We believe that much of the conversion time is spent translating an ASCII representation of a real number into the computer's internal representation. The solution times are the times to reach the convergence criterion $||\Pi_i^{(k+1)} - \Pi_i^{(k)}||_\infty < 10^{-12}$ described above, and are roughly twice the generation times. This shows that the solution process does not take a disproportionate amount of time more than the state generation or conversion process.

Another interesting observation of this model is that in the case where $N = 6$, the transition-rate matrix generated by the GSPN state generator (a sparse textual representation of the matrix) would be larger than 2 Gbytes, which is larger than the maximum allowable file size on our workstation. To solve this system, we rounded the rates to 6 decimal places. This obviously affects the accuracy of the solutions. There are obvious and simple ways to use multiple

	$N=1$	$N=2$	$N=3$	$N=4$	$N=5$	$N=6$
λ	74.3467	120.372	150.794	172.011	187.413	198.919
P_{send}	0.01011	0.01637	0.02051	0.02334	0.02549	0.02705
P_{recv}	0.98141	0.96991	0.96230	0.95700	0.95315	0.95027
P_{sess1}	0.00848	0.01372	0.01719	0.01961	0.02137	0.02268
P_{sess2}	0.92610	0.88029	0.84998	0.82883	0.81345	0.80197
$P_{transp1}$	0.78558	0.65285	0.56511	0.50392	0.45950	0.42632
$P_{transp2}$	0.78871	0.65790	0.57138	0.51084	0.46673	0.43365

Table 5. Reward variables for Courier protocol model.

files to avoid this problem; we simply state this observation to give the reader
a feel for the size of the data that the tool is manipulating. Also, of the 144
Mbytes necessary to compute the solution, 118 Mbytes of it are needed just to
hold the solution vector.

In Table 5 we show several of several of the reward variables in the model as
N varies from 1 to 6. The λ we compute here corresponds to measuring λ_{lsp} in the
model, which corresponds to the user's message throughput rate. The measures
λ_{frg} can easily be computed as $\lambda_{frg} = \lambda q_1/q_2$. Similarly, $\lambda_{ack} = \lambda_{lsp} + \lambda_{frg}$. From
this, we can see how the packet throughput rate (λ) increases as the window size
increases. Other reward variables are explained in [8], and they correspond to the
fraction of time different parts of the system are busy. We note that the values
we computed here differ from those Li found by approximate techniques [8, 14].
We suspect that Li used a fragmentation ratio in his approximation techniques
that is different (and unpublished) from the ratio for which he gives "exact"
solutions because we were able to reproduce the exact solutions.

5 Conclusion

We have described a new tool for solving Markov models with very large state
spaces. By devising a method to efficiently store the state-transition-rate matrix
on disk, overlap computation and data transfer on a standard workstation, and
utilize an iterative solver that exhibits locality in its use of data, we are able to
build a tool that requires little more memory than the solution vector itself to
obtain a solution. This method is completely general to any model for which one
can derive a state-transition-rate matrix. As illustrated in the paper, the tool can
solve models with 10 million states and 100 million non-zero entries on a machine
with only 128 Mbytes of main memory. Because we make use of an innovative
implementation using two processes that communicate via shared memory, we
are able to keep the compute process utilizing the CPU approximately 80% of
the time.

In addition to describing the tool, we have illustrated its use on two large-
scale models: a Kanban manufacturing system and the Courier protocol stack
executing on a VME bus-based multiprocessor. For each model, we present detailed results concerning the time and space requirements for solutions so that

our tool may be compared with existing and future tools. The results show that the speed of solution is much faster than those reported for implementations based on Kronecker operators. These results show that our approach is the current method of choice for solving large Markov models if sufficient disk space is available to hold the state-transition rate matrix.

References

1. G. Ciardo, "Advances in compositional approaches based on Kronecker algebra: Application to the study of manufacturing systems," in *Third International Workshop on Performability Modeling of Computer and Communication Systems*, Bloomingdale, IL, Sept. 7–8, 1996.
2. G. Ciardo and M. Tilgner, "On the use of Kronecker operators for the solution of generalized stochastic Petri nets," ICASE Report #96-35 CR-198336, NASA Langley Research Center, May 1996.
3. D. D. Deavours and W. H. Sanders, " 'On-the-fly' solution techniques for stochastic Petri nets and extensions," to appear in *Petri Nets and Performance Models*, 1997.
4. S. Donatelli, "Superposed generalized stochastic Petri nets: Definition and efficient solution," in R. Valette, editor, *Application and Theory of Petri Nets 1994, Lecture Notes in computer science 815 (Proc. 15th Int. Conf. on Application and Theory of Petri Nets, Zaragoza, Spain)*, pp. 258–277, Springer-Verlag, June 1994.
5. G. Horton, "Adaptive Relaxation for the Steady-State Analysis of Markov Chains," ICASE Report #94-55 NASA CR-194944, NASA Langley Research Center, June 1994.
6. P. Kemper, "Numerical analysis of superposed GSPNs," in *Proc. Int. Workshop on Petri Nets and Performance Models (PNPM'95)*, pp. 52–61, Durham, NC, Oct. 1995. IEEE Comp. Soc. Press.
7. P. Kemper, "Numerical Analysis of Superposed GSPNs," in *IEEE Transactions on Software Engineering*, 1996, to appear.
8. Y. Li, "Solution Techniques for Stochastic Petri Nets," Ph.D. Dissertation, Department of Systems and Computer Engineering, Carleton University, Ottawa, Ontario, May 1992.
9. J. F. Meyer, A. Movaghar, and W. H. Sanders, "Stochastic activity networks: Structure, behavior, and application," In *Proc. International Workshop on Timed Petri Nets*, pp. 106–115, Torino, Italy, July 1985.
10. A. Movaghar and J. F. Meyer, "Performability modeling with stochastic activity networks," In *Proc. 1984 Real-Time Systems Symp.*, Austin, TX, December 1984.
11. W. H. Sanders, W. D. Obal II, M. A. Qureshi, F. K. Widjanarko, "The *UltraSAN* modeling environment," in *Performance Evaluation*, pp. 89–115, Vol. 24, 1995.
12. W. J. Stewart, "Introduction to the Numerical Solution of Markov Chains," Princeton University Press, 1994.
13. A. S. Tanenbaum, *Modern Operating Systems*, Prentice Hall, 1992.
14. C. M. Woodside and Y. Li, "Performance Petri Net Analysis of Communications Protocol Software by Delay-Equivalent Aggregation," in *Proc. Fourth Int. Workshop on Petri Nets and Performance Models*, pp. 64–73, Melbourne, Australia, Dec. 2–5, 1991.

Efficient Transient Overload Tests for Real-Time Systems

Guillem Bernat[1], Alan Burns[2] and Albert Llamosí[3]

[1] Dept. Matemàtiques i Informàtica, Univ. de les Illes Balears, Spain
[2] Dept. Computer Science. Univ. of York, England
[3] Dept. Enginyeria Informàtica, Univ. Rovira i Virgili, Tarragona, Spain
e-mail: dmigbn0@ps.uib.es burns@minster.york.ac.uk
allamosi@etse.urv.es

Abstract. Timing requirements of real-time systems are usually specified in terms of deadlines which are often classified as being either *hard, firm* or *soft*. A hard task must always meet its deadline while a soft or firm one can occasionally miss them. When a task may miss a deadline, traditional scheduling tests do not provide information on the number of deadlines the task may miss. It may just miss a single deadline or may not meet a deadline at all. In this paper we introduce the *any n* in *m* and *row n* in *m* temporal constraints to model the transient overload a task may suffer. They express that in *m* consecutive invocations there are at least *n* deadlines met in any order or in a row. With these temporal constraints we can capture both hard, firm and soft requirements. We present a worst case response time based formulation to compute whether a given set of real-time tasks scheduled under fixed priority meets its *n* in *m* temporal constraints.

Keywords: Real-time systems, transient overload, schedulability analysis.

1 Introduction

Real-time systems are those in which the time at which the results are produced is important; the system not only has to meet the functional requirements but also the non functional ones expressed in the form of timing constraints [9]. Real-time systems are usually classified as being hard, firm or soft. Hard real-time systems are those in which missing a deadline can be catastrophic, on the other hand soft real-time systems are those where providing a late result is still useful. Firm real-time systems are those where, in general, providing a late result is useless, but the consequences of missing a deadline are not catastrophic [2] so a certain number of missed deadlines can be tolerated.

There are different techniques for analysing the temporal behaviour of real-time systems. Soft real-time systems are usually analyzed for their average case behaviour with simulation techniques or queuing networks [9]. Those techniques are not applicable to hard real-time systems because probabilistic guarantees of the timing constraints are not sufficient; there always exists a probability greater than zero that a timing constraint is not met.

Temporal constraints are usually specified in terms of deadlines and the problem of guaranteeing that all deadlines will be met is reduced to the problem of scheduling and guaranteeing that in the worst case all tasks will meet their deadlines. The obvious problem of worst case dimensioning of the system is that it leads to low processor utilization due to the difference between the average and worst case.

For hard real-time systems, transient overloads are not acceptable but for firm real-time systems, where some deadlines can be missed, they may occur and be accepted. For example, the robustness of general control algorithms can tolerate some degree of missed deadlines in the same way that some deadlines missed in a digital video player can not be noticed by the user if they do not last for too long. Traditional worst case scheduling techniques can not be applied directly to analyze systems that may accept a transient overload because they address the problem of guaranteeing that *all* deadlines have to be met.

This paper addresses the problem of determining *a priori* if a set of real-time tasks may suffer a transient overload . More specifically, we introduce (a) a temporal constraint on real-time tasks that allow us to specify the number and the pattern of missed deadlines a given task may suffer and (b) worst case schedulability tests for those constraints. We introduce the n in m temporal constraints to define the bounds of a transient overload. It means that a given task meets n deadlines in every window of m invocations. These temporal constraints are based on the (m, k)−firm deadline temporal constraint, presented by Hamdaooui and Ramanathan in [7]. Traditional temporal constraints used in specifying real-time systems, like guaranteeing a maximum percentage of deadlines missed, are not appropriate to model transient overloads. A temporal constraint like "90% of the deadlines met" could either mean, miss 1 deadline and then meeting the following 9 or miss 100 deadlines and then meeting the following 900, which is quite different. The analysis is applicable to systems that are deemed to be bounded but not schedulable in the traditional sense. By bounded we mean a system in which there exists an upper bound on the response time of any invocation of a task.

With this temporal constraint, we are able to extend the class of systems that can be analyzed by considering those that are not schedulable in the traditional sense but have a bounded transient overload. We say that a task set with n in m temporal constraints is schedulable in the weak sense if there are tasks that may miss the deadlines but the temporal constraints are guaranteed.

The structure of the paper is as follows: in section 2 the process model is introduced, followed by the formal definitions of the temporal constraints shown in section 3. After that, in section 4, the analysis to test the temporal constraints is developed, with the addition of the proofs of boundedness and complexity of the analysis. The paper follows in section 5 with the analysis of the properties of some particular cases. Finally, conclusions are presented in section 6.

2 Process model

We follow the traditional hypotheses of task sets [12, 6]. We consider a real-time system with N periodic tasks $\tau_1, \ldots, \tau_N$. Each task is defined by $\tau_i = (T_i, D_i, C_i, O_i)$. A task τ_i is invoked every T_i time units, called the period, and it starts with an offset of $O_i < T_i$ and executes for at most C_i units of time, including the cost of the context switch. After a task is invoked, it has to finish within the following D_i time units, called the deadline. We assume that the tasks have a fixed unique priority with τ_1 being the highest priority task and τ_N the lowest priority task. The run-time system is controlled by a preemptive scheduler that always runs the highest priority runable task. Tasks only suspend themselves at the end of each invocation.

The hyperperiod HP is the least common multiple of the periods of the tasks. The release pattern will be repeated at every hyperperiod. We can also consider the hyperperiod at level i: HP_i. The hyperperiod of the task τ_i as the least common multiplier of the periods of the tasks of higher (or equal) priority than task τ_i. From the point of view of a task at level i the pattern of invocations of higher priority tasks is repeated every HP_i time units. The number of invocations of a task in its hyperperiod is given by $s_i = \frac{HP_i}{T_i}$. The number of invocations of a task in the hyperperiod is $s'_i = \frac{HP}{T_i}$.

We compute for each task, $F_i(k)$, the worst case finalization time of the kth invocation of the task. $S_i(k) = (k-1)T_i + O_i$ is the invocation time and $R_i(k) = F_i(k) - S_i(k)$ is the worst case response time of the task at invocation k. It is said that the task meets the deadline D_i at invocation k if $R_i(k) \leq D_i$. Otherwise, we say that the task has missed the deadline. We define the μ-pattern M, of a task τ_i as the pattern of missed and met deadlines. We denote with 1 a met deadline and with 0 a missed deadline, so the task's μ-pattern is given by:

$$M_i(k) = \begin{cases} 1 \text{ if } R_i(k) \leq D_i \\ 0 \text{ } Otherwise \end{cases} \qquad (1)$$

3 Temporal Constraints

We are interested in analysing tasks that may miss deadlines at some invocations, therefore we need to introduce metrics to specify bounds on the number of deadlines; and the pattern of consecutive deadlines a task may miss. By considering deadlines missed or met in any order or consecutively, we introduce the following four temporal constraints:

Definition 1. A task "meets row n in m" deadlines if in any window of m consecutive invocations, there are at least n consecutive invocations that meet the deadline. ($n, m > 0 \wedge n \leq m$)

Definition 2. A task "meets any n in m" deadlines if in any window of m consecutive invocations, there are at least n invocations *in any order* where the deadline is met. ($n, m > 0 \wedge n \leq m$)

Definition 3. A task "misses row n" deadlines if the task does not miss the deadline in more that n consecutive invocations. ($n > 0$)

Definition 4. A task "misses any n in m" deadlines if in any window of m consecutive invocations, the task misses the deadline in any order in, at most, n invocations within that window. ($n, m > 0 \wedge n \leq m$)

For example, consider the following task set with tasks τ_1 and τ_2: $T_1 = 45$, $D_1 = 38$, $C_1 = 30$, $O_1 = 0$, $T_2 = 77$, $D_2 = 72$, $C_2 = 25$, $O_2 = 0$. The task set is not schedulable in the ordinary sense because although task τ_1 meets all of the deadlines, task τ_2 does not. Figure 1(a) shows the μ-pattern of the first invocations of task τ_2. The task meets *any 2 in 10* deadlines because if we consider any 10 consecutive invocations of the task there are at least 2 deadlines met. Note that in the first 10 invocations 3 deadlines are met but at a later time there exists a window of 10 invocations where only two deadlines are met. We can also say that τ_2 *misses any 3 in 4*. In any window of four invocations no more than 3 deadlines are missed. Figure 1(b) shows the μ-pattern of task τ_3 of the task set $\tau_1, \ldots, \tau_3$. $T_1 = 26$, $D_1 = 13$, $C_1 = 6$, $O_1 = 0$ $T_2 = 32$, $D_2 = 19$, $C_2 = 3$, $O_2 = 0$ $T_3 = 55$, $D_3 = 34$, $C_3 = 24$, $O_3 = 0$. In this case task τ_3 meets *row 5 in 13*. In any window of 13 consecutive invocations of the task, a row of at least 5 deadlines is met.

(a) 001001,0001,0010001001000...

(b) 001,1111000011111,0000111...

Fig. 1. (a) Task *meets any 2 in 10* and *misses any 3 in 4* deadlines. (b) Task *meets row 5 in 13*

The example shows that, in general, the worst case does not happen at $t = 0$, even with $O_i = 0$ and therefore the analysis of all invocations of the tasks in the hyperperiod is required. We later characterize the task sets where such worst case happens at $t = 0$. Note that the strict schedulability constraint can be represented by *any n in n*, *row n in n*, *miss any 0 in n*, etc.

Other temporal constraints traditionally used in specifying real-time systems, like guaranteeing a percentage of the deadlines missed (or met), are not appropriate for this context. Take, for example, a temporal constraint of the form: "90% of deadlines met". It is intuitively correct but it could mean: missing one deadline and then meeting the next 9, or missing 100 deadlines and then meeting the next 900, which is clearly quite different. In order to overcome this problem we specify the two dimensional temporal constraint, the degree of deadlines missed and met and the locality where this measure has to be provided. Also note that this two dimensional temporal constraint provides more information than, for instance, the maximum duration d of a transient overload because it also bounds the *distance* between two transient overloads.

4 Tests for n in m temporal constraints

Given a task set with temporal constraints of the n in m type, it is required to solve the following problem

Problem *Given a priority ordering on the tasks, can the system meet all the temporal constraints?*

That is, does every task meet its temporal constraints of the n in m type?. We show that for the general case it is required to test all invocations within the hyperperiod at level i. Fortunately for some particular cases we can derive a formulation that has a pseudopolynomial complexity with the same order of complexity as the traditional scheduling test.

Please note that the maximum window of deadlines missed in a row does not always contain the invocation where the task suffered the maximum interference. For instance, in figure 1(a), task τ_2 suffers its maximum interference at $t = 0$ where it misses two consecutive deadlines but at a later time it misses three in a row. This task meets the last invocation in the hyperperiod.

This result shows that the worst case scenario for temporal constraints of the n in m type does not happen when a task suffers its maximum interference (even when the worst case response time happens at $t = 0$, when $O_i = 0$ for all tasks). Taking into account these results, we propose a solution based on computing the worst case finishing time of all invocations of a task within the hyperperiod, building the task μ-pattern and then testing all the windows for the temporal constraint. In the rest of this section we prove that it is only required to compute the response times of a task within its hyperperiod and we present an effective way to compute $R_i(k)$.

4.1 Bounded systems

The pattern of invocations is repeated every hyperperiod. We show that the worst case response times of the tasks at each invocation is also repeated at every hyperperiod. We first consider $O_i = 0$ and then generalize the result for $O_i \neq 0$.

Definition 5. (Bounded) A task is *bounded* if an upper bound exists on the response time of any invocation of the task; otherwise it is *unbounded*. $\exists B > 0 \mid R_i(k) \leq B \ \forall i = 1, \ldots, N, \ k = 1, 2, \ldots$

By extension, we say that a system is bounded if every task in the task set is bounded.

Definition 6. (Overrun) A task with $O_i = 0$ suffers an overrun over the hyperperiod, if the last invocation of the task before the hyperperiod, finishes after the hyperperiod.

If a task suffers an overrun over the hyperperiod then the worst case response time is no longer within the first hyperperiod because at $t = HP$ there is pending computation time. This additional interference could affect subsequent task invocations. The following theorem allows us to ascertain that the behaviour of the system is closed within the hyperperiod:

Theorem 7. *For a task set defined in section 2 with $O_i = 0$,*
Bounded $\Leftrightarrow U \leq 1 \Leftrightarrow$ Not Overrun.

This result says that if the system has a utilization less than or equal to 1 then the last invocation of every task in the hyperperiod finishes before the start of the next hyperperiod. Therefore the pattern of worst case response times, and the μ-pattern is repeated in each hyperperiod.

For task sets where $O_i \neq 0$ for some tasks, similar results can be derived. For task sets with offsets we show that: *Bounded* $\Leftrightarrow U \leq 1$. This can be demonstrated by viewing the task set equivalent to another one where offsets are removed and then applying theorem 7. Please note that the worst case response time of the tasks does not occur at the start of the hyperperiod as it happens when $O_i = 0$. Also note that with offsets it is possible that a task finishes the last invocation in the hyperperiod after the hyperperiod, thus interfering with tasks invocations in the following hyperperiod. At the end of the first hyperperiod there may be some pending computation time d that will have to be performed in the second one. It can be easily shown that if $U \leq 1$ at the end of the second hyperperiod the amount of pending computation time is at most d (if it were greater, it would increase at each hyperperiod, in contradiction with the hypotheses that the system is bounded). Therefore the worst case response times of the tasks can be computed by calculating the worst case finalization time of the invocations in any hyperperiod but the first one, for instance, the *second* hyperperiod.

4.2 Number of invocations

We now turn to the computation of the number of invocations to test. In the general case, it is required to test all invocations within the hyperperiod for all tasks. The longest string of missed and met deadlines does not start at $t = 0$. With offsets, it is even worse. The worst case response time does not happen at $t = 0$ as figure 2 shows. The task set is : $T_1 = 10, D_1 = 2, C_1 = 2, O_6 = 0$ $T_2 = 15, D_2 = 5, C_2 = 4, O_2 = 0$. The lower priority task τ_2 misses the second deadline but not the first one.

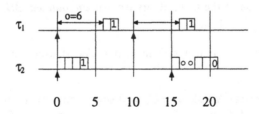

Fig. 2. Worst case response time of task τ_b does not happen at $t = 0$, it happens at $t = 15$.

The pattern of missed and met deadlines is repeated at the hyperperiod at level i, therefore it is required to compute $F_i(k)$ for $k = 1, \ldots, s_i$ (actually, for the general case k should range from $k = s_i + 1, \ldots, 2s_i$ but for notation simplification we keep the range of k from 1 to s_i). This number depends on the relative periods of the tasks. This number can be quite large if periods are co-prime. It is considered a good engineering practice to choose the periods of the tasks so that the hyperperiod (and the number of invocations of each task in the hyperperiod) is kept small. This can be easily done by choosing, whenever possible, the periods of the tasks as multiples of each other or with common prime factors. Note that the number of invocations to test depends on the hyperperiod at level i and not on the hyperperiod.

$F_i(k)$ could also be computed by constructing the schedule of the tasks from $t = 0$ until $t = 2HP$. But for non-trivial task sets it is impractical because this computation can be quite large. For example, Locke in [13], describes a typical case study of an avionics platform application made of 16 tasks with periods ranging from 1 to 1000. The hyperperiod of the task set is 236000. If a simulation based tool were used to build the schedule and to compute $F_i(k)$ for $k = s_i + 1, \ldots, 2s_i$, it should have to process about 679000 task invocations. With the formulation presented in this article, the computation of each $F_i(k)$ is harder but, it is necessary to compute only 1200 task invocations. The simulation based tool would require to compute more than 560 times the number of invocations that the worst case based formulation does. This example shows that even when hyperperiods are large the number of invocations to test is small. It is therefore reasonable to conclude that it is a practical computation method.

4.3 Test for *any* and *row*

Given a μ-pattern $M_i(k)$ for $k = 1 \ldots s_i$, the test for *any* n in m is a counting algorithm. We have to test if in a string of 0's and 1's there are at least n 1's in any window of m successive characters. It can be done in linear time $O(s_i)$. The algorithm for testing *row* n in m is similar. We have to test if, in a string of 0's and 1's, there are at least n 1's in a row in any window of m successive characters. This algorithm can be also implemented in linear time with the number of invocations in the hyperperiod. Because the pattern of missed and met deadlines is repeated in each hyperperiod, it is only necessary to compute $M_i(k)$ within the hyperperiod and when considering invocations over the hyperperiod, perform a *wrap-around*.

4.4 Formulation

To test the n in m temporal constraint it is necessary to compute the worst case finalization time of each invocation of the tasks within its hyperperiod. We are interested in the derivation of analytical formulation partially based on [15, 1] work on computing the worst case response time of a task set. It is only required to compute the finalization time of the invocations of the hyperperiod at level i, because a task may only be interfered by higher priority tasks. In this section, we provide the formulation for efficiently and effectively computing the worst case response time of all invocations of a task within its hyperperiod. Firstly the formulation is developed for a basic model with $O_i = 0$ and later extended to the general case.

The response time of the first invocation of a task τ_i, defined by $F_i(1)$, is given by:

$$F_i(1) = \min \{ t > 0 \mid t = C_i + Intf_i(t) \} \tag{2}$$

where the $Intf_i(t)$ is the interference of tasks of higher priority than τ_i during interval $[0, t]$ and is given by

$$Intf_i(t) = \sum_{j \in hp(i)} \left\lceil \frac{t}{T_j} \right\rceil C_j \tag{3}$$

Where $hp(i)$ is the set of tasks of higher priority than τ_i. The equation in (2) can be computed with the recurrence formula: $t_{n+1} = C_i + Intf_i(t_n)$. Starting with $t_0 = C_i$. The succession $\{t_i\}_{i \geq 0}$ increases monotonically. The iteration finishes when $t_n = t_{n+1}$ (This upper bound exists if $U \leq 1$) or when exceeds a maximum value $t_n > \mathcal{B}$ for a given $\mathcal{B}$ (for instance, the deadline). For the process model in section 2, the formulation in (2) can be extended to compute the finalization time of the kth invocation of a task.

Definition 8. ($Idle_i(t)$) The Idle time at level i is the amount of time the processor can be used by tasks of lower priority than τ_i during period of time $[0, t)$.

It can be computed by adding a virtual task $\bar{\tau}$ with lower priority than τ_i with a period and deadline equal to the time t. $\bar{\tau} = (\bar{T} = t, \bar{D} = t, \bar{C})$. The maximum time the processor can be used by tasks of lower priority than τ_i is the maximum computation time that makes task $\bar{\tau}$ meet its deadline. Formally:

$$Idle_i(t) = \max \left\{ \bar{C} \mid \bar{\tau} \text{ is schedulable} \right\} \tag{4}$$

The scheduling test in (4) is done by solving the next equation for t. In this, j counts for all the tasks of higher or equal priority than τ_i plus the virtual task $\bar{\tau}$.

$$t = \sum \left\lceil \frac{t}{T_j} \right\rceil C_j \tag{5}$$

and checking if $t \leq \bar{D}$. Again, it can be computed by a recurrence relation producing the succession of values of t: $\{t_i\}_{i \geq 0}$. If $t_n = t_{n+1}$ and $t_n \leq \bar{D}$ then the idle time at level i is at least equal to $\bar{C}$. If $t_n > \bar{D}$ then the idle time is smaller than $\bar{C}$. For notation simplification, $Idle_i(k) \equiv Idle_i(S_i(k))$

The possible values of $\bar{C}$ range from 0 to t and can be computed by a dicotomic search. The number of values to test is of the order $O(\log_2 n)$ where n is the size of the interval. After $F_i(k)$ there exist a window of level i idle time $\kappa_i(k)$, that can be used as an effective lower bound for the computation of the idle time between $F_i(k)$ and $S_i(k+1)$.

$$\kappa_i(k) = \begin{cases} S_i(k+1) - F_i(k) \\ \min_{j \in hep(i)} \left\lceil \frac{F_i(k)}{T_j} \right\rceil T_j - F_i(k) \end{cases} \tag{6}$$

The bounds on the possible values of $Idle_i(k)$

$$Idle_i(k-1) + \kappa_i(k-1) \leq Idle_i(k) \leq Idle_i(k-1) + S_i(k) - F_i(k-1) \tag{7}$$

4.5 Finishing time of the kth invocation: $F_i(k)$

The computation of the finishing time of the kth invocation of the task τ_i is the time required for k invocations of the task, plus the time the processor is used by lower priority tasks plus the interference due to higher priority tasks. The finishing time is given by:

$$F_i(k) = \min\{t > 0 \mid t = kC_i + Intf_i(t) + Idle_i(k)\} \tag{8}$$

After $S_i(k)$ no processor time will be spent with tasks of lower priority than τ_i and therefore it is only necessary to compute the amount of idle time left during the period $[0, S_i(k))$. Note that $Idle_i(k)$ is constant (it does not depend on t)

Extending the formulation with offsets. The offset O_i of a task is the time after the start of the period when a task is invoked. A task should finish D_i time units after the invocation. We incorporate offsets in the formulation in the following way: the formulation to compute the finish time of the kth invocation is the same as before, we update the interference function and Idle time function. The interference a task suffers from higher priority tasks is given by:

$$Intf_i(t) = \sum_{j \in hp(i)} \left\lceil \frac{t - O_j}{T_j} \right\rceil C_j \tag{9}$$

and the idle time function is updated as follows:

$$Idle_i(t) = \max\{\bar{C} \mid \bar{\tau} \text{ is schedulable}\} \tag{10}$$

Where $\bar{\tau}$ is defined as in (4). The scheduling test in (5) of the virtual task $\bar{\tau}$ is updated for (10) as follows:

$$t = \sum \left\lceil \frac{t - O_j}{T_j} \right\rceil C_j \tag{11}$$

Note that the net effect is that the interference has been reduced and the idle time increased in the same amount.

5 Particular cases

In this section we consider some particular cases that allow us to reduce considerably the number of invocations to test and the computation cost of the test. We consider (a) tasks sets without offsets (b) tasks with temporal constraints of the *any 1 in m* type.

When $O_i = 0$, all tasks behave with a coordinated execution pattern and all tasks are released simultaneously at $t = 0$. This is the point when all tasks suffer their maximum interference [1]. Using the fact that the worst case scenario is known for all tasks it is possible to reduce considerably the number of invocations to test.

For hard tasks (*any 1 in 1*), it is only required to test for the first invocation. If it meets the first deadline, then it will meet all of them. The test is equivalent to the strong schedulability test.

For *any|row n in m* temporal constraints, if a task meets the first deadline then it meets *any 1 in 1* deadlines. Therefore it will meet *any or row n in m*. Therefore it is not required to test all invocations within the hyperperiod. Only in the case where the first deadline is missed it is required to compute the finalization time of all invocations within the hyperperiod for that task. As shown above, the worst case transient overload, the maximum number of deadlines missed in a row does not necessarily happen when task suffers its maximum interference, therefore it is not enough to test the window of invocations around $t = 0$.

For tasks with a temporal constraint of the *any 1 in m* type and with $D_i = T_i$ the worst case scenario happens when the tasks suffers the maximum transient overload that happens when all tasks are released simultaneously. In this case, it is only necessary to test the first m invocations for missed deadlines. If the task does not miss the first m deadlines then the task meets *any 1 in m* deadlines. The proof is based on two points, the first one is that the task does meet the deadline on the last invocation within the hyperperiod and the second that we can transform the task into an equivalent one with a temporal constraint of the *any 1 in 1* type. Theorem (7) says that the system is bounded, and that all tasks finish their computation before (or at) the hyperperiod. In the case where $D_i = T_i$ this is equivalent to say that if a task meets a deadline, it will meet the last deadline before the hyperperiod. Therefore the largest window of missed deadlines starts with the first invocation in the hyperperiod. With $D_i = T_i$, missing a deadline implies that the finish time is greater than the period and therefore the start of the next invocation so that a task interferes with the following invocation. Therefore there is no time left for lower priority tasks between the invocation that miss the deadline and the next one. For $m - 1$ consecutive invocations that miss the deadline it means that there has not been time left for lower priority tasks. This situation is equivalent to having a task with a period m times the period of the original task and requiring m times the computation time. Formally, given a task: $\tau_i = (T_i, D_i, C_i)$, the task meets *any 1 in m* deadlines if the equivalent task, $\bar{\tau}_i = (\bar{T}_i = mT_i, \bar{D}_i = mD_i, \bar{C}_i = mC_i)$ is schedulable (meets *any 1 in 1*). We have shown that for hard tasks it is only required to test the first invocation .

6 Conclusion

This paper has introduced a new temporal constraint, the n in m, as a measure of the transient overload a real-time task may accept. Analytical models have been provided to analyze real-time systems scheduled by a fixed priority scheduler. The analytical model requires less computation power than an equivalent event-driven simulation model and applying some particular cases the computation time can be reduced even more thus making a feasible and practical analysis tool. Further research includes the definition and implementation of tests for more general process models to include, blocking, sporadic tasks, imprecise computations and fault-tolerant process models and optimal priority orderings.

7 Acknowledgments

This research was partially funded with a grant from "Caixa de Balears. Sa Nostra". The authors wish to thank the computer science department of the University of Wales at Aberystwyth where part of this research was carried on. Specially, professor Ian C. Pyle and Philip G. K. Reiser for their encouragement and valuable comments in all the stages of this research. We will also wish to thank Julián Proenza and Carlos Juiz for the comments on an earlier draft of this paper.

References

1. N. C. Audsley. Flexible scheduling in hard real-time systems. *PhD theses. Department of Computer Science, University of York*, 1993.

2. N. C. Audsley, A. Burns, R. I. Davis, K. W. Tindell, and A. J. Wellings. Fixed priority pre-emptive scheduling: An historical perspective. *Real-Time Systems*, 8, 1995.

3. N. C. Audsley, A. Burns, M.F. Richardson, and Wellings A.J. Stress: A simulator for hard real-time systems. *Software-Practice and Experience*, 24(6), June 1994.

4. N. C. Audsley, A. Burns, M.F. Richardson, and A.J. Wellings. Hard real-time scheduling: The deadline monotonic approach. In *Proceedings of the 8th IEEE Workshop on Real-Time Operating Systems and Software. Atlanta.*, May 1991.

5. N.C. Audsley, R.I. Davis, and A. Burns. Mechanisms for enhacing the flexibility and utility of hard real-time systems. In *15th Real Time System Symposium, December 1994.*, December 1994.

6. A. Burns. Scheduling hard real-time systems: A review. *Software Engineering Journal*, 6(3), 1991.

7. M. Hamdaoui and P. Ramanathan. A dynamic priority assignment technique for streams with (m,k)-firm deadlines. *IEEE Transactions on Computers*, 44(12), December 1995.

8. M. Joseph and P. Pandya. Finding respone times in a real time system. *BCS Computer Journal*, 29(5), October 1986.

9. C. Juiz and R. Puigjaner. Approximate performance models of real time software systems. In *Proceedings of MASCOTS 95, IEEE Computer Society Press*, January 1995.

10. J.P. Lehoczky, L. Sha, and V. Ding. The rate monotonic scheduling algorithm: Exact characterization and average case behavior. Technical report, Tech. Report. Department of Statistics, Carnegie-Mellon, 1987.

11. J.Y.T. Leung and J. Whitehead. On the complexity of fixed-priority scheduling of periodic, real-time tasks. *Performance Evaluation (Netherlands)*, 2(4), December 1982.

12. C. L. Liu and J. W. Layland. Scheduling algorithms for multiprogramming in a hard-real-time environment. *Journal of the ACM*, 20(1), January 1973.

13. C.D. Locke, D.R. Voge, and R.J. Mesler. Building a predictable avionics platform in ada: A case study. In *Real-Time Systems, San Antonio, Texas*, 1991.

14. L. Sha, R. Rajkumar, and J.P. Lehoczky. Priority inheritance protocols: An approach to real-time synchronisation. *IEEE Transactions on Computers*, 39(9), September 1990.

15. K.W. Tindell. Fixed priority scheduling of hard real-time systems. *PhD theses. Department of Computer Science, University of York*, 1993.

Towards an Analytical Tool for Performance Modelling of ATM Networks by Decomposition

Gerhard Haßlinger

TH Darmstadt, Alexanderstr. 10, D-64283 Darmstadt, Germany

Abstract: The analysis of open queueing networks by decomposition has developed to include more detailed and generalized representation forms of traffic. We investigate this method concerning its preconditions and requirements for ATM network modelling. We use discrete time semi-Markovian processes (SMP) to characterize traffic with short-term as well as long-term autocorrelation, and to evaluate the performance of ATM switches with non-renewal input. Basic results are summarized for the autocorrelation function of semi-Markov processes, which show how to represent autocorrelated traffic by an adequate SMP model of limited size.

Keywords: ATM networks, semi-Markov processes, SMP/G/1 analysis in discrete time, autocorrelation function, self-similar traffic.

1. Introduction

ATM traffic is generated by a broad variety of services, each producing loads of different shape. Often the behaviour over several time scales must be taken into account, which has essential influence on queues and waiting times. For speech sources we can distinguish cell, burst and call level. The performance of switches loaded with speech traffic superposed from many sources has been evaluated by the queueing network analyser tool [24] and afterwards by several different approaches, for a semi-Markovian model see [8]. Video sources show a high variability due to the motion and changing of scenes, which is described including the autocorrelation function [15]. Measurement of traffic in data networks reveal self-similar structures [14, 18] which give rise to new approaches in the traffic characterization. Thus an adequate modelling of ATM traffic is difficult and must include a detailed representation of the interarrival time distributions and of their autocorrelation function.

Advances in the analysis of open queueing networks by decomposition have been made using phase-type representations of renewal traffic [1, 10] and exploiting Ph/Ph/1 queueing models for the nodes, which has been generalized to non-renewal input forms [2]. In this paper we present the current developements and capabilities of discrete time traffic models in comparison to phase-type ones. We use results from previous work, including

- an investigation of the decomposition approach for renewal traffic represented by discrete arrival and service time distributions with finite support [9], which allow for efficient analysis methods of GI/G/1 single server nodes [5, 6] and

- the extension of both discrete time analysis methods to SMP/G/1 queues with semi-Markovian input [7, 8, 21].

We discuss implications of the decomposition approach for ATM networks in section 2. Properties of the SMP autocorrelation are summarized in sections 3 and 4, accompanied by examples of the performance evaluation of ATM switches for input having a self-similar structure and input consisting of superposed ON-OFF traffic.

2. Decomposition approach in ATM networks

A queueing network analyser was proposed by Kühn [13] and Whitt [26] using decomposition. The main principles of their approach for open queueing networks are

- the representation of external and internodal traffic flows as renewal processes,

- isolated treatment of each network node as a single server GI/G/1-system,

- transformations of the traffic flows by three basic steps
  - the superposition of flows at the input of a node,
  - departure process construction from given input and service process,
  - the splitting of departures into substreams directed to other nodes or to external destinations according to probabilistic routing, i.e. the routes of departures from a node are mutually independent, leading to each of the subsequent nodes with predefined probabilities.

The initial works [13, 26] used the first and second moment of the interarrival times as the only information about internodal traffic and already determined feedback flows by an iteration of the entire network analysis.

Recent investigations extended the decomposition approach in several ways, improving its broad applicability as a tool in the area of communication networks as well as manufactoring systems.

Bitran and Dasu introduce non-renewal phase-type representations of traffic, socalled super-Erlang chains [1, 2], with special emphasis on approximate modelling of superposed traffic.

Pourbabai [19] and Haverkort [10] also include loss systems with finite buffers and study the impact of loss on the departure processes again in a phase-type traffic representation.

Alternatively, discrete time modelling of traffic in queueing networks is addressed by Haßlinger and Rieger [9]. This includes deterministic multiserver nodes $(\cdot/D/c)$ by exploiting the equivalence to a system of c identical single server queues $(\cdot/D/1)$ in parallel with cyclic assignment of arrivals from a common input. In addition to probabilistic routing, departures may be switched depending on previous ones, with cyclic switching as a special case.

Basic preconditions for a decomposition approach to work are

- stochastical independence of all traffic flows, which are superposed at the input of a node

- a representation of internodal traffic flows allowing for efficient analysis methods to determine performance measures at the nodes and to obtain approximate representations of their output process from given input and service processes.

When the independence property is violated by merging flows with strong mutual correlation, e.g. within immediate feedback loops, then the decomposition approach may fail, as already demonstrated in examples by Kuehn [13]. In ATM networks, links are loaded with virtual circuits and paths from different origin. Traffic flows with mutual correlation caused by feedback or fork-join routing are unlikely to appear in ATM. On the contrary, ATM networks are designed to make use of statistical multiplexing, where the gain in bandwidth reduction is largest for links carrying numerous independent circuits of bursty traffic.

The absense of feedback at the ATM layers also removes the need for iteration of the complete network analysis, since all input processes to the nodes can be determined straightforwardly, starting from nodes which have only external inputs. Thus ATM traffic is in accordance with the prepositions for a decomposition analysis and even simplifies its execution.

2.1 Representation of renewal traffic

The two-moments approach assumes renewal processes characterized by the mean and variance of their interarrival times. The rates and thus the mean interarrival times of superposed and switched flows are obtained due to flow conservation, whereas the variance in a superposition depends on the complete interarrival time distributions of all components. The second moment of the single server GI/G/1 departure process also depends on the complete arrival and service time distribution. Nevertheless, the two-moments approach yields an efficient approximation [13, 26] of the mean queue size. The complete queue size distribution and its percentiles are not included, which are an important measure of ATM quality-of-service parameters, especially for the cell loss rate and for the permissable delay.

The representation of renewal traffic by the complete distribution of arrival and service intervals as studied in [1, 9, 10] allows for an exact GI/G/1 analysis to evaluate the waiting time and queue size distribution at each network node. Besides better accuracy, the detailed renewal representation leads to a consistent execution of the decomposition approach, since the complete interarrival time distributions are again obtained by each of the three basic transformation steps, which determine the GI/G/1 output, the superposition and the splitting processes [9]. But the consistency is restricted to renewal traffic, whereas the output of a GI/G/1 server and superposed processes are generally non-renewal, even if all involved components are renewal. Thus the approach has inherent requirements to include processes with correlated intervals.

2.2 Phase-type versus discrete time distribution functions

Efficient analysis procedures of the GI/G/1 queue are known for phase-type and discrete time distributions of the arrival and service times. Matrix-geometric approaches [16] and polynomial factorization [6] are applicable in both cases and a workload-oriented algorithm [5] serves as fast discrete time method. Phase type or discrete time representations are appropriate for approximations of arbitrary distribution functions, whose accuracy can be improved by increasing the number of phases or equidistant discretization steps, at the expense of a more complex performance analysis. The computational effort in the solution of discrete time systems using the workload-based algorithm [5] or polynomial factorization [6] is bounded by a quadratic increase in the number of discretization steps. Providing 100 discretization steps for the arrival and service time distribution, which seems sufficient for many cases, the run time of the workload-based algorithm is about 0.08 seconds and polynomial factorization requires no more than 0.3 seconds in our implementation on a Sun Sparc 10 workstation.

However, a detailed approximation of arbitrary distribution functions by phase-type ones seems to be subject to considerable computational effort [12]. When used within the decomposition approach, phase-type distributions are restricted to a simplified form [1, 10] depending on only a few parameters. On the contrary, the discretization of a given distribution function is fairly trivial and allows for a scalable adaptation of accuracy versus run time requirements [9].

In ATM networks an even stronger argument in favour of discrete time modelling emerges from the prevalent presence of deterministic servers, which produce output processes and internodal traffic of discrete time shape. Deterministic distributions are handled as the simplest case in discrete time domain, whereas adequate phase-type representations involve a large number of states.

2.3 Finite versus infinite buffer models

A design decision has to be made on the usage of queueing analysis for finite or infinite buffer systems. Finite buffer systems ask for an iterative fixed-point approach in the global network analysis as pointed out in [10] to determine the influence of losses on traffic flows. In ATM networks demands for cell loss are typically in a range from 10^{-3} to 10^{-10} in order to minimize the quality-of-service reduction imposed on transmitted data, which makes the impact of cell loss on internodal traffic neglegible. We prefer infinite capacity systems, since they allow for more elegant and faster steady state analysis methods. Especially low buffer overflow probabilities can be bounded [9] and accurately estimated [25] from the infinite buffer analysis.

3. Semi-Markovian representation of non-renewal traffic

As already mentioned, output and superposition processes are generally non-renewal in open queueing networks. In addition, the integration of data, speech and video sources into ATM networks generates traffic of very different shape, which is usually far from renewal. The ATM application layer specifies constant bit rate as well as available and even unspecified bit rate services including high burstiness. Investigations of video sources [15] have established the autocorrelation function as a main traffic descriptor.

Measurements in local [14] as well as wide area networks [18] show a self-similar, fractal-like behaviour of traffic, which isn't foreseen in classical performance analysis. The autocorrelation is observed to reach over several time scales with strong effect on queueing processes and especially on tail probabilities of queues. Recent investigations [17] conclude, that even if performance analysis exploits the self-similar structure, it remains insufficient to consider only a few parameters e.g. the arrival rate, burst factor and the hurst parameter. It is not surprising, that the variability of traffic demands for a detailed modelling of manysided situations.

In the sequel, we consider semi-Markovian representations as a scalable extension of renewal processes. The arrival instants of a SMP are associated with states of a finite Markov chain. The distribution of interarrival times as well as the arrival rates depend on the current state. The states carry all information about the past at arrival instants and enable a SMP to express correlation. State dependent source and network load models, see e.g. [20], may be directly transferred into a SMP model. SMP include bursty traffic with strong positive correlation of arrival intervals as well as periodic traffic.

3.1 Definitions

A series $\{R_T, \sigma_T\}$ $(T \in I\!N)$ of random variables forms a semi-Markov process (SMP) in discrete time $R_T \in I\!N_0$, $\sigma_T \in \{1, \ldots, M\}$, if

$$\Pr\{R_{T+1} = k, \sigma_{T+1} = j \,|\, R_1, \ldots \sigma_1, \ldots\} = \Pr\{R_{T+1} = k, \sigma_{T+1} = j \,|\, \sigma_T\}. \quad (1)$$

R_T denote the interarrival times or intervals of the process and σ_T is referred to as *underlying Markov chain* with notation SMP(M) to indicate the number M of states. State dependent distributions of the intervals are sufficient to determine a SMP in steady state $(i, j \in \{1, \cdots, M\}; k \in I\!N_0)$:

$$r_{ij}(k) \overset{\text{def}}{=} \Pr\{R_{T+1} = k, \sigma_{T+1} = j \,|\, \sigma_T = i\}; \quad r_i(k) \overset{\text{def}}{=} \sum_{j=1}^{M} r_{ij}(k);$$

$$p_{ij} \overset{\text{def}}{=} \Pr\{\sigma_{T+1} = j \,|\, \sigma_T = i\} = \sum_k r_{ij}(k); \quad \mathbf{P} \overset{\text{def}}{=} (p_{ij}). \quad (2)$$

The transition matrix $\mathbf{P}$ is assumed to be irreducible. The stationary probabilities $p_1, \cdots, p_M$ of the underlying Markov chain are then uniquely determined. As the limit for stationary distributions we use regardless of periodicity $p_i \overset{\text{def}}{=} \lim_{N \to \infty} \sum_{T=1}^{N} \Pr\{\sigma_T = i\}/N$ and have to solve the equations

$$p_i = \sum_{j=1}^{M} p_j \, p_{ji}; \qquad \sum_{i=1}^{M} p_i = 1; \qquad r(k) \overset{\text{def}}{=} \sum_{i=1}^{M} p_i \, r_i(k). \quad (3)$$

In the sequel we refer to $r(k)$ as stationary distribution of the SMP intervals and to $r_i(k)$ or $r_{ij}(k)$ as state dependent distributions with corresponding means denoted as $E(R), E_i(R)$ and $E_{ij}(R)$.

In our considerations of the SMP autocorrelation, we restrict to special SMP, denoted as SSMP, such that $\forall j : r_{ij}(k) = p_{ij} \, r_i(k)$ holds, i.e. an interarrival time and the following transition are mutually independent and both depend only on the current state i. Since a SMP(M) of general form can be equivalently represented as a SSMP(M^2), SSMP do not introduce a loss of generality. The state space of an equivalent SSMP(M^2) consists of pairs (σ_T, σ_{T+1}), combining the current and the subsequent state of the SMP(M).

3.2 SMP modelling of autocorrelated ATM traffic

An important, but to the author's knowledge only scarcely investigated problem is the representation of a given autocorrelated traffic as a SMP of limited size. Without state space limitation, exact or detailed approximate SMP models seem possible for almost any traffic type, but their performance evaluation often becomes intractable. Detailed SMP representations have been proposed for the superposition of traffic by Elsayed [4], where the underlying chain extends to an enormous size.

To describe autocorrelated traffic, we include the stationary distribution of its interarrival times and its autocorrelation function with n-th order coefficient κ_n defined as

$$\kappa_n \overset{\text{def}}{=} E\big((R_T - E(R))(R_{T+n} - E(R))\big) / \text{Var}(R) \qquad \text{for } n \geq 1, \qquad (4)$$

where $E(R)$ and $\text{Var}(R)$ denote the mean and variance of intervals R_T.

3.3 Basic properties of the SSMP autocorrelation

The autocorrelation of a SSMP can be expressed in the form

$$\kappa_n = \left(\sum_{i=1}^{M} \sum_{j=1}^{M} p_i \, E_i(R) p_{ij}^{(n)} E_j(R) - E^2(R) \right) \Big/ \text{Var}(R) \qquad \text{for } n \geq 1, \ (5)$$

$$\kappa_0 \overset{\text{def}}{=} \left(\sum_{i=1}^{M} p_i \, E_i^2(R) - E^2(R) \right) \Big/ \text{Var}(R) \qquad (6)$$

where $E_i(R)$ is the state dependent mean of an interval at state i and $p_{ij}^{(n)}$ denote the n-step transition probabilities of the underlying chain ($p_{ij}^{(1)} = p_{ij}$). Formula (5) was already derived by Ding [3], who constructed discrete time SSMP(2) processes to match the stationary distribution of intervals and their first and second order coefficient κ_1 and κ_2 of the autocorrelation. In addition, we define κ_0 for SSMP processes in continuation of equation (5) where $p_{ij}^{(0)} = 1$ if $i = j$, as opposed to $\kappa_0 = 1$ resulting from the general definition (4). Then κ_0 is a bound of the complete autocorrelation function [7] $\forall n \in \mathbb{N} : |\kappa_n| \leq \kappa_0$, and thus a key parameter of the SSMP autocorrelation, indicating the capability of a SSMP to express correlation.

In case of a two-state underlying chain the autocorrelation function is geometrical [3]. Using the previous notation we obtain the SSMP(2) autocorrelation in the short form

$$\kappa_n = \kappa_0 \, (1 - p_{12} - p_{21})^n.$$

Ding [3] adapts a SSMP(2) according to given first and second order coefficients κ_1 and κ_2. When the complete autocorrelation of a considered process is known, we can include the long term correlation. Let

$$C_0 \overset{\text{def}}{=} \sum_{n=1}^{\infty} \kappa_n \qquad \text{and} \qquad C_i \overset{\text{def}}{=} \sum_{n=1}^{\infty} n^i \kappa_n / C_0 \qquad \text{for } i \in \mathbb{N} \qquad (7)$$

denote the sum of coefficients C_0 and the moments C_i of the autocorrelation function. The definitions presume ergodicity of the underlying chain to assure convergence of the infinite sums, which is not valid e.g. in periodic chains. For the SSMP(2) adaptation we obtain

$$C_0 = \kappa_0 \, (1 - p_{12} - p_{21})/(p_{12} + p_{21}) \quad \text{and} \quad C_1 = 1/(p_{12} + p_{21}).$$

Figure 1 depicts an example of a SSMP(2) adaptation to some traffic with uniformly distributed interarrival times $F_R(t) = Prob\{R \le t\} = t/T$ for $0 \le t \le T$ and a geometrical autocorrelation function $\kappa_n = 0.75 \, (1 - 2\beta)^n$, where $0 < \beta \le 1$.

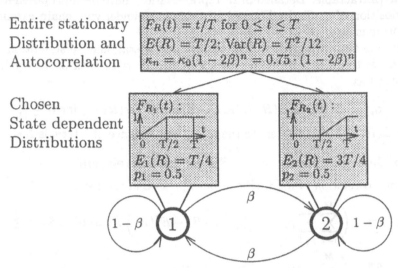

Figure 1: SSMP(2) adaptation to traffic with given chararcteristic

SSMP adaptations in general offer several degrees of freedom in the choice of the state dependent distributions $F_{R_i}(t)$ and of the transition matrix (p_{ij}). But we are also aware of bounds, which restrict the autocorrelation function of arbitrary SSMP(M) models depending on their stationary distribution $F_R(t)$. In the example, the parameter $\kappa_0 = 0.75$ is at a maximum for any SSMP(2) with uniform $F_R(t)$. Thus SSMP(2) models do not include bursty traffic with correlation coefficients close to 1, since the bound for κ_0 extends to the complete autocorrelation function ($|\kappa_n| \le \kappa_0$). We can determine the bounds $\overline{\kappa}_0(M)$ of κ_0 in a SSMP model of size M for a given stationary distribution.
Table 1 compares the bounds for uniform and exponential distributions, which are obtained explicitly $\overline{\kappa}_0(M) = 1 - M^{-2}$ in the first case and from recursive equations in the second:

Distribution	$M =$	2	5	10	20	50	100
Uniform	$\overline{\kappa}_0(M) \approx$	0.750	0.960	0.9900	0.9975	0.9996	0.9999
Exponential	$\overline{\kappa}_0(M) \approx$	0.648	0.927	0.9798	0.9947	0.9991	0.9998

Table 1: Bounds of κ_0 for SSMP(M) with uniform and exponential distribution

From the results a minimum size M of the underlying chain of SSMP(M) representations is obtained for traffic of high burstiness with correlation coefficients approaching 1.

3.4 A SSMP model of self-similar traffic

We consider an example of a SSMP model for traffic revealing a self-similar structure over several time scales. The SSMP has 2^n states ($n = 4$ in the example), which are denoted as binary vectors $(s_n, \cdots, s_2, s_1)$. States are numbered by interpreting the vector as a binary number $S = \sum_{i=1}^{n} s_i\, 2^{i-1}$. A component $s_i \in \{0, 1\}$ characterizes the process at the i-th level in the time scale. Therefore the transition matrix has to handle the components s_i independent of each other and at different rates.

In our example we assume a component s_i to switch between 0 and 1 with probability $1/t_i = 1/4^{i+1}$ at each arrival, such that the mean number t_i of arrivals until a component changes its current state is in the range from medium ($t_1 = 16$) to long-term correlation ($t_4 = 1024$). The transition matrix of the SSMP is given by

$$p_{(s_n, \cdots, s_1)(\tilde{s}_n, \cdots, \tilde{s}_1)} = \prod_{i=1}^{n} q_i \quad \text{where} \quad q_i = \begin{cases} 1/t_i & \text{if } s_i \neq \tilde{s}_i \\ 1 - 1/t_i & \text{if } s_i = \tilde{s}_i. \end{cases} \quad (8)$$

All states are entered with equal probability 2^{-n}. The interarrival times are assumed to be constant at each state and are given by the product $1/\lambda_S = \prod_{i=1}^{n}(s_i + 1)$. Thus the rate is doubled, when any of the components s_i switches from 1 to 0, which causes a similar but independent behaviour of the process in each time scale.

The total mean interarrival time is $1/\lambda = 81/16 = 5.0625$. The autocorrelation function of the SSMP shows strong short-term and long-term correlation, as can be seen from the coefficients $\kappa_1 \approx 0.952$, $\kappa_2 \approx 0.909$ and the sum $C_0 \approx 133.1$ and first moment $C_1 \approx 483.9$ of the coefficients.

We evaluate an ATM switch with input of the previously given self-similar form. The analysis assumes a deterministic single server SSMP/D/1 system and is performed by the workload-based discrete time method [7, 8] in extension of the algorithm proposed in [5]. The service times vary in the range from 1 to 4.75 with corresponding utilization ρ form 20/81 to 76/81. The run time is 203.4 seconds on the average per example, where a refined discretization is applied when the service times are not integer-valued with double or 4-times the number of steps at half or quarter step width.

Figure 2 shows results for the mean waiting time $E(W)$ and the percentiles of the waiting time. W^{-k} denotes the waiting time, which is exceeded with probability 10^{-k}. The percentiles are averaged over the complete SMP state space, whereas the mean waiting time is separately averaged over sets of four states, each with identical components s_3 and s_4. Queueing effects are observed to creep into the states 0..3 at low utilization without influence on the other states. With increasing utilization the queue size enlarges and swaps over even to the states 12..15, although their interarrival times remain longer than the service time and the queue decreases in those states.

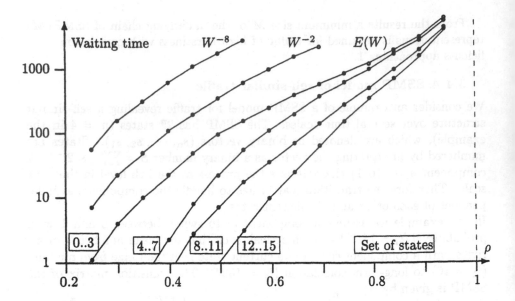

Figure 2: Percentiles and state dependent mean of the waiting time

The difference between the states 4..7 and states 8..11 is remarkable. Their interarrival times are pairwise identical, but the first set of states occures in a long-term period of high arrival rate indicated by $s_4 = 0$ as opposed to $s_4 = 1$ for the states 8..11.

SSMP modelling of traffic with varying behaviour in different time scales can be generalized from the considered example by varying the factors t_i/t_{i-1} for the distance between the time scales and by providing larger sets of more than two states for the components describing the behaviour at each time level, as far as the state space remains tractable for the analysis. The constant arrival intervals in each state can be replaced by arbitrary discrete time distributions, which results in a further level of short term burstiness.

4. Adaptation of SSMP in the modelling of traffic

We state some properties, which help to adapt a SSMP(M) to some given autocorrelation. First we consider two modifications of the transition matrix, which allow to match any sum C_0 of autocorrelation coefficients.

1. Modification to increase autocorrelation

When the transition matrix $\mathbf{P} = (p_{ij})$ of a SSMP is modified into

$$\tilde{p}_{ij} = \begin{cases} (1 - \beta)\, p_{ij} & \text{for } i \neq j \\ \beta + (1 - \beta)\, p_{ij} & \text{for } i = j \end{cases} \quad \text{i.e.} \quad \tilde{\mathbf{P}} = (1 - \beta)\, \mathbf{P} + \beta\, \mathbf{I} \quad (9)$$

for some $\beta \in (0, 1)$, then the autocorrelation function of the modified SSMP is given by

$$\tilde{\kappa}_n = \sum_{l=0}^{n} \binom{n}{l} \beta^{n-l} (1 - \beta)^l \kappa_l. \quad (10)$$

The modified sum $\tilde{C}_0$ and first moment $\tilde{C}_1$ are obtained as

$$\tilde{C}_0 = \frac{C_0 + \beta\kappa_0}{1-\beta} \quad \text{and} \quad \tilde{C}_1 = \frac{C_1 C_0 + \beta C_0 + \beta\kappa_0}{(C_0 + \beta\kappa_0)(1-\beta)}, \tag{11}$$

which allows to match any parameter $\tilde{C}_0 > C_0$ or $\tilde{C}_1 > C_1$.

2. Modification to decrease autocorrelation

Let $\tilde{\mathbf{P}} = (\tilde{p}_{ij})$ be defined by $\tilde{p}_{ij} = \gamma p_j + (1-\gamma)p_{ij}$ for $\gamma \in (0,1]$. Then $\tilde{\kappa}_n = (1-\gamma)^n \kappa_n$ is the autocorrelation function of the modified SSMP.

The results are derived by substitution of the modified n-step transition probabilities into (5), which are obtained for the first and second case as

$$\tilde{p}_{ij}^{(n)} = \sum_{k=0}^{n} \binom{n}{k} \beta^k (1-\beta)^{n-k} p_{ij}^{(n-k)} \quad \text{and} \quad \tilde{p}_{ij}^{(n)} = (1-(1-\gamma)^n)p_j + (1-\gamma)^n p_{ij}.$$

A general representation of the n-step transition matrix of a Markov chain given by Hunter [11] reveals the useful form of a linear combination of geometrical series for the SSMP(M) autocorrelation. The n-step transition probabilities of the underlying chain of size M are expressed as

$$p_{ij}^{(n)} = \sum_{l=1}^{M} \alpha_l x_{il} y_{lj} z_l^n; \quad \alpha_l = 1/\sum_{r=1}^{M} y_{lr} x_{rl}; \quad i,j \in \{1, \cdots, M\} \tag{12}$$

where $z_1, \cdots, z_M$ are the eigenvalues of the transition matrix $\mathbf{P}$ with elements $x_{1l}, \cdots, x_{Ml}$ and $y_{l1}, \cdots, y_{lM}$ of the corresponding right and left eigenvectors [11]. Substitution into (5) results in a simple linear combination of the form

$$\kappa_n = \sum_{l=1}^{M-1} \beta_l z_l^n \quad \text{for } n \in \mathbb{N}_0, \quad \text{including} \quad \kappa_0 = \sum_{l=1}^{M-1} \beta_l, \tag{13}$$

with a term for each eigenvalue except for $z_M = 1$. For a SSMP(2) we again have a geometrical autocorrelation [3], whereas complex-valued parameters are involved for $M > 2$.

4.1 The splitting of ATM traffic in SSMP representation

Substreams, which are partitioned from a renewal process by probabilistic routing, are again renewal [9, 10]. This also holds for SSMP(M) instead of renewal processes. On the other hand, probabilistic routing does not match the switching process in ATM networks in a satisfactory manner. The splitting of a virtual path into several flows is related to their previous superposition at a different starting point of a common transmission line. The in-sequence-delivery in ATM networks preserves mutual cell scattering among superposed flows within a transmission path, and consequently the cells leave a virtual path in the same order as they came in. The distribution of the number of cells, which are inserted from superposed flows in between successive cells of a considered flow, is of importance for the interarrival times in a splitted flow behind the separation point of a path [22]. When traffic of increasing burstiness is involved, the switching process more and more deviates from probabilistic routing.

4.2 Superposition of ATM traffic in SSMP representation

A general treatment of superposition processes is a main difficulty in network modelling without hope for exact solutions. Detailed modelling of superposed traffic is possible but leads to state space explosion for phase type as well as SMP representations [2, 4], which have to be compensated by approximate state space reduction schemes [2]. For discrete time SSMP a reduction scheme to construct an approximate SSMP of smaller size is discussed in [8], which contracts sets of states of the underlying chain into a corresponding single state. The reduction preserves the distribution of the interarrival times but deviations of the autocorrelation are inevitable. The modifications considered at the start of the section can restore some parameters of the autocorrelation function. There is often a potential for a SSMP reduction starting from a large underlying chain, but on the other hand performance measures are sensitive to deviations in the autocorrelation function.

4.3 The output from ATM switches

Output processes also reveal difficulties for a general representation. The $SMP(M)/D/1$ departure process arising in ATM switching models is characterized by alternating idle and busy periods, the latter producing constant departure intervals. The workload-based analysis [7] is capable of determining the moments of busy periods and the distributions of the following idle time, both depending on the state of the arrival process at the start of the busy period. This suggests to build up approximate SSMP submodels for the course of a busy period based on known moments and appended with an idle time, and to combine the submodels for all states of the arrival process. A state space reduction may again be required to limit the size of the detailed representation.

4.4 Switches with superposed ON-OFF input and varying capacity

In another example, we apply a SMP/G/1 model to traffic composed of identical ON-OFF sources. State i $(0 \leq i \leq M)$ of the underlying chain indicates the number of active sources. Arrival intervals are assumed to have constant length T/i at state i, taking into account, that each active source generates arrivals at constant rate $\lambda = 1/T$.

The transitions in the underlying chain consider the probability p^-, that a source becomes inactive immediately after having generated an arrival, which decrements the number of active sources. During an interarrival time T/i at state i, we assume the number $A(T/i)$ of inactive sources, which become active again, to be binomially distributed $Pr\{A(T/i) = j\} = b_j(M - i, \tilde{p})$ where

$$b_j(l, p) \stackrel{\text{def}}{=} \binom{l}{j} p^j (1-p)^{l-j}; \quad b_j(l, p) \stackrel{\text{def}}{=} 0 \text{ if } j < 0 \text{ or } j > l$$

and $\tilde{p} = 1 - (1 - p^+)^{1/i} \approx p^+/i$ for small p^+. p^+ is the probability, that an inactive source is activated within time span T. The corresponding transition probabilities for $i = 1, \cdots, M$ and $j = 0, \cdots, M$ are

$$p_{ij} = p^- \, b_{j+1-i}(M - i, \tilde{p}) + (1 - p^-)b_{j-i}(M - i, \tilde{p}).$$

Since no arrivals occure at state 0, its interarrival times last until an arrival at a subsequent state. Thus $r_0(k)$ and the transition probabilities p_{0j} must be treated separately.

Table 3 shows results for SMP models of $M = 24$ superposed sources with varying p^+, p^-. A service time to forward a packet is set to $2T/M$, which is also the time unit for discretization. The mean waiting time $E(W)$ is obtained together with the probability of no waiting $Pr\{W = 0\}$ and the percentiles W^{-k} of the waiting time, which are exceeded with tail probabilities $\leq 10^{-k}$. The first four rows give examples with constant ratio p^+/p^- and constant utilization ρ, but with increasing correlation as indicated by the sum C_0 of correlation coefficients. The last four rows depict results for an increasing mean number of active sources and thus increasing utilization ρ.

p^+	p^-	Utiliza-tion ρ	Correla-tion C_0	Waiting time			
				$E(W)$	$Pr\{W = 0\}$	W^{-3}	W^{-5}
0.16	0.32	0.6667	10.68	0.104	0.9444	8	20
0.08	0.16	0.6667	21.72	0.256	0.9260	19	44
0.04	0.08	0.6667	43.81	0.562	0.9141	41	89
0.02	0.04	0.6667	87.54	1.173	0.9067	79	177
0.09	0.15	0.7500	23.61	0.943	0.8184	34	70
0.10	0.14	0.8333	24.52	3.287	0.6301	64	120
0.11	0.13	0.9167	24.36	13.23	0.3531	149	257
0.115	0.125	0.9583	23.82	35.83	0.1846	313	531

Table 3: Performance results for a switch with superposed ON-OFF input

While the previous example gives a view on ON-OFF sources comparing the effect of autocorrelation and utilization on the waiting time distribution, another SSMP adaptation is discussed in [8] for a classical ON-OFF source model introduced by [24] with comparision to simulation and other analytical approaches.

Finally, the workload-oriented SMP/G/1 analysis extends to SMP/SMP/1 servers with state dependent arrival and service process, provided that state transitions always occure at arrival instants. The underlying chain may in general provide two components, one for the arrival and one for the service process.

We consider the example of a traffic flow with constant arrival intervals, passing through an ATM switch, whose capacity is shared among traffic arising from other links, too. The switch provides $M = 24$ output lines and is modelled as a D/SMP/1 system, such that state i of the underlying chain gives the number of available output lines for the considered arrival process. Accordingly, constant service times T/i are valid at each state i, where T is the time to forward a packet on an output line. We assume, that each available output line is no longer available until the next arrival with probability p^- and in reverse, each unavailable line becomes available again during an arrival interval with probability p^+. The transition matrix (p_{ij}) is then determined from binomially distributed decrease $b_j(i, p^-)$ and increase $b_j(M-i, p^+)$ of available lines during an interarrival time.

p^-	p^+	Utiliza- tion ρ	Corre- lation	Waiting time			
				$E(W)$	$Pr\{W = 0\}$	W^{-3}	W^{-5}
0.16	0.24	0.8333	1.5	0.898	0.7949	25	48
0.08	0.12	0.8333	4	1.952	0.7695	55	107
0.04	0.06	0.8333	9	4.088	0.7531	116	225
0.02	0.03	0.8333	19	8.375	0.7433	239	464
0.10	0.30	0.6667	1.5	0.0045	0.9973	1	8
0.13	0.27	0.7500	1.5	0.1087	0.9563	9	22
0.1778	0.2222	0.9000	1.5	3.7765	0.5460	54	94
0.1895	0.2105	0.9500	1.5	12.898	0.2948	124	211

Table 4: Results for an ATM switch with varying capacity assignment

Table 4 shows a series of examples with constant utilization and increasing autocorrelation and another with increasing utilization and constant autocorrelation, where the indicated autocorrelation concerns the service rates.

5. Conclusion

We have studied representation forms of ATM traffic, which are capable of adaptations to the distribution of the intervals and to the autocorrelation function, while also allowing for an efficient performance analysis when considered as input to ATM switches. Discrete time semi-Markovian processes serve as a suitable model covering a number of typical ATM traffic types even with autocorrelation over several time scales. SMP representations are a promising feature to extend the decomposition approach for open queueing networks to a tool for quality-of-service evaluation in ATM networks.

Remaining difficulties and challenges for further research are undeniable with regard to an adequate representation of superposition and departure processes.

References

[1] G.R. Bitran and S. Dasu, *A review of open queueing network models of manufacturing systems*, Queueing Systems 12 (1992) 95-134.

[2] G.R. Bitran and S. Dasu, *Approximating nonrenewal processes by Markov chains: Use of super-Erlang (SE) chains*, Opsn. Res. 41 (1993) 903-923.

[3] W. Ding, *A unified correlated input process model for telecommunication networks*, Proc. 13. Internat. Teletraffic Congress, Copenhagen, eds. A. Jensen and V.B. Iversen (1991) 539-544.

[4] K.M. Elsayed, *On the superposition of discrete-time Markov renewal processes and application to statistical multiplexing of bursty traffic sources*, Proc. IEEE GLOBECOM (1994) 1113-1117.

[5] W.K. Grassmann and J.L. Jain, *Numerical solutions of the waiting time distribution and idle time distribution of the arithmetic GI/G/1 queue*, Operations Research 37 (1989) 141-150.

[6] G. Haßlinger, *A polynomial factorization approach to the discrete time GI/G/1/(N) queue size distribution*, Performance Evaluation 23 (1995) 217–240.

[7] G. Haßlinger, *Semi-Markovian modelling and performance analysis of variable rate traffic in ATM networks*, to appear in Telecommunication Systems, selected paper issue of the 3. INFORMS Telecom. Conf.

[8] G. Haßlinger and M. Adam, *Modelling and performance analysis of traffic in ATM networks including autocorrelation*, Proc. IEEE Infocom'96 Conference, San Francisco (1996) 1460-1467.

[9] G. Haßlinger and E.S. Rieger, *Analysis of open discrete time queueing networks: A refined decomposition approach*, J. Opl. Res. Soc. 47 (1996) 640-653.

[10] B.R. Haverkort, *Approximate analysis of networks of Ph/Ph/1/K queues: Theory & tool support*, Proc. Performance Tools/MMB '95, Lecture Notes in Comp. Sci. 977, Springer (1995) 239-253.

[11] J.J. Hunter, *Mathematical techniques of applied probability*, Vol. 1/2, Academic Press, New York (1983).

[12] M.A. Johnson, *An empirical study of queueing approximations based on phase-type distributions*, Commun. Statist.-Stochastic Models 9, (1993) 531-561.

[13] P.J. Kühn, *Approximate analysis of general queueing networks by decomposition*, IEEE Trans. on Com. COM-27 (1979) 113–126.

[14] W.E. Leland, M.S. Taqqu, W. Millinger and D.V. Wilson, *On the self-similar nature of ethernet traffic*, IEEE/ACM Trasnsactions on Networking 2 (1994) 1-15.

[15] B. Maglaris, D. Anastassiou, P. Sen, G. Karlsson and J. Robbins, *Performance Models of Statistical Multiplexing in Packet Video Communications*, IEEE Trans. on Com. COM-36 (1988) 834–843.

[16] M.F. Neuts, *Matrix-Geometric Solutions in Stochastic Models*, J. Hopkins (1981)

[17] M. Parulekar and A. Makowski, *Tail probabilities for a multiplexer with self-similar traffic*, Proc. IEEE Infocom'96 Conference, San Francisco (1996) 1452-1459.

[18] V. Paxson and S. Floyd, *Wide area traffic: The failure of Poisson modelling*, IEEE/ACM Trasnsactions on Networking 3 (1995) 226-244.

[19] B. Pourbabai, *Tandem behaviour of a telecommunication system with repeated calls: A Markovian case with buffers*, J. Opl. Res. Soc. 40 (1989) 671-680.

[20] S.V. Raghavan, D. Vasukiammaiyar and G. Haring, *Hierarchical approach to building generative networkload models*, Computer Networks and ISDN Systems 27 (1991) 1193-1206.

[21] E.S. Rieger and G. Haßlinger, *An analytical solution to the discrete time single server queue with semi-Markovian arrivals*, Queueing Systems 18 (1994) 69-105.

[22] F. Schwarzkopf, *Cell scattering among bursty ATM traffic on virtual circuits and paths* (in german) diploma thesis, TH Darmstadt (1995).

[23] B. Sengupta, *The semi-Markovian queue: Theory and applications*, Commun. Statist.-Stochastic Models 6 (1990) 383-413.

[24] K. Sriram and W. Whitt, *Characterizing superposition arrival processes in packet multiplexers for voice and data*, IEEE J. Sel. Areas in Com. SAC-4 (1986) 833–846.

[25] H.C. Tijms, *Heuristics for the loss probability in finite-buffer queues*, Proc. Conf. on Appl. Prob. in Engineering, Computer and Comm. Sciences, Paris (1993) 156-157.

[26] W. Whitt, *The queueing network analyser*, Bell Syst. Techn. J. 62 (1983) 2779-2843.

An Embedded Network Simulator to Support Network Protocols' Development

Luigi Rizzo

Dip. di Ingegneria dell'Informazione, Università di Pisa
via Diotisalvi 2 – 56126 Pisa (Italy) – email: l.rizzo@iet.unipi.it

Abstract. The development of network protocols, especially if designed for use in very large scale networks, generally requires extensive simulation and tests in operational environments to assess their performance and correctness. Both approaches have limitations: simulation because of possible lack of accuracy in modeling the system (and, especially, traffic generators), tests in operating networks because of the difficulty of setting up and controlling the experimental testbed.

In this paper we propose to embed network simulators in operational systems, so as to get the advantages of both simulators and real testbeds. Such simulators can be built with minimal modifications to existing protocol stacks. They work by intercepting communications of the protocol layer under test and simulating the effects of finite queues, bandwidth limitations, communication delays, noisy channels. As a result, experiments can be run on a standalone system, while simulating arbitrarily complex networks. Thanks to the ability of using real traffic generators and protocol implementations, doing experiments becomes as simple as running the desired set of applications on a workstation.

An implementation of such a simulator, targeted to TCP and compatible with BSD-derived systems, is available from the author.

Keywords: Protocol evaluation, TCP/IP, simulation

1 Introduction

Network protocols, especially if designed to be used on very large scale systems such as the Internet, require careful analysis, both in design and implementation, to ensure that they can work properly even in unusual operating conditions. Almost unavoidably, theoretical analysis must be accompanied or followed by simulations and tests in operational systems to evaluate the actual performance.

Experimental testbeds, when available, are extremely useful because they allow testing real implementations of the protocol, and with real applications used as traffic generators. This way, no effort is required in modeling any part of the system under test, increasing the confidence in the tests' results. On the other hand, often testbeds are hard to setup with the desired features, because of cost or unavailability of suitable hardware/software. Also, experiments done in real testbeds might suffer from the lack of adequate control over operating conditions (queue sizes, delays, external traffic sources).

Simulations have complementary properties. They make it possible to overcome the lack of a testbed with the desired features, at the expense of a greater effort in modeling the whole system under test. As an example of the difficulties in building an accurate simulator, consider a simple FTP transfer over TCP. The flow of data is regulated by a number of factors, such as the speed of disks at the sender and the receiver side, the scheduling of processes at the two nodes, the size of send and receive windows, the acknowledgement generation policy. The latter, in turn, depend on the behaviour of different protocol layers, or even on the result of previous communication.

In many cases, building an accurate model of a system is an extremely challenging task, and the unavoidable simplifications that are introduced might possibly result in inaccurate or unreliable results. Also, simulated environments might not be available to debug and test the final implementation of a protocol, when it is easy to introduce subtle implementation bugs. Nevertheless, the difficulties of setting up a real testbed with the desired features has stimulated the development of a number of network simulators, such as REAL [1], Netsim [2, 3] and ns [4]. The x-kernel framework [5] has also been used for the implementation and testing of network protocols.

Experiments on network protocols are usually aimed to determine protocols' behaviour in complex networks made of many nodes, routers and links, with different queueing policies, queue sizes, bandwidths, propagation delays. The problems discussed above in building and/or modeling complex environments, and, especially, in interpreting experimental results obtained in such settings, often suggests the use of simplified networks such as the ones shown in Figure 1. There, a bottleneck router followed by a link with given bandwidth and delay models the overall features of the network, and additional nodes simply generate background traffic on the network.

Quite often, in experiments on real testbeds, the bottleneck router is also modified to act as a "flakeway", introducing artificial delays, random packet losses and reordering. In some cases, the effects of bandwidth limitations can be simulated [6].

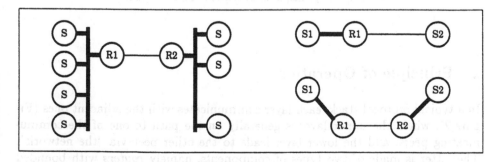

Fig. 1. Typical settings used in the study of network protocols. The thin line represents the bottleneck link.

In this paper we extend the concept of a flakeway in order to build a testbed which gives the advantages of both simulation and real-world testing. Our proposal consists in embedding a flexible network simulator into an operational protocol stack. Under normal operating conditions, the simulator is disabled and introduces a negligible overhead in system's operations. When running experiments, the simulator can be configured to simulate arbitrary networks with the desired features. Hence, experiments can be run on a standalone system, without the need of a real testbed. Yet, real traffic generators and protocol implementations can be used to run experiments. This allows the tests to cover the final implementation as well, something that is not generally possible by using simulators. Also, the researcher has full control over the testbed, which makes experimental results easier to understand.

In the next section we show the principle of operation of our simulator, showing the way to simulate its basic components (routers and links). Section 3 shows how arbitrary networks can be built with a proper composition of the basic components. Finally, we present some examples showing the ease of use and the little intrusivity of the simulator, and illustrate some possible applications.

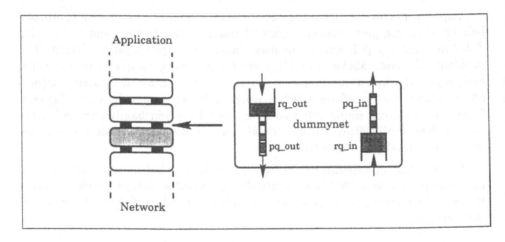

Fig. 2. The principle of operation of our simulator

2 Principle of Operation

In a typical protocol stack, each layer communicates with the adjacent ones (Figure 2), where the upper layer is generally on the path to one of the communicating peers, and the lower layer leads to the other peer via "the network". The latter is made of two types of components, namely *routers* with bounded queue size and a given queueing policy, and communication links (*pipes*) with given bandwidth, delay and loss rate. A network is an arbitrary graph of routers and pipes, and the presence of multiple paths between two nodes can lead to out-of-order delivery of packets.

The simplest topologies used in experiments usually include just two routers and one pipe. Both elements can be easily modeled (see Figure 2) by two pairs of queues, **rq** and **pq**, inserted at some point in the protocol stack (typically, below the transport layer). Let k be the maximum size of **rq**, B and t_p the bandwidth and propagation delay of the pipe, respectively. Traffic exchanged between the two layers is then subject to the following processing:

1. packets are first inserted in **rq**; insertions are bounded by the maximum queue size, k, and are performed according to the queueing policy of choice (usually FIFO with tail-drop, but other policies are also possible, such as RED [7]).
2. packets are moved from **rq** to **pq** at a maximum rate of B bytes per second. **pq** uses a FIFO policy;
3. packets remain in **pq** for t_p seconds, after which they are dequeued and sent to the next protocol layer. Random losses can be introduced at this stage, by dropping packets according to the loss rate instead of delivering them to the next stage.

Steps 2 and 3 can be performed by running a periodic task whose period T is a suitable submultiple of t_p. In this case, at each run at most BT bytes are moved from **rq** to **pq**, while packets remain in **pq** for t_p/T cycles.

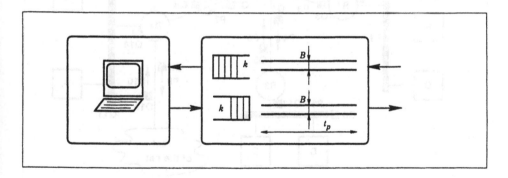

Fig. 3. Structure of a node using the basic simulator

The basic component of our simulator comprises two pairs **rq/pq** and is inserted between protocol layers as shown in Figure 2. Since most systems implement a loopback at the bottom of the stack, local communication (through the loopback) is also subject to the queueing and delay introduced by the simulated network, and the resulting system looks like the one in Figure 3. The presence of the loopback is what lets experiments to be run on standalone systems, without the need for a real network. By using such a simple setting, we can simulate most of the settings used in the literature on TCP congestion control [5, 8, 9, 10, 11, 12].

3 Simulating Arbitrary Networks

More complex structures, involving multiple queues and links, can also be simulated, even when the simulator is running on a single node. To this purpose, a model of the system must be defined in terms of queues and links. On each router, and possibly on each simulated node, queues of bounded size are associated to the output links (or, depending on the buffer-management policy used in the router, a single queue may be used for all output links). Unidirectional pipes with given bandwidth and delay are used to simulate communication links: two pipes are used for full-duplex links (e.g. a point-to-point connection), while a single one suffices for half-duplex, shared links such as an Ethernet LAN (in this case, we implicitly assume that all nodes transmitting to the shared medium queue their data into an additional, shared queue). Routing tables must also be defined, so that traffic can be forwarded through the appropriate paths depending on the source and destination addresses. The system where the experiment is run can be assigned multiple addresses in order to simulate a complete network on a standalone system, or it can use a single address and simply simulate the effect of different paths to different destinations.

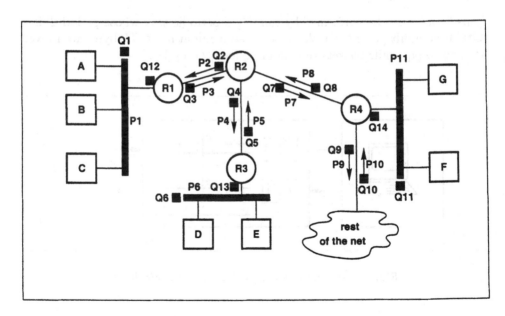

Fig. 4. A sample network and the corresponding structure of the modules.

Figure 4 presents a sample topology, with three Ethernet networks (between A, B, C and R1; D, E and R3; F, G and R4), and four point-to-point links. In order to run a standalone simulation, the system is assigned seven addresses, corresponding to the simulated end-nodes A..G. A total of 11 unidirectional pipes is used to represent the various links and Ethernets. Queues are assigned to the outputs of each router (and to the link coming from the rest of the network, P10). Q1, Q6 and Q11 are the queues associated with the three Ethernets in the system, whereas we have not provided queues for the end nodes. Finally, a routing table is associated to the output end of each pipe to determine the flow of packets, depending on source and destination addresses, and the direction of flow in the protocol stack (e.g. from TCP to IP or from IP to TCP).

Traffic is routed in the following way. Packets generated and received by "internal" nodes (A..G) are subject to queueing and delay on one direction only (e.g. going from TCP to IP). Once they have reached the destination queue, they are forwarded to the lower protocol layer. From here, through the loopback interface, they move upwards and straight to the final destination. Packets originating from or directed to an external destination (the cloud labeled "rest of the net") are subject to queueing and delays in the inbound and outbound path, respectively.

4 Limitations

Our simulation technique produces, of course, only an approximate model of a real network with given features. Most of the approximations introduced by our technique derive from the granularity, T, and the precision of the operating system's timer, and in many cases they have little influence on the experiments.

T sets the resolution of all timing-related measurements. On modern systems, a granularity of 1 ms or even smaller is easy to achieve, and is suitable for the vast majority of networks except, perhaps, those with very high bandwidths and short pipes.

On a non real-time system there is no guarantee that deadlines are honored; thus, depending on the overall system's load, the periodic task might be run late, or even miss one or more ticks. In our experiments, however, these events have been extremely rare even on a relatively slow system running FreeBSD, which is not a real-time OS. Besides, the same errors affect all protocol timers, which are driven by the same clock interrupt.

Finally, it should be noted that network-related events occur synchronously with the system's timer. This might hide or amplify some real-world phenomena which occur because of race conditions. Such a problem can only be of some concern in very special situations.

The accuracy of the simulation also depends on the correct computation of packet sizes (needed in the computation of the simulated bandwidth). Our technique makes it possible to account for link-layer "overheads", including the effect of link-layer compression, a feature which makes the link appear as a variable-bandwidth channel, and might have significant effects on performance.

5 A Sample Implementation

We have developed a basic simulator [13] using the technique described in this paper, working at the interface between TCP and IP; it intercepts calls to `ip_output()` made by TCP modules, and those to `tcp_input()` made by the protocol demultiplexer in IP. All the basic functionalities required to build arbitrary networks are included in less than 300 lines of kernel code.

When disabled (i.e. no buffering, delay or bandwidth limitation is required), the overhead introduced by our tool corresponds to one function call per packet. This is a negligible overhead, and allows one to have the simulator compiled into the kernel at all times. When enabled, the overhead is directly proportional to the work required to route packets through the simulated network: all queue manipulations are in fact constant time operations, and no copies of data are done at all. As it is shown from Figure 6, even when the simulator is enabled the available communication bandwidth still remains much larger than the typical Ethernet bandwidth, so that no sensible performance degradation is perceived.

There are only two practical limitations in running a simulation: the CPU power required by all producers/consumers to generate the required traffic, and the memory required to buffer all packets in transit (both in queues and pipes).

Since the simulator only intercepts calls between selected protocol layers, other traffic is left unmodified. As an example, our implementation does not interfere with UDP traffic, allowing a system to mount disks using NFS over UDP, yet leaving a clean simulation environment with only TCP traffic.

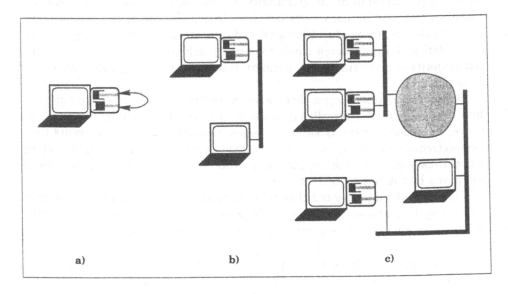

Fig. 5. Various configurations used for experiments

5.1 Examples of use

Depending on the complexity of the simulated network, different techniques can be used to configure the simulator. For the simple case shown in this Section, comprising one pipe and one router, the operating parameters (k, B, t_p) are set using a single kernel variable (net.inet.tcp.dummynet). The sysctl command allows an easy setting of the parameters. The value of net.inet.tcp.dummynet is given as the decimal number BBBBkkddd, where BBBB is the bandwidth in KB/s, kk is the queue size, ddd is the value of t_p in units of T seconds (1 ms in our case). For more complex setups, such as those shown in Section 3, a more flexible setup utility is required, to define the structure of the simulated network and set up the routing tables.

The simplest way of doing an experiment consists in running a communication between two processes on the same system. Since the loopback occurs at the end of the pipe (Figure 5a), buffering and delays occur twice, and buffers are shared by traffic in the two directions.

An example of use of this setting is shown in Figure 6, where some FTP transfers are done using ncftp; for each configuration (except for the last three), we show the average throughput value of 10 tests, to compensate for the variations deriving from concurrent network and CPU activities. Lines beginning with --- are normally part of the system's logfile. The system used for the experiments is a Pentium100 with 32MB RAM, running FreeBSD 2.1. During the experiments, both client and server were running on the same system (the author's workstation), together with the usual workload consisting of an X Server, a number of X applications, a Web server and various other applications.

TCP communications use a 16KB window in this example, so in some cases the throughput is limited by the window size rather than the available bandwidth. The MSS for the interface is set to a low value, which limits performance further but allows a larger number of packets to fit in the window in use.

In the first test, bandwidth and queue limits are set to a large value in order to determine the maximum throughput. The second experiment limits the bandwidth to 200KB/s, but the actual throughput is lower because the channel is shared by data and ACKs, and the TCP header (including RFC1323 and RFC1644 extensions) consumes a portion of the bandwidth. In the third experiment a short propagation delay is introduced, which has negligible effect on the throughput. Increasing the delay to 50 ms (making the RTT 200 ms) causes the connection to be limited by the window size (roughly one window per RTT or 80 KB/s, with various overheads and the cost of slow start reducing the throughput even further). The next two experiments are run with very limited queue sizes: here, frequent overflows occur which reduce the throughput significantly. In the last run, Selective Acknowledgments are enabled.

In single-system experiments, both communication peers usually run the same implementation of a protocol (unless the system allows the protocol parameters to be set individually for each process). Interoperability tests can be done by using two nodes on the same LAN, with the simulator running on one of them (Figure 5b). This resembles the typical setting for protocol evaluation in real networks, consisting in two nodes on different LANs connected by one or two routers and a bottleneck link. Finally, more complex simulation settings can be built by using several systems, some of which use the simulator configured

```
prova# ifconfig lo0 127.0.0.1 mtu 576 # small packets --> large windows
prova# ncftp -u localhost
...
ncftp> !sysctl -w net.inet.tcp.dummynet=999900000
--- 0 ms, 9999 KB/s, 0 buffers
ncftp> get 1M a
a: 1048576 bytes received in 0.66 seconds, 1552.17 K/s.

ncftp> !sysctl -w net.inet.tcp.dummynet=20000000
--- 0 ms, 200 KB/s, 0 buffers
ncftp> get 1M a
a: 1048576 bytes received in 6.17 seconds, 166.10 K/s.

ncftp> !sysctl -w net.inet.tcp.dummynet=20000001
--- 1 ms, 200 KB/s, 0 buffers
ncftp> get 1M a
a: 1048576 bytes received in 6.21 seconds, 165.01 K/s.

ncftp> !sysctl -w net.inet.tcp.dummynet=20000050
--- 50 ms, 200 KB/s, 0 buffers
ncftp> get 1M a
a: 1048576 bytes received in 15.53 seconds, 65.96 K/s.

ncftp> !sysctl -w net.inet.tcp.dummynet=20007050
--- 50 ms, 200 KB/s, 7 buffers
ncftp> get 1M a
--- tcp_ip_out drop, have 7 packets (3 times)
a: 1048576 bytes received in 28.01 seconds, 36.56 K/s.

ncftp> !sysctl -w net.inet.tcp.dummynet=20007001
--- 1 ms, 200 KB/s, 7 buffers
ncftp> get 1M a
--- tcp_ip_out drop, have 7 packets (40 times)
a: 1048576 bytes received in 10.88 seconds, 94.09 K/s.

ncftp> !sysctl -w net.inet.tcp.sack=0x10 # enable SACK
ncftp> get 1M a
--- tcp_ip_out drop, have 7 packets (40 times)
a: 1048576 bytes received in 10.14 seconds, 101.01 K/s.
```

Fig. 6. A sample session showing the use of the simulator

with different parameters (Figure 5c).

One would expect that the use of our simulation technique – especially when working on a single workstation – leads to completely deterministic and reproducible results, since the behaviour of the network is simulated. These expectations are wrong, because the traffic sources and, especially, their interactions with the simulator, are not fully deterministic.

5.2 Applications

The simulation technique used in this paper has been used extensively in the development of Selective Acknowledgement options for TCP [14, 15], and is being actively used in experiments on new congestion control strategies. These two applications reflect the typical cases where such a simulated environment is most useful. In the former (implementation of a protocol extension), building a real testbed would be hard because it would require the availability of other implementations. In the latter (analysis of the behaviour of a modified or new protocol), tests needs to be done first in a controlled environment, in order to get a better understanding of the protocol's behaviour; only at a later time the effects of (unknown) external traffic can be accounted for. In both cases, it is also very important to make sure that the final implementation has no undesired interaction with other mechanism already present in the protocol stack. Such experiments will be more and more necessary in the development of new protocols such as IPv6, or multicast extensions, because of the unavailability of a suitable infrastructure.

We would like to remark that, since the network simulator we have shown introduces very little overhead, it can also be used during normal operations, e.g. as a tool to provide rate-limitation for selected traffic.

6 Conclusions

We have shown how experiments on network protocols can be done easily on a standalone system using real world applications as traffic generators. Our approach gives the advantages of both real-world testing and simulation: simplicity of use, high control over operating parameters, high accuracy, no need for complex hardware settings, no overhead for running simulations. Especially, experiments can be run using a single workstation and do not require the presence of a real network or expensive devices such as routers and delay emulators.

The convenience of use and the little intrusivity of the technique described in this paper really encourages in having the network simulator available as a standard part of the system, so that experiments with different system configurations can be done as soon as there is a need, without requiring long times to setup a suitable testbed. The simulator is especially useful when developing completely new protocols, as a suitable testbed might simply not exist. The use of our technique can speed up dramatically the analysis and development of protocols, making the simulation environment readily available in a production environment and easily interfaced with other working systems.

Acknowledgements

The work described in this paper has been supported in part by the Commission of European Communities, Esprit Project LTR 20422 – "Moby Dick, The Mobile Digital Companion (MOBYDICK)", and in part by the Ministero dell'Università e della Ricerca Scientifica e Teconologica of Italy.

References

1. S.Keshav: "REAL: A Network Simulator", Technical Report 88/472, Dept. of Computer Science, UC Berkeley, 1988.
   Available as (http://netlib.att.com/~keshav/papers/real.ps.Z)
   Simulator sources available as ftp://ftp.research.att.com/dist/qos/REAL.tar
2. A.Heybey: "The network simulator", Technical Report, MIT, Sept.1990
3. J.Hoe: "Startup dynamics of TCP's Congestion Control and Avoidance Schemes", Master's Thesis, MIT, June 1995
4. S.McCanne, S.Floyd: ns-LBNL Network Simulator.
   Available from (http://www-nrg.ee.lbl.gov/ns/)
5. N.C.Hutchinson, L.L.Peterson: "The x-kernel: An architecture for implementing network protocols", IEEE Trans. on Software Engineering, 17(1):64-76, Jan.1991.
6. E.Limin Yan: "The Design and Implementation of an Emulated WAN", Tech. report, CS Dept., USC, 1995.
   Available from http://catarina.usc.edy/lyan/delayemulator.tar.gz
7. S.Floyd, V.Jacobson: "Random Early Detection Gateways for Congestion Avoidance", IEEE/ACM Trans. on Networking, 1(4):397-413, Aug.1993.
   Available from http://www-nrg.ee.lbl.gov/nrg-papers.html
8. V.Jacobson, "Congestion Avoidance and Control", *Proceedings of SIGCOMM'88* (Stanford, CA, Aug.88), ACM.
9. Z. Wang, J. Crowcroft, "Eliminating Periodic Packet Losses in the 4.3-Tahoe BSD TCP Congestion Control Algorithm", ACM Computer Communications Review, Apr '92.
10. L.S.Brakmo, L.Peterson: "Performance Problems in BSD4.4. TCP", 1994.
    Available as ftp://cs.arizona.edu/xkernel/Papers/tcp_problems.ps
11. L.S.Brakmo, S.W.O'Malley, L.Peterson: "TCP Vegas: New Techniques for Congestion Detection and Avoidance", *Proceedings of SIGCOMM'94 Conference*, pp.24-35, Aug.94. Available as ftp://ftp.cs.arizona.edu/xkernel/Papers/vegas.ps
12. K. Fall, S.Floyd: "Comparison of Tahoe, Reno and SACK TCP", Tech. Report, 1995. Available from http://www-nrg.ee.lbl.gov/nrg-papers.html
13. L.Rizzo, Simulator's sources.
    Available as http://www.iet.unipi.it/~luigi/dummynet.diffs
14. M. Mathis, J. Mahdavi, S. Floyd, A. Romanow: "RFC2018: TCP Selective Acknowledgement Option", Oct.1996.
15. L.Rizzo: Sources for a SACK implementation for FreeBSD.
    Available as http://www.iet.unipi.it/~luigi/sack.diffs

Synchronized Two-Way Voice Simulation Tool for Internet Phone Performance Analysis and Evaluation[1]

Adrian E. Conway

Racal-Datacom, 1601 North Harrison Parkway, Sunrise, FL 33323, USA

Sue B. Moon

Department of Computer Science, University of Massachusetts at Amherst, Amherst, MA 01003, USA

Paul Skelly

GTE Laboratories Incorporated, 40 Sylvan Road, Waltham, MA 02254, USA

Abstract: A simulation tool is developed for the performance analysis and evaluation of Internet phone applications. The tool can be used off-line to simulate real two-way phone conversations under different Internet loss and delay conditions. The simulation model includes access links that connect an Internet service provider to the Internet, as well as background Internet phone and data traffic. It also includes details of Internet phone implementations such as encoding, packetization, silence detection, and the IP, UDP, and RTP protocols. An original feature of the simulator is that it takes into account explicitly the synchronization of talkspurts in a two-way conversation. Example results of two-way conversations under various delay and loss conditions are provided in audio files. Pointers to download the files are at http://www-net.cs.umass.edu/~sbmoon/synch.html.

1. Introduction

Internet phone has recently gained much attention as a computer-to-computer application for conducting voice conversations over the Internet. Software products are now available commercially or as freeware. Examples of commercial packages include Cooltalk 1.0 by Netscape Comm. Corp and Internet Phone 3.2 by VocalTec Inc. A recent survey of existing products is given in [VEN]. Examples of freeware packages include `nevot` and `vat`. The present main attractive feature of Internet phone is that there are basically no direct charges associated with the calls that are made. One can use it to make local, long-distance, or international phone calls between computers on the Internet without any significant service charges. Systems are also being developed currently to interconnect Internet phone calls with the public switched telephone network. The present main disadvantage of internet phone is that

---

[1] Work carried out at GTE Laboratories Incorporated.

it relies on the best effort service that is provided by the existing Internet. Consequently, the perceived quality of the voice communication is variable. Measurements on routes indicate that end-to-end Internet packet losses can be quite high [BOL,SAN]. Losses in the range of 30 - 50% are not atypical [YAJ]. The delay is also quite variable, depending not only on the existing traffic but also on the number of routers and 'firewalls' that may be traversed. When the conditions are favorable, however, near toll quality can be reached. Another disadvantage is that, except for a few experimental audio conferencing tools, most commercial products are incompatible and standards do not yet exist.

At this point in time, it is unclear what the future may hold for Internet phone. The extent to which it evolves depends, of course, on how the Internet evolves in terms of bandwidth and real-time service offerings. A variety of opinions can be heard in the press and in the computer-communications and telecommunications communities. At one extreme, Internet phone is viewed as a novelty with no real potential. At the other extreme, it is viewed as the 'third-generation' of telephony - the first generation being that based on analogue circuit-switching and the second being that based on digital circuit-switching. Whatever the opinions may be today, the reality is that Internet phone is growing in use among Internet users. It will also be offered as a 'value-added' feature by a growing number of Internet service providers (ISPs) in the near future.

In order for an ISP to offer Internet phone service at a certain level of quality either over a private 'engineered' network or subnetworks that are owned or operated by other organizations, it is necessary that one have an understanding of the limits of packet loss and delay that can reasonably be tolerated. In the case of a private network, one can then dimension and plan the network appropriately to meet the traffic demands of Internet phone customers and satisfy the loss and delay limits. In the case where an ISP is providing Internet phone service using the subnetworks of other organizations, one can then plan out a loss and delay 'budget' for the subnetworks that are to be traversed so that the end-to-end loss and delay limits are satisfied and the desired overall level of quality is achieved. In the standards making process, it is also necessary that one be able to quantify these limits.

The determination of the loss and delay limits for telephony of a reasonable quality over the Internet is not a simple problem. For circuit-switched voice, the maximum tolerable delay is well known to be 400ms or less [ITU]. This delay limit is dependent on the end-to-end delay that can be tolerated before a voice conversation becomes awkward. It also depends on the limits that can be handled by echo cancellers. In computer-to-computer Internet telephony, however, the delay and loss are variable and there is a full-duplex end-to-end channel so that there is no echo problem (in the traditional sense). Playout algorithms [MOO,RAM] at the receivers are also used to compensate to a certain extent for variable delay. The quality that is expected of Internet telephony may also be lower than that of conventional telephone service depending on the price that a user may be charged by an ISP in the future. Hence, the delay and loss limits may be significantly different from those associated with conventional public telephone quality. Moreover, Internet phone is designed to be simply a voice communication device. Therefore, it does not need to faithfully reproduce the signals required to support analogue modem and fax devices.

The delay and loss requirements of packet voice have been studied extensively in the past (see, for example, [COH,JAY,MON]). However, given the particularities of the Internet architecture, the implementation details of different products, and the recent evolution of networking and computing, it is now necessary to re-examine the issues in a more modern context. Details that now need to be considered include the packetization period, Internet architecture, protocol stack overheads of IP, UDP, and RTP [SCH3], silence/talkspurt detection algorithms, playout delay adjustment algorithms, encoding and compression schemes, and error recovery mechanisms. To evaluate the delay and loss limits for different parameter settings, it is necessary to evaluate the voice quality under a multitude of scenarios. This should be done in a controlled experiment. There are two possible approaches in which such an experiment might be carried out. In the first approach, we could build a *real-time* simulator and have pairs of users evaluate voice quality in real-time as a function of network loss and delay. In the second approach, we could build an *off-line* simulator, record voice conversations, run them through the simulator off-line for various loss and delay scenarios, and then evaluate the resulting voice quality off-line. A basic problem with the first approach is that real-time simulation is, in general, not feasible since too much processing is required if we want to include the effects of, for example, a multitude of background Internet phone calls and other data traffic, complex loss and delay processes, or multiple routers and subnetworks. The problem with the second approach is that if we simply run recorded voice conversations through an off-line simulator, then we cannot properly capture the effect that the end-to-end delay has on the interaction between the speakers.

In this paper, we develop a *two-way* voice simulation tool for Internet phone performance analysis and evaluation. The tool can be used off-line to simulate two-way phone conversations while taking into account implementation details, parameter choices, user-specifiable Internet loss and delay characteristics, other background Internet phone traffic and data traffic, and the effect of multiplexing at the access links connecting an ISP to the Internet. Since the actual simulation is done off-line, the tool is along the lines of the second approach described above. Apart from being of use to determine the delay and loss limits for Internet phone, the simulation tool can also be used for the qualitative validation of analytically based sizing models for access links and other multiplexing points. In other words, we can use the simulator to get a feeling for what real voice conversations sound like when they pass through a multiplexing point that has been sized using some mathematical model.

The principal novel contribution in the simulator is the notion of modeling explicitly the inter-speaker synchronization that exists between the talkspurts in the original unperturbed two-way voice conversation. By doing this, we are able to simulate more realistically the effect that variable end-to-end delays have on the interaction between the speakers, vary the experiment in a controlled manner, and thereby better determine in a qualitative manner the delay and loss limits for reasonable phone quality. To the best of our knowledge, such a two-way synchronized voice simulation technique has not been considered previously. Of course, the simulator has certain limitations since it cannot capture how delay and loss affects the information *content* (e.g. extra interruptions and repetitions due to excessive delay) in a two-way interaction. The idea for the two-way simulation technique was inspired by [BRA2], where an analytical Markov model is developed for talkspurt generation in a *two-way* voice conversation. This model is a generalization of the *one-way* two-state Markov model that has been adopted almost invariably in analytical packet voice studies to date (see, for example, [DAI,GRU,HEF,LEE,SRI]). The two-way model is much more complex than the one-way model but it is an attempt to capture in an analytical model the synchronization of talkspurts in a two-way conversation.

In the following section, we first provide a functional view of the Internet phone simulation tool and explain in general terms how a two-way phone conversation is synchronized in the simulation. In Section 3, we then go into more detail and describe how we first record two-way voice conversations using a pair of Sun SPARCstations and process the resulting audio files. We also explain how silence detection and packetization is carried out. In Section 4, we explain in more detail how we synchronize the talkspurts in the simulated two-way conversation. In Section 5, we provide a complete logical block diagram of the simulation tool to show how we proceed from collecting audio samples to processing the simulation output and constructing the final audio files that can be played out and evaluated. We also describe in more detail the parameters that may be changed in the simulation. In Section 6, we present some example simulation results to demonstrate two-way conversations under different loss and delay conditions. The results are in audio files that are in Sun audio file format. Pointers to download the files are located at http://www-net.cs.umass.edu/~sbmoon/synch.html. Finally, in Section 6, we make some concluding remarks and indicate some directions in which the present work is being extended.

2. Internet Phone Simulation Model

An overall functional view of our simulation model is provided in Fig. 1. In the figure, we have Speakers *A* and *B* at computers who conduct a two-way voice conversation using an Internet phone application. The voice signal of each speaker is sampled, encoded, and packetized by the computer. The resulting packet stream is then transmitted over the access link and the Internet. Sampling, encoding, and packetization is described in more detail in Section 3. The simulation is driven by the packet voice streams that are generated by the two speakers (see a–a and b–b in Fig. 1). These streams are generated prior to running the simulation by recording a direct two-way telephone conversation and then processing the voice signals off-line. The recording procedure and processing is described in more detail in Section 3. When the packet voice traffic arrives at its destination, the received packets are played out according to a certain playout algorithm, as shown in Fig. 1. During the simulation,

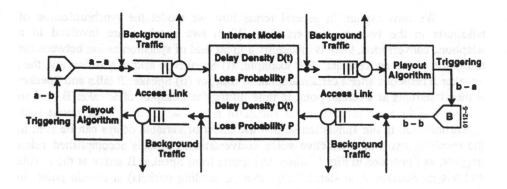

Fig. 1. Internet Phone Simulation Model

we store the playout times of packets at each side (see b–a and a–b in Fig. 1). We also store the transmission times of packets at each side (see a–a and b–b in Fig. 1). The voice signals are then reconstructed off-line after the simulation is finished using the original voice samples and the stored packet transmission and playout time information.

The access links to the Internet are full-duplex. Each link is modeled by two finite buffer FIFO queues, one for each direction of transmission. The links could be, for example, T1 links with a data payload transfer rate of 1.344 Mbits/s. At the access links, we can also incorporate other background traffic. This is meant to take into account the presence of other Internet phone traffic and data traffic, such as web browsing, that is multiplexed on the same access links. For instance, an ISP multiplexes the traffic from many customers onto one or more access links to the rest of the Internet. Note that, in the model, this background traffic only passes through the FIFO queues. We do not include the background traffic in the Internet model itself since the intent of our simulation tool is to evaluate the performance of an Internet phone conversation for different access link scenarios and *existing* or *projected* Internet traffic conditions. The generation of the background traffic is described further in Section 5.

In the center of Fig. 1, we have the Internet model. In the present version of this model, the Internet impairments are represented simply by an end-to-end delay density function $D(t)$ and a loss probability P. The delay density includes propagation delays. The delay and loss processes are assumed to be independent. The impairments in the two directions are also assumed to be independent. The sampling of delays from the given density function presents a packet ordering problem that we shall revisit in Section 5.

We now explain in general terms how we model the synchronization of talkspurts in the two-way conversation. When two speakers are involved in a telephone conversation, there is inherently a great deal of synchronization between the talkspurts of the conversants. For example, (i) Speaker A asks a question and then Speaker B responds after a certain amount of time, or (ii) Speaker B talks and Speaker A then interrupts at a certain point in time during the talkspurt of Speaker B, and so on. One of the main features of our simulator is that we explicitly incorporate such synchronization in our simulation so that the effect of variable delays can be seen in the resulting two-way interactive voice conversation. This is accomplished using triggers, as illustrated in Fig. 1, where talkspurts from Speaker B arrive at the A side and trigger Speaker A to start talking (that is, sending packets) at certain points in time, and *vice versa*. Further details are provided in Section 4.

3. Recording and Packetization of Two-Way Voice Conversations

To record a two-way voice conversation, it is necessary that the two speakers be isolated acoustically so that the voice signals can be recorded separately without any mixing. This is done by placing the two speakers in separate offices that each contain a Sun SPARCstation and a conventional telephone. The two Suns are connected by a LAN. The two-way voice conversation between the speakers is then made using the telephones that are connected through the local PBX. At each telephone, we attach the Sun SPARCstation microphone in close proximity to the microphone in the telephone hand-set. The voice signal at each end can then be recorded separately. The recording should be done with no silence detection activated so that different silence detection algorithms can be applied off-line to the voice recordings, as desired.

The recording of the voice signal at each Sun can be carried out easily using `audiotool` that is available on SPARCstation 20 with Solaris 2.4. A problem with simply using `audiotool`, however, is that we need to synchronize the time at which the recordings are started on both sides since we will need to establish the timing relationships between the talkspurts of the two speakers, say Speakers 'A' and 'B'. Such a synchronization facility is not available in `audiotool`. To circumvent this problem, we can instead use `nevot` [SCH2] to make the recordings since the source code is available and we can modify it readily to produce a timestamp at the beginning of an audio file when a recording is started. In order to synchronize the clocks on the two Suns, we use NTP [MIL1]. This protocol provides clock synchronization "to within a few tens of milliseconds" [MIL2] in the Internet of today. The procedure is then to record the voice signals on both sides using the modified version of `nevot` and then delete the timestamps and a part of one of the audiofiles so that the voice samples of the two speakers are synchronized. Let T_x denote the timestamp in the audiofile for Speaker x, let δ denote the voice sampling period, and assume without loss of generality that $T_A \leq T_B$. Then the number of samples that should be deleted from the audio file for Speaker A is $\lceil (T_B - T_A)/\delta \rceil$. This is an approximate number since NTP provides a coarser granularity of timing than audio samples, but it is a good enough approximation for the present purposes since a time shift of several milliseconds in the playout of talkspurts is imperceptible. Let the resulting synchronized audio files be denoted by a.au and b.au.

In the recording of voice traces using nevot, we can specify either 64 Kbit/s 8-bit PCM μ-law, 64 Kbit/s 8-bit PCM A-law, 8KHz 13Kbit/s GSM, 8KHz 32Kbit/s DVI, or 8KHz 5.6Kbit/s LPC, to name a few encoding schemes. We can also specify 16KHz and 44.1KHz encoding but the use of these schemes depends on the machine. By simply modifying the nevot software, virtually any other standardized or proprietary encoding and compression scheme can be incorporated in our simulation tool. Hence, the tool also enables us to compare the performance of Internet phone applications with different voice encoding and compression schemes. In the simulation runs that we have carried out so far, we have used 64 Kbit/s 8-bit PCM μ-law.

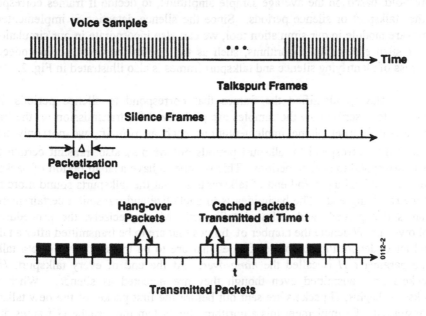

Fig. 2. Talkspurt/Silence Detection and Packetization of Voice Samples

Having obtained the synchronized voice sample files a.au and b.au, the next step is to perform silence detection on these files. Silence detection is used in packet voice to reduce the number of packets that need to be sent. To detect silence periods, we first divide the sample stream into frames, where each frame consists of a set of consecutive samples that is to be packetized, as illustrated in Fig. 2. The number of samples in a frame depends on the packetization interval Δ that is selected.

This parameter is a software variable that can be adjusted in our simulation tool. In [JAY], it is recommended that Δ be set in the range of 16 to 30ms. In the experiments that we have carried out so far, we have used $\Delta = 20$ms. Note that nevot uses $\Delta = 20$ms. Audio devices on Sun SPARCstations and SGI workstations generate a block of audio samples every 20ms if the sampling rate is set at 8KHz. This is why most voice applications use 20ms as the default packetization interval. Nevertheless, it is still adjustable. It can also be noted that 20ms of 64Kbit/s 8-bit PCM is a relatively long period for voice. It corresponds to 160 octects of voice data per packet. In contrast, we can note that in ATM there is at most only 48 octets of voice data in each cell (48 octets is an upper bound when no AAL is used). By making Δ larger, we reduce the packet transmission rate and the overall protocol overhead at the expense of an increase in packetization delay.

To decide which frames correspond to silence periods, we use the adaptive silence detection algorithm that is used in nevot. This algorithm uses a running threshold, based on the average sample amplitude, to decide if frames correspond to either talkspurt or silence periods. Since the silence detection is implemented as a software module in our simulation tool, we can also incorporate in our simulation tool other silence detection algorithms, such as the one in the GSM audio codec. The process of identifying silence and talkspurt frames is also illustrated in Fig. 2.

Having identified the frames that correspond to silence periods, it now remains to describe how the samples are packetized for transmission on the Internet. In certain Internet phone implementations such as nevot, we not only transmit frames that correspond to talkspurt periods but we may also transmit certain frames that correspond to silence periods. This is done to have a small period of background noise at the beginning and end of talkspurts so that the talkspurts sound more natural at the receiving end. The basic idea is to packetize and transmit a certain number of frames that precede and follow a talkspurt. More precisely, the procedure is as follows. Let H denote the number of frames that are to be transmitted after a talkspurt and let G denote the number of frames that are to be transmitted before a talkspurt. The parameter H is called the *hang-over*. At the end of every talkspurt, H more packets are transmitted even though they are detected as silence. When a new talkspurt begins, G packets are sent out before the first packet of the new talkspurt is transmitted. To implement this algorithm, the system must cache G frames during a silence period. The procedure is illustrated in Fig. 2 for $H=2$ and $G=2$. Note that all silence periods up to H+G frames in length are effectively eliminated. By changing H and G, we can take into account different implementation details in our simulator. nevot, for example, uses the default values $H=2$ and $G=3$, but these parameters can be modified.

Each frame that is to be packetized for transmission is sent in an individual packet. To this data, we add a 20 octet IP header, an 8 octet UDP header, and a 12 octet RTP header [SCH3], as illustrated in Fig. 3. This is the packetization procedure that is followed in nevot. With $\Delta = 20$ms and 64Kbps 8-bit PCM, the protocol overhead is 20%. By modifying the packetization process, we can also consider other protocol stack implementations in our simulation. Note that the RTP header contains a timestamp and a sequence number that is used in the playout algorithms.

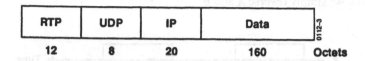

RTP	UDP	IP	Data	
12	8	20	160	Octets

Fig. 3. Internet Packet Format and Protocol Overheads ($\Delta = 20$ms)

4. Synchronization of Talkspurts in Two-Way Conversation

We now describe in more detail how the talkspurts of the two speakers are synchronized in the simulation. Consider the timing diagrams in Fig. 4. These illustrate the timing between Speaker B talkspurts and how the talkspurts of Speaker B are related to those of Speaker A in the *original* two-way conversation. Each talkspurt actually consists of a packet stream at rate Δ^{-1} packets/s. In Case 1 of Fig. 4, Speaker A finishes talking and B then starts talking after t seconds. In Case 2, Speaker A starts talking and Speaker B interrupts t seconds later when Speaker B 'hears' packet x from Speaker A. In Case 3, B talks, falls silent, and then starts talking again after t seconds. In Case 4, both speakers happen to start talking at the same time, t seconds after Speaker B stopped talking. If we reverse A and B in Fig. 4, then we have timing diagrams that illustrate the timing between Speaker A talkspurts and how the talkspurts of Speaker A are related to those of Speaker B in the original conversation.

In the simulation, we use the above defined timing relationships to reproduce the synchronization that exists between talkspurts in the original voice conversation. This is done as follows. We first consider how the synchronization is performed at the side of Speaker B. There are several cases that need to be defined.

(1) *Case 1 in Fig. 4*: A talkspurt from Speaker A finishes arriving at the side of Speaker B at time t_a and Speaker B is silent. The next talkspurt from Speaker B is then *triggered* to begin at time $t + t_a$.

(2) *Case 2 in Fig. 4*: A talkspurt from Speaker A is in the process of arriving at the B side and Speaker B is silent. The arrival of packet x from Speaker A then *triggers* the transmission of the (interruption) talkspurt from Speaker B.

(3) *Case 3 in Fig. 4*: A talkspurt from Speaker B finishes when Speaker A is silent. Speaker B then falls silent at time t_b. The next talkspurt from Speaker B is then *scheduled* to be sent out starting at time $t_b + t$.

117

(4) *Case 4 in Fig. 4*: Both speakers are silent and then both speakers send out talkspurts at the same time. The talkspurt from Speaker B is then scheduled to be sent out at time $t_B + t$. This is also done in the case where $t_a > t_b$.

The synchronization performed at the side of Speaker A is also as described above except that we simply reverse A and B.

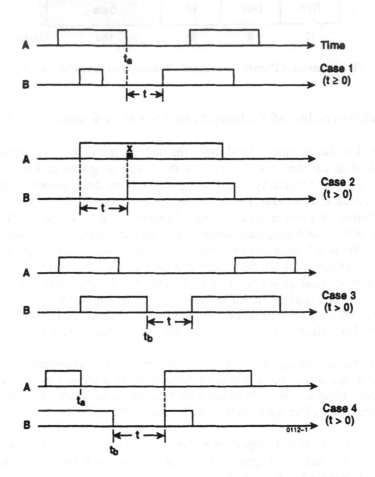

Fig. 4. **Timing Diagrams for Generation of Speaker B Talkspurts**

5. Logical Block Diagram and Model Parameters

The complete simulation model depicted in Fig. 1 has been programmed in C. We make use of C subroutines from SIMUL [SCH1] that simplify the construction of the discrete-event simulation program. Subroutines from SIMUL are also used to gather performance statistics such as the delay and loss at the finite buffer FIFO queues. A logical block diagram of the simulation tool is illustrated in Fig. 5. This shows the entire sequence of processing required from collecting voice samples to reproducing the conversation that is heard on either the *A* or *B* side.

In Fig. 5, we first use the `nevot` program to record voice samples in a file. As mentioned previously, the `nevot` software can be modified to consider different encoding schemes. The output of `nevot` is a `.tau` file. This file contains the voice samples as well as the timestamp that indicates when the recording was started. The `filter` program then takes as input the `a.tau` and `b.tau` files, removes the timestamps, and deletes a portion of one of the files, as described in Section 3, to synchronize the two voice traces. The synchronized voice samples are contained in the `.au` files. Following this, the `ts` program is run to detect the talkspurt frames in the voice sample files. The `ts` program can be modified to incorporate virtually any silence detection algorithm. The output of `ts` is a `.nevot` file. The `.nevot` file specifies which frames correspond to talkspurt periods. Following this, the `a.nevot`

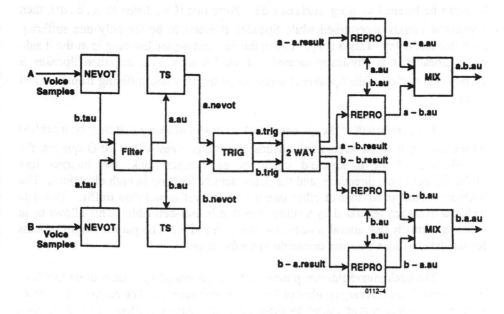

Fig. 5. Logical Block Diagram of Simulation Tool

and `b.nevot` files are processed by `trig` to determine all the triggering and scheduling information that is required to synchronize the talkspurts at both sides in the simulation. The output of `trig` is `a.trig` and `b.trig`.

The central part of the tool is the discrete-event simulation program `2way` that simulates the queueing system depicted in Fig. 1. This program takes `a.trig` and b.trig as inputs and outputs the .result files. The file a-a.result is a record of the departure times of Speaker A packets from the A side. The file a-b.result is a record of the playout times of Speaker B packets at the A side (after the playout algorithm). The definitions of b-b.result and b-a.result are apparent. The 2way program contains many parameters of the queueing system model that may be modified by the user. These will be described further below.

It now remains to construct audio files corresponding to a-a.result, a-b.result, b-b.result, and b-a.result. The .result file only contains packet playout times. Hence, it is necessary to build audio files by effectively filling the packets with voice samples. The program repro takes a .result file as input and builds an audio file using the voice samples that are contained in a .au file. The pair of audio files corresponding to each side is then mixed using the program mix. The audio file a.b.au is then a reproduction of the two-way conversation as seen at the A side. The file b.a.au is the two-way conversation as seen at the A side. These files can be listened to using audiotool. Note that if we listen to a.b.au, then Speaker A sounds unperturbed while Speaker B seems to be the only one suffering from loss and delay. This is simply due to the fact that we are listening in at the A side where Speaker A is physically located. If we listen to b.a.au, then Speaker B sounds unperturbed while Speaker A seems to be the only one suffering from loss and delay.

The parameters of the queueing system model in 2way that may be modified by the user include the access link speeds, the buffer sizes of the FIFO queues, the specification of the background traffic at each access link, the Internet loss probabilities in both directions, and the delay density function in both directions. The background traffic consists of other Internet phone traffic and data traffic. The data traffic arrivals are generated by a subroutine that is user-definable. This allows us to consider virtually any arrival process for the data traffic. The packet length process for the data traffic is also user definable in a subroutine.

The background Internet phone traffic is generated by a subroutine in which we can specify an arbitrary number of Internet phone sources. The packet traffic from each phone source is synthesized by generating talkspurts and silence periods using a well-known and widely adopted two-state Markov model for voice (see, for example, [HEF,SRI]). The talkspurts are then packetized, as in Section 3. Hang-over packets and cached packets are also added in, as in Section 3. In the Markov model, the talkspurt and silence periods are independent and exponentially distributed. The mean talkspurt and silence lengths are 352ms and 650ms, respectively [SRI]. The subroutine generates the packet process for each source, superimposes the resulting packet streams, and then presents the aggregate phone traffic to the FIFO queue. We use separate and independent background Internet phone traffic generators for each FIFO queue.

The Internet loss is generated simply using an independent Bernoulli trial with probability P. The 2way program can, however, be modified easily to accommodate more complex loss processes such as burst losses. The end-to-end delay is generated from a delay density function $D(t)$ that is user definable. When a packet is presented to the Internet model, the delay is drawn from the specified density function. Although this seems simple enough, there is a reordering problem. Suppose that packet i arrives at the Internet model at time t_i and the sampled delay is d_i and then packet $i+1$ arrives at time t_{i+1} and the sampled delay is d_{i+1}, where $t_{i+1} > t_i$. If $t_i+d_i > t_{i+1}+d_{i+1}$, then packet $i+1$ arrives at the destination end of the Internet before packet i. In other words, the sequencing of the packets is lost. To avoid this problem, we keep resampling d_{i+1} until $t_i+d_i > t_{i+1}+d_{i+1}$ is satisfied. The unused samples are stored for later use. When we determine the delay for subsequent packets, we first try to use the largest stored sample that does not lead to missequencing before generating any new delay samples from $D(t)$. To find the largest sample that can be used among the stored samples, we use a binary search. Since this delay generation procedure uses samples that are generated directly from $D(t)$, the marginal density function for the Internet delay is generated as specified.

6. Example Simulation Results

We now present some simulation results to demonstrate some two-way voice conversations under different delay and loss conditions. The results are in audio files that are in Sun audio file format. Pointers to download the files are located at http://www-net.cs.umass.edu/~sbmoon/synch.html. These files can be played out using audiotool. In all the examples, the access links are T1 links. We use the parameters Δ=20ms, H=2, and G=3. We consider six examples. In the first two examples, there is background phone traffic at the access links. In the remaining examples, we eliminate the background traffic completely and set the buffers at a large size so as to be able to concentrate on the effects of the Internet model impairments. In the examples, we use four different delay distributions D_1, D_2, D_3 and D_0. In D_1, the delays are in the range (0.1, 1.0) and the mean is 0.46 seconds. In D_2, the range is (0.5, 1.5) and the mean is 0.96 seconds. In D_3, the range is (1.0, 1.9) and the mean is 1.47 seconds. In D_0, there is no delay.

In the first example, the number of buffers at each FIFO queue is set at 30 packets. There are 25 background phone sources at each FIFO queue. The file adrian-paul.au is an original conversation between Adrian and Paul with no impairments. The file adrian-paul.delay1.0.ex1.au is the resulting conversation between Adrian and Paul, as heard at Adrian's side, with delay distribution D_1 and P=0%.

In the second example, the number of buffers at each FIFO queue is set at 30 packets and there are 30 background phone sources at each FIFO queue. The file adrian-paul.delay2.0.ex2.au is the conversation between Adrian and

Paul, as heard at Adrian's side, with D_2 and P=0%. The respective conversations at Paul's side are in the files `paul-adrian.delay1.0.ex1.au`, `paul-adrian.delay2.0.ex2.au`. Listening to these audio files, we can hear that the quality of the conversation is quite good in the case of `delay1.0.ex1`. In the case of `delay2.0.ex2`, the quality is relatively bad.

In the third example, the number of buffers at each queue is set at 100 and there is no background traffic. We consider a conversation between Adrian and Sue with no delay and P=33%. The conversation at Sue's side is in the file `sue-adrian.delay0.33.ex3.au`. The fourth example is the same as the third except that P=50%. The conversation at Adrian's side is in the file `adrian-sue.delay0.50.ex4.au`. Listening to these last two files, we can hear that, even with 33% loss, the speaker is still quite intelligible. At 50% loss, however, the speaker is very difficult to understand.

In the fifth example, the number of buffers at each queue is set at 100 and there is no background traffic. The conversation is between Adrian and Paul with D_1 and P=10%. The conversation at Paul's side is in the file `paul-adrian.delay1.10.ex5.au`. The last example is the same as the fifth except that we use D_3 and P=25%. The conversation at Paul's side is in the file `paul-adrian.delay3.25.ex5.au`. Listening to these files, we can hear that the case `delay1.10.ex5` is acceptable while the case `delay3.25.ex5` is very difficult to understand.

7. Concluding Remarks

A simulation tool has been developed to evaluate off-line the performance of Internet phone applications under various scenarios and parameter settings. The simulation includes Internet access links, background Internet phone and data traffic, and Internet loss and delay modeling. The main original feature of the simulator is that it takes into account the synchronization between talkspurts in two-way conversation. Example results of two-way conversations under different delay and loss conditions may be downloaded from a web page.

References

[BOL] J. Bolot, End-to-End Packet Delay and Loss Behaviour in the Internet, in *Proc. ACM SIGCOMM'93*, San Francisco, CA, pp. 289-298, Sept. 1993.

[BRA1] P.T. Brady, A Statistical Analysis of On-Off Patterns in 16 Conversations, *The Bell System Technical Journal*, 47, pp. 73-91, 1968.

[BRA2] P.T. Brady, A Model for Generating On-Off Speech Patterns in Two-Way Conversation, *The Bell System Technical Journal*, 48, pp. 2445-2472, 1969.

[COH] D. Cohen, Issues in Transnet Packetized Voice Communication, *in Proc. Fifth Data Communications Symposium*, pp. 6.10-6.13, Snowbird, UT, Sept. 1977.

[DAI] J.N. Daigle, and J.D. Langford, Models for Analysis of Packet Voice Communications Systems, *IEEE Journal on Selected Areas in Communications*, 4, 6, pp. 847-855, 1996.

[GRU] J.G. Gruber, A Comparison of Measured and Calculated Speech Temporal Parameters Relevant to Speech Activity Detection, *IEEE Transactions on Communications*, 30, 4, pp. 728-738, 1982.

[HEF] H. Heffes, and D.M. Lucantoni, A Markov Modulated Characterization of Packetized Voice and Data Traffic and Related Statistical Multiplexer Performance, *IEEE J. Selected Areas in Communications*, 4, 6, pp. 856-868, 1986.

[ITU] Telecommunication Standardization Sector of ITU, *ITU-T Recommendation G.114 Technical Report*, International Telecommunication Union, March 1993.

[JAY] N.S. Jayant, Effects of Packet Loss on Waveform Coded Speech, in *Proc. Fifth Int. Conference on Computer Communications*, Atlanta, GA, pp. 275-280, Oct. 1980.

[LEE] H.H. Lee, and C.K. Un, A Study of On-Off Characteristics of Conversational Speech, *IEEE Transactions on Communications*, 34, 6, pp. 630-637, 1986.

[MIL1] D.L. Mills, Network Time Protocol (Version 3) Specification, Implementation and Analysis, *Network Working Group Report RFC-1305*, University of Delaware, pp. 113, March 1992.

[MIL2] D.L. Mills, Improved Algorithms for Synchronizing Computer Network Clocks, *IEEE/ACM Transactions on Networking*, 3, 3, pp. 245-254, 1995.

[MON] W. A. Montgomery, Techniques for Packet Voice Synchronization, *IEEE Journal on Selected Areas in Communications*, 6, 1, pp. 1022-1028, 1983.

[MOO] S. B. Moon, J. Kurose, and D. Towsley, Packet Audio Playout Delay Adjustment: Performance Bounds and Algorithms, to appear in *ACM/Springer Multimedia Systems*.

[RAM] R. Ramjee, J. Kurose, D. Towsley, and H. Schulzrinne, Adaptive Playout Mechanism for Packetized Applications in Wide-Area Networks, in *Proc. of IEEE INFOCOM '94*, Toronto, Canada, pp. 680-688, June 1994.

[SAN] D. Sanghi, A.K. Agrawala, O. Gudmundsson, and B.N. Jain, Experimental Assessment of End-to-End Behaviour on Internet, in *Proc. IEEE INFOCOM'93*, San Francisco, CA, pp. 867-874, March 1993.

[SCH1] H. Schulzrinne, SIMUL Discrete Event Simulation Package, University of Massachusetts at Amherst, 1991.

[SCH2] H. Schulzrinne, Guide to NeVoT 3.33, 1995.

[SCH3] H. Schulzrinne, S. Casner, R. Frederick, and V. Jacobson, *RFC 1889*, RTP: A Transport Protocol for Real-Time Applications, Audio-Video Transport Working Group, IETF.

[SRI] K. Sriram, and W. Whitt, Characterizing Superposition Arrival Processes in Packet Multiplexers for Voice and Data, *IEEE Journal on Selected Areas in Communications*, 4, 6, pp. 833-846, 1986.

[VEN] G. Venditto, Internet Phones, *Internet World*, pp. 40-52, June, 1996.

[YAJ] M. Yajnik, J. Kurose, and D. Towsley, Packet Loss Correlation in the Mbone Multicast Network, *Global Internet Miniconference*, in conjunction with *IEEE GLOBECOM '96*, London, UK, Nov. 1996.

SPNL: Processes as Language-Oriented Building Blocks of Stochastic Petri Nets

Reinhard German

Technische Universität Berlin, Prozeßdatenverarbeitung und Robotik, Franklinstr. 28/29, 10587 Berlin, Germany, rge@cs.tu-berlin.de

Abstract. This paper presents a modeling paradigm which combines graphical and textual elements for the structured specification of performance and dependability models based on stochastic Petri nets. The aim is to manage the complexity of model specification. In the proposed framework processes are encapsulated submodels which are building blocks as known from modular programming languages. Process interaction is possible via ports, rewards, and result measures. Ports are arcs crossing the process boundaries. Rewards and result measures represent the internal state and actions of a process and are defined in a unified structured manner. A modeling example of a wireless LAN MAC protocol is given to illustrate the flexibility of the approach.

1 Introduction

Petri nets represent a flexible modeling paradigm which allows to build general models by a small number of graphical primitives. A strong point of Petri nets is their ability to model system aspects like concurrency and synchronization and to represent these aspects graphically. Furthermore, models are represented in a compact way and have a well-defined underlying semantics. Due to these reasons Petri nets with stochastic extensions, *stochastic Petri nets* (SPNs) [2], were found to be useful for model-based performance and dependability evaluations. However, a problem which has limited user acceptance is the complexity of model specification and evaluation. In larger applications the number of places, transitions, and arcs grows to a size which makes the model nearly incomprehensible. Additionally, numerical analysis and simulation becomes expensive in terms of run time and memory.

Several approaches have been proposed for managing the complexity. Structuring concepts are known from various fields, e.g., programming languages, other (graphical) specification techniques, and simulation languages and tools. A number of extensions facilitating the specification process were already introduced in *generalized stochastic Petri nets* (GSPNs) [2], *stochastic reward nets* (SRNs) [6] and *stochastic activity networks* (SANs) [13]. These extensions include immediate transitions, priorities, inhibitor arcs, guards, and marking-dependent properties. In SRNs and SANs reward variables are understood as an integral part of the model and allow a flexible definition of performance, dependability, and performability measures. Various kinds of high-level nets (HLNs) have been introduced which use typed tokens for an increased specification convenience, with *coloured Petri nets* [11] as one example. Different hierarchy concepts have also been suggested for HLNs, e.g., refinement and fusion of elements [11]. In [3], a language called PROTOB was presented in which HLNs are combined with concepts known from modular programming languages. Elements for defining building blocks in a language-like fashion are provided.

In this paper a language called SPNL (SPN Language) is defined which combines textual and graphical modeling primitives. *Processes* are used as language-like building blocks for a structured description of SPN performance and dependability models. The approach is similar to PROTOB, but the language is especially tailored to performance and dependability modeling. Furthermore, the interaction mechanisms between subnets are different. The concept of rewards is taken from SANs and SRNs [13, 6] and is adapted to the hierarchical process structure. The syntax for parameter, marking-dependent, and reward expressions is unified and is basically motivated by the syntax for marking-dependent and result measure expressions in GreatSPN [5]. The specification of the behaviour of transitions by attributes is motivated by [4]. The preemption policies are taken from [14].

A process is composed of subprocesses and of ordinary SPN elements (places, transitions, and arcs). Interaction between processes is possible via three different elements: *ports*, *rewards*, and *measures*. Ports are arcs crossing the process boundary, rewards depend on the internal states and actions of the process, and measures origin from stochastic operations on rewards. A process consists of an *interface* and a *body*. In the interface internal objects can be made visible for the environment. The body represents the internal structure in a *graphical part* which can be supplemented by *textual declarations*. Processes can be either declared as single entities or as *process types* and *process instances* supporting reuse of building blocks. Process instances can be customized by actual parameters. A *module* is given by a collection of declarations in a separate file.

SPNL also provides a unified structured reward concept. Rewards are based on rate and impulse rewards associated with the states and actions of a process, respectively. They can be used both for the specification and observation of process behaviour. The specification of marking-dependent properties and guards is facilitated by reward variables and expressions, which can be passed as parameters between processes. Result measures are defined as stochastic operations on rewards. Result measures can be passed as parameters between processes. Thus, SPNL provides a formal framework for expressing hierarchical and iterative models, which have to be solved by fixed-point iteration in case of cyclic dependencies [12]. It is furthermore possible to specify various attributes of transitions which are important for correct performance and dependability models: priorities, general firing time distributions, marking-dependency (dependent on the marking in the instant of enabling or varying during enabling), preemption policy (preemptive repeat different, preemptive resume, preemptive repeat identical [14]), and concurrency degree (single/infinite server).

In SPNL graphical and textual elements are "balanced": the internal structure of a process is graphically represented, other model elements are textually represented: parameters, rewards, distributions, etc. Each textual element has a well defined location in the language-oriented model, a confusing "overloading" of figures with textual inscriptions is therefore avoided. Furthermore, a clear distinction is made between syntax and semantics of the language. A syntactical model description in SPNL can be compiled into an internal SPN representation which is subject to analysis and simulation. The semantics of an SPNL model is defined for the language and does not depend on a tool environment.

The rest of the paper is organized as follows. In Sec. 2, SPNL is introduced by examples. Sec. 3 discusses the syntax and model representation and Sec. 4 tests the applicability of SPNL in a larger modeling examples: a wireless local area network (LAN) medium access control (MAC) protocol. More details about SPNL and a formal definition of the syntax can be found in [8].

2 Introductory Examples for the Usage of SPNL

A queueing system consisting of n M/M/l/k queueing systems which share a pool of m servers is considered. In the following this system is described in SPNL in a structured fashion. The description is divided into two *modules*. Fig. 1 shows the module "queueing" which contains a *process type* "mmlk". Fig. 2 shows the main module "sharing" which describes the entire system. The process type in module "queueing" is a description of one M/M/l/k queueing system. The process type *declaration* contains a *formal parameter list*, an *interface*, and a *body*. In the interface, externally visible objects are declared. Such public objects may be *reward* and *measure variables* as well as *ports*. Ports may be considered as cut arcs which have to be connected with suitable external places and transitions. In each port declaration its type has to be given (e.g., "**t<-p**" indicates that an input arc to an internal transition is crossing the boundary).

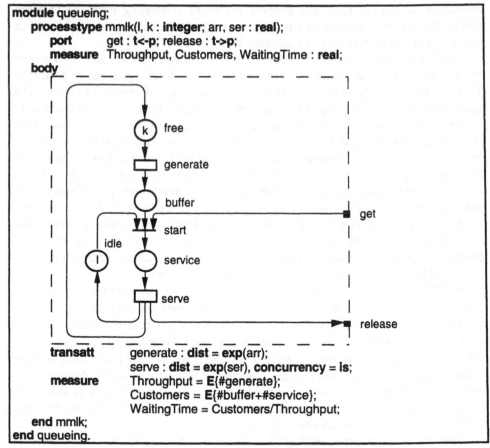

Fig. 1. Module "queueing"

The body represents the internal structure and contains a graphical part which is supplemented by textual declarations. In the example, the graphical part consists of customary Petri net elements. The ports which have been declared in the interface are visualized as small black squares. The graphical part is augmented by textual declarations: the firing times of transition "generate" are exponentially distributed, the rate is given by the formal parameter "arr". Transition "serve" also has an exponential firing time distribution with rate "ser", its degree of concurrency is infinite-server. Measure expressions are based on reward expressions. In the example, the throughput (expected value of an impulse reward), the mean queue length (expected value of a rate reward), and the mean waiting time (Little's law) is defined.

Declarations in other modules can be made visible by *imports*. The process declaration in main module "sharing" of Fig. 2 is similar to a process type declaration and represents the top level of the model. The body contains the declaration of process instances. An instance is shown in the graphical part as a rectangle with thick lines. The ports are depicted as small black squares and are connected by Petri net arcs. In the interface, again a measure "WaitingTime" is declared. In the body, it is defined as the arithmetic mean of the measures of the process instances. Reference to those measures is given by instance name qualifiers. In order to increase specification convenience further, arrays of identical process instances can also be defined. An example is given in Sec. 4, details are described in [8].

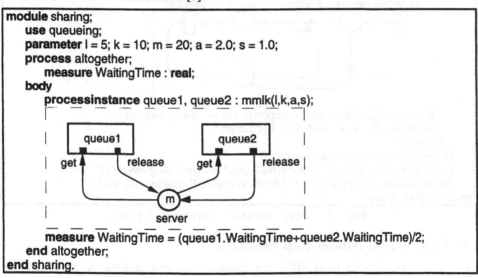

Fig. 2. Main module "sharing"

To illustrate the ability of SPNL to model hierarchical and iterative models, a system of two layers of a communication protocol is considered. Packets arrive at several queues of layer 2 and are passed to one queue of layer 1. The service time of each queue at layer 2 is given by the waiting time in the queue of layer 1 and the arrival rate to the queue at layer 1 is given by the throughput of the queues at layer 2. Fig. 3 shows a main module "protocol_layers" defining the model. A process type "mm1k" represents an M/M/1/K queueing system. Measures throughput "S" and mean waiting time "W" are public. Two processes "layer2" and "layer1" are declared as

127

instances of the process type representing two SPN models. Measures of both processes are mutually used as actual parameters. Thus, an iterative model is represented which has to be solved by fixed-point iteration. The initial guess of the measures are indicated by the keyword **"guess"**, similarly as in [7].

SPNL provides also the possibility to use the same process in the bodies of different processes (thus, processes can be fused, like places and transitions in coloured Petri nets [11]). Such a process usage can be declared by **"useprocess** UseId : ProcId;"**, where "ProcId" must be the name of a visible process. The semantics is that in the underlying model all arcs connected with ports of the used process are added. Furthermore, rewards can be used as an interaction mechanism. For this purpose, in a process type a formal parameter is preceded by the keyword **"reward"** and in the process instance declaration a reward expression is passed as actual parameter. Examples for process usages and process interaction via rewards will be given in Sec. 4.

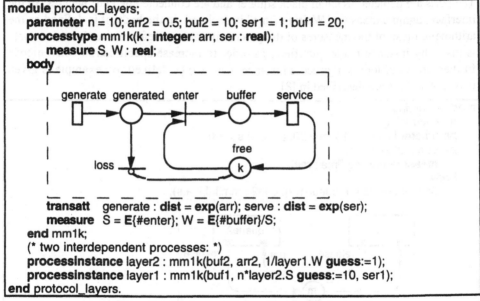

```
module protocol_layers;
    parameter n = 10; arr2 = 0.5; buf2 = 10; ser1 = 1; buf1 = 20;
    processtype mm1k(k : integer; arr, ser : real);
        measure S, W : real;
    body
```

generate generated enter   buffer   service

free

loss   k

```
    transatt   generate : dist = exp(arr); serve : dist = exp(ser);
    measure    S = E{#enter}; W = E{#buffer}/S;
    end mm1k;
    (* two interdependent processes: *)
    processinstance layer2 : mm1k(buf2, arr2, 1/layer1.W guess:=1);
    processinstance layer1 : mm1k(buf1, n*layer2.S guess:=10, ser1);
end protocol_layers.
```

Fig. 3. Main module "protocol_layers"

3 Syntax and Model Representation

Some syntactical aspects of SPNL are discussed in this section. A more detailed definition of syntax, semantics as well as more examples can be found in [8].

The internal structure of a process or process type is mainly represented by the graphical part. The graphical part is an implicit declaration of objects, given by their identifier, type, and certain attributes. These graphical declarations also have a textual representation. Therefore the entire model description can be stored in ASCII format and used for tool-independent model exchange. Fig. 4 shows the textual representation of the graphical part of process type "mmlk" in Fig. 1.

The graphical part can be augmented by textual declarations of arcs, transitions attributes, processes, parameters, distributions, rewards, and measures. If an attribute is not explicitly defined, default values are assigned. For transitions it is possible to define the *priority* (cardinal number), the *firing time distribution*, the *weight* (real number), the *marking-dependency* (constant **"constant"**, scaling **"scaling"**, enabling-dependent **"enabdep"**), the *policy* (preemptive repeat different **"prd"**, preemptive resume **"prs"**, preemptive repeat identical **"pri"**), the *degree of concurrency* (single server "**ss**", infinite server "**is**"), and a guard.

```
graphbegin
    place    free : k; buffer, service; idle : l;
    trans    generate, serve : timed; start : imm;
    arc      a1 : (free, generate); a2 : (generate, buffer); a3 : (buffer, start);
             a4 : (start, service); a5 : (service, serve); a6 : (serve, free);
             a7 : (serve, idle); a8 : (idle, start); a9 : (get, start); a10 : (serve, release);
    graphplace    free : center = (35, 70), name = (40, 70), mark = (35, 70); ...
    graphtrans    generate : center = (35, 65), name = (40, 65), orient = 90; ...
    grapharc      a10 : viapos = ((35, 5), (10, 5), (10, 95)); ...
    graphport     get : center = (110, 50), name = (115, 70); ...
graphend;
```

Fig. 4. Textual representation of the graphical part in Fig. 1

Reward and Measure Specification

In SPNL, a unified structured reward concept is used both for the specification and observation of model behaviour. Rewards are based on *rate* and *impulse rewards* [13, 6]. A rate reward is a value which is collected during the process spends time in a marking and an impulse reward is a value which is collected when a transition fires. Both reward types can be considered in the same mathematical framework if rate rewards are continuous functions in time and impulse rewards are discrete functions in time [9]. The operator "#" applied to a place denotes a rate reward: the number of tokens in that place (e.g., "#service" gives the number of tokens in place "service"). Applied to a transition, it gives the impulse reward equal to one if the transition fires and zero otherwise (e.g., "#serve" gives a Dirac impulse with an area equal to one when "serve" fires).

More complicated reward expressions can be formed by arithmetic operators, e.g., "#free+#start+#serve", "-((#service+#idle)/#buffer)*3/N". Rewards can also be conditioned on the marking: rate rewards may depend on the marking and impulse rewards may depend on the marking in the instant before firing. Conditional reward expressions are formed by predicates. Predicates are formed by comparisons between reward expressions and by boolean operators and evaluate to true or false, e.g., "**not**((#buffer>0) **and** (#idle=l))". Examples for conditional reward expression are: "**if** #buffer<10 **then** 0 **elsif** #buffer<20 **then** 10 **else** #buffer", in "**if** #buffer>10 **then** #generate" an impulse reward is obtained if "buffer" has more then 10 tokens and "generate" fires.

Reward expressions may either be used directly or in a reward variable declaration. In the latter case, reference to the reward expression is possible by using the identifier of the variable, e.g., "**reward** insystem = #buffer + #service". Reward expressions and variables provide a flexible method of specifying marking-dependent model elements: it is possible to use rewards in other expressions, e.g., "**transatt** serve : **dist** = **exp**(**if** insystem<5 **then** ser **else** 2*ser)". If reward expressions are used in other expressions, like in predicates or distributions, they must not contain impulse rewards.

Result measure definitions are based on rewards which are similar to random variables. A result measure expression is a stochastic operator applied to a reward expression. "E" denotes expectation, e.g., "E{insystem}", "E{**if** #free = 0 **then** 1}", and "E{#start+#serve}" give the expected values of the corresponding rewards. The stochastic operation can be conditioned on a predicate, e.g., "E{#free **given** #service>0}" denotes the expected value of tokens in "free" given that at least one token is in "service". Conditional stochastic expressions and conditional marking expressions should not be confused: "E{**if** #free > 0 **then** 1 **given** #service>0}" denotes the expected value that "free" is nonempty given that "service" is nonempty.

Observable rewards are a function of the internal state and actions of a process. These rewards can be passed to other processes and can there be used for the specification of model behaviour, e.g., in guards and marking-dependent firing rates. Rewards provide therefore a communication mechanism between processes. In a tool environment, the values of these reward variables can be displayed during animation, analysis, and simulation. Observable measure variables provide information about the stochastic behaviour of the process and can be displayed during/after the evaluation.

4 Modeling Example: IEEE 802.11 Wireless LAN

Recently, different mechanisms have been proposed for medium access control (MAC) in wireless local area networks (LANs). Radio channels provide a lower data rate and are less reliable than wired media. Furthermore, collision detection as employed in the common IEEE 802.3 (CSMA/CD) MAC protocol is physically not possible. Therefore, mechanisms for *collision avoidance* (CA) have been developed which reduce the collision probability. In this section, an SPNL model of the proposal of the IEEE 802.11 working group [10] is presented. The model is partly motivated by the GSPN model of CSMA/CD presented in [1].

We consider the *distributed coordination function* (DCF) of the protocol which is the basic access method used for asynchronous traffic. A station wishing to transmit senses the medium and may transmit after the medium is free for a period called DCF interframe space (DIFS). If the medium is busy or becomes busy during DIFS, the transmission is deferred by a random backoff time. The receiving station immediately sends back a positive acknowledgement. If no acknowledgement is obtained, the packet is retransmitted after a random backoff time. If after a successful transmission the next packet is already waiting, a backoff time has to be inserted before the next transmission.

The model consists of three modules "TrafficSources", "WLANParts", and "WLAN" (main module) shown in Fig. 5 – 10. Module "TrafficSources" in Fig. 5 provides a process type "MMPPT" (a Markov modulated Poisson process) for the generation of traffic. "TrafficSources" could be extended to a library of typical traffic generators. Module "WLANparts" provides the necessary building blocks in order to compose the entire model: some general network parameters, process types "BackoffT", "AckHandlerT", "WLANstationT", and a process "Channel".

```
module TrafficSources;
    processtype MMPPT(rlow, rhigh, rl2h, rh2l : posreal);
        port      put : t->p;
        measure   MeanRate, Burstiness : posreal;
    body
```

```
    transatt   l2h : dist := exp(rl2h); h2l : dist := exp(rh2l);
               generate : dist := exp(if #low = 1 then rlow else rhigh);
    measure    MeanRate := (rlow*rh2l+rhigh*rl2h)/(rl2h+rh2l);
               Burstiness := rhigh/MeanRate;
    end MMPPT;
end TrafficSources.
```

Fig. 5. Module "TrafficSources"

```
module WLANparts;
    use TrafficSources;
    parameter   (* bits per time unit = 1 ms*)
                PacketLength := 1000*8 (* bits *); Bandwidth := 2000
                TransTime := PacketLength/Bandwidth; AckTime := 0.081;
                SlotTime := 0.05; DIFS := 0.125;
                rlow := 0. 00001, rhigh := 0.0001, rl2h := 0.0001, rh2l := 0.0001;
                K := 50 (* buffer size *);
    processtype BackoffT(reward rep, ch : cardinal);
        (* backoff procedure for packet transmissions *)
        port get : p<-t; put : t->p;
    body
```

```
    reward     max := if rep<=10 then rep else 10;
    transatt   startDIFS : guard := ch=0;
               defer1, defer2 : guard := ch>0;
               TDIFS : dist := det(DIFS);
               TBackoff : dist := discreteuniform(1, 2^max, SlotTime), policy := prs;
    end BackoffT;
```

Fig. 6. Module "WLANparts", process type "BackoffT"

131

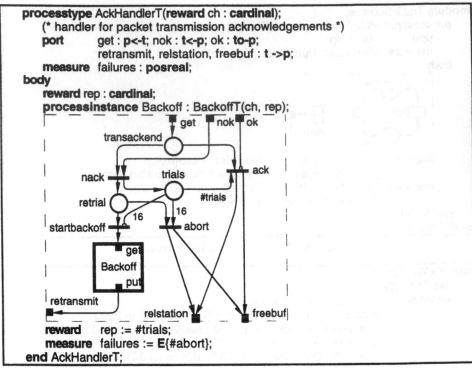

Fig. 7. Module "WLANparts", process type "AckHandlerT"

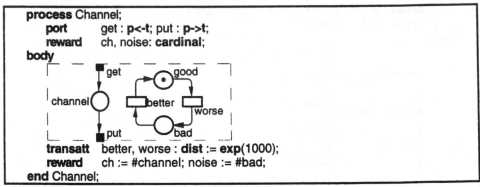

Fig. 8. Module "WLANparts", process "ChannelP"

Process type "WLANstationT" in Fig. 9 represents the DCF access performed by each station. A generated packet (modeled by a token generated by process "Source") is stored in place "buffer". After a new transmission request has been initiated by the firing of transition "startnew", either transition "free" or "busy" fires depending on the channel state (observable by public reward "ch" of process "Channel"). After the firing of "busy", the backoff procedure is started. If after the firing of "free" the channel remains free for a time equal to DIFS, transitions "TDIFS" and "transstart" fire and start the transmission of the packet. Otherwise the backoff procedure is started. If during the transmission and acknowledgement the packet is destroyed (due to transmissions of other stations or channel noise), a token is put in place "Pdestroy".

```
process type WLANstationT;
   measure MaxLoad, OfferedLoad, Throughput, MeanDelay : posreal;
body
   useprocess          ChannelU : Channel;
   processinstance     Source : MMPPT(rlow, rhigh, rl2h, rh2l);
                       Backoff : BackoffT(0, Channel.ch);
                       AckHandler : AckHandlerT(Channel.ch);
```

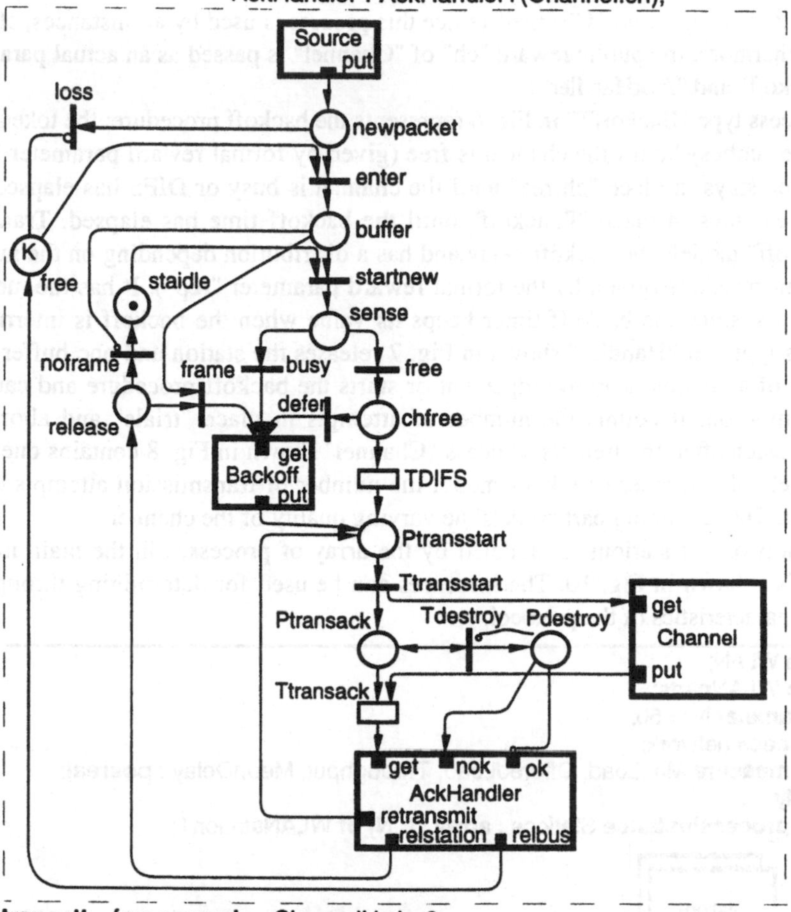

```
transatt   free : guard := ChannelU.ch=0;
           busy, defer : guard := ChannelU.ch>0;
           Tdestroy : guard := ChannelU.ch>1 or ChannelU.noise>0;
           TDIFS : dist := det(DIFS);
           Ttransack : dist := det(TransTime+AckTime);
   measure GenaratedLoad := Source.MeanRate*PacketLength/Bandwidth;
           OfferedLoad := E{#transstart}*PacketLength/Bandwidth;
           Throughput := E{#enter}*PacketLength/Bandwidth;
           MeanDelay := (K-E{#free})/Throughput;
   end WLANstationT;
end WLANparts.
```

Fig. 9. Module "WLANparts", process type "WLANstationT"

After transmission and acknowledgement transition "Ttransack" fires and process "AckHandler" handles the possible cases. In case of a successful transmission the station and one buffer place are released. If at this moment a new packet is already waiting in place "buffer", the backoff procedure is initiated. Note that different instantiations of "WLANstationT" have independent subprocesses "Source", "Backoff", and "AckHandler" (since these are declared in "WLANstationT"), but share the identical subprocess "Channel" (since this process is used by all instances, cf. Sec. 2). Furthermore, the public reward "ch" of "Channel" is passed as an actual parameter to "Backoff" and "AckHandler".

Process type "BackoffT" in Fig. 6 represents the backoff procedure: the token stays in place "chbusy" until the channel is free (given by formal reward parameter "ch"), the token stays in place "chfree" until the channel is busy or DIFS has elapsed, and the token stays in place "Pbackoff" until the backoff time has elapsed. Transition "Tbackoff" models the backoff delay and has a distribution depending on the number of retransmissions (given by the formal reward parameter "rep"). It has the memory policy prs, since the backoff timer keeps its value when the backoff is interrupted. Process type "AckHandler" shown in Fig. 7 releases the station and one buffer place in case of a positive acknowledgement or starts the backoff procedure and causes a retransmission. It counts the number of attempts in place "trials" and aborts the transmission after 16 attempts. Process "Channel" shown in Fig. 8 contains one place "channel", the number of tokens model the number of transmission attempts on the channel. The remaining part models the varying quality of the channel.

A network of stations is modeled by the array of processes in the main module "WLAN" shown in Fig. 10. The measures can be used for determining throughput-delay characteristics of the protocol.

```
module WLAN;
    use WLANparts;
    parameter N := 50;
    process network;
        measure MaxLoad, OfferedLoad, Throughput, MeanDelay : posreal;
    body
        processinstance Stations : array [1..N] of WLANstationT;

        ┌─────────────────┐
        │  ┌───────────┐  │
        │  │           │  │
        │  │ Stations  │  │
        │  │           │  │
        │  └───────────┘  │
        └─────────────────┘

        reward    GeneratedLoad := ArithmeticMean(Stations.MeanRate);
                  OfferedLoad := ArithmeticMean(Stations.OfferedLoad);
                  Throughput := ArithmeticMean(Stations.Throughput);
                  MeanDelay := ArithmeticMean(Stations.MeanDelay);
    end network;
end WLAN.
```

Fig. 10. Module "WLAN"

5   Conclusions

Model-based performance, dependability, and performability evaluation of large systems suffers from the lack of tools which can support the "model engineering" during the whole design process with its different steps of refinements and abstractions. We proposed a mixed textual/graphical modeling paradigm called SPNL in which concepts of modular programming languages are used in order to specify building blocks of an SPN. The language is based on processes which can interact via ports, rewards, and measures. Process declarations may be distributed over modules. The generic concept of processes and ports can be used for the representation of refinement and fusion of SPN elements and of synchronous and asynchronous communication. The reward concept is adapted to the structure of the language. The syntax, model representation, and semantics of SPNL have been discussed. Furthermore, we have given a modeling example in order to illustrate the flexibility of the approach: a wireless LAN MAC protocol.

References

[1] M. Ajmone Marsan, G. Chiola, A. Fumagalli. An Accurate Performance Model of CSMA/CD Bus LAN. 1987.

[2] M. Ajmone Marsan, G. Balbo, G. Chiola, S. Donatelli, G. Franceschinis. *Modeling with Generalized Stochastic Petri Nets*. John Wiley & Sons, 1995.

[3] M. Baldarassi, G. Bruno. PROTOB: An Object Oriented Methodology Based on Hierachical Colored Petri Nets. In K. Jensen, G. Rozenberg (eds.): *High-level Petri Nets, Theory and Application*. Springer-Verlag, pp. 624–648, 1991.

[4] F. Bause, P. Kemper, P. Kritzinger. Abstract Petri Net Notation, In F. Bause, H. Beilner (eds.): Perfomance Tools Model Interchange Formats, Research Report 581/1995, Universität Dortmund, Informatik IV.

[5] G. Chiola. GreatSPN 1.5 Software Architecture. In G. Balbo, G. Serazzi (eds.): *Computer Performance Evaluation*, North-Holland, pp. 121–136, 1991.

[6] G. Ciardo, A. Blakemore, P.F. Chimento, J.K. Muppala, and K.S. Trivedi. Automated Generation of Markov Reward Models using Stochastic Reward Nets. *Linear Algebra, Markov Chains, and Queueing Models*, Vol. 48 of IMA Volumes in Mathematics and its Applications, Springer Verlag, 1993.

[7] G. Ciardo, A. S. Miner. SMART: Simulation and Markovian Analyzer for Reliability and Timing. *Proc. 2nd IEEE Int. Computer Performance & Dependability Symp.*, Urbana-Champaign, Illinois, USA, p. 60, 1996.

[8] R. German. SPNL: Processes as Language-Oriented Building Blocks of Stochastic Petri Nets. Technical Report 96-37, Technical University Berlin, Computer Science Department, 1996.

[9] R. German, A. P. A. van Moorsel, M. A. Qureshi, W. H. Sanders. Expected Impulse Rewards in Markov Regenerative Stochastic Petri Nets. *Proc. 17th Int. Conf. on Application and Theory of Petri Nets*, pp. 172–191, Osaka, Japan, Springer-Verlag, LNCS 1091, 1996.

[10] IEEE. P802.11. Draft Standard for Wireless LAN Medium Access Control (MAC) and Physical Layer (PHY) Specification, May 1996.

[11] K. Jensen. *Coloured Petri Nets, Basic Concepts, Analysis Methods and Practical Use*. Vol. 1, Springer-Verlag, 1992.

[12] V. Mainkar, K. S. Trivedi. Fixed Point Iteration Using Stochastic Reward Nets. *Proc. 6th Int. Workshop on Petri Nets and Performance Models (PNPM)*. Durham, North Carolina, USA, pp. 21–30, 1995.

[13] W. H. Sanders, J. F. Meyer. A Unified Approach for Specifying Measures of Performance, Dependability, and Performability. *Dependable Computing for Critical Applications*, 4 (1991) 215–237, Springer-Verlag.

[14] M. Telek, A. Bobbio, A. Puliafito. Steady State Solution of MRSPN with Mixed Preemption Policies. *Proc. 2nd IEEE Int. Computer Performance & Dependability Symp.*, Urbana-Champaign, Illinois, USA, pp. 106–115, 1996.

Performance Engineering Evaluation of Object-Oriented Systems with *SPE•ED*™

Connie U. Smith
Performance Engineering Services
PO Box 2640
Santa Fe, NM 87504

Lloyd G. Williams
Software Engineering Research
264 Ridgeview Lane
Boulder, CO 80302

Abstract

Although object-oriented methods have been shown to help construct software systems that are easy to understand and modify, have a high potential for reuse, and are relatively quick and easy to implement, concern over performance of object-oriented systems represents a significant barrier to its adoption. Our experience has shown that it is possible to design object-oriented systems that have adequate performance *and* exhibit the other qualities, such as reusability, maintainability, and modifiability, that have made OOD so successful. However, doing this requires careful attention to performance goals throughout the life cycle. This paper describes the use of *SPE•ED*, a performance modeling tool that supports the SPE process, for early life cycle performance evaluation of object-oriented systems. The use of *SPE•ED* for performance engineering of object-oriented software is illustrated with a simple example.

1.0 Introduction

Object-oriented development (OOD) methods have been shown to be valuable in constructing software systems that are easy to understand and modify, have a high potential for reuse, and are relatively quick and easy to implement. Despite the demonstrated successes of OOD, many organizations have been reluctant to adopt object-oriented techniques, largely due to concerns over performance.

Our experience has shown that it is possible to design object-oriented systems that have adequate performance *and* exhibit the other qualities, such as reusability, maintainability, and modifiability, that have made OOD so successful [Smith and Williams, 1993]. However, doing this requires careful attention to performance goals throughout the life cycle. Failure to build-in performance from the beginning can result in the need to "tune" code, destroying the benefits obtained from a careful object-oriented design. In addition, it is unlikely that "tuned" code will ever equal the performance of code that has been engineered for performance. In the worst case, it will be impossible to meet performance goals by tuning, necessitating a complete re-design or even cancellation of the project.

Software Performance Engineering (SPE) for object-oriented systems is especially difficult since functionality is decentralized. Performing a given function is likely to require collaboration among many different objects from several classes. These interactions can be numerous and complex and are often obscured by polymorphism and inheritance, making them difficult to trace. Distributing objects over a network can compound the problem.

One of the principal barriers to the effective use of SPE with OOD is the gap between the designers who need feedback on the performance implications of design decisions and the performance specialists who have the skill to conduct comprehensive performance engineering studies with typical modeling tools. This gap means that extra time and effort is required to coordinate design formulation and analysis, effectively limiting the ability of designers to explore design alternatives.

The ideal long-term solution to providing SPE assessments during the design stage is an evolution of today's CASE tools to provide decision support for many facets of the design including correctness, completeness, performance, reliability, and so on. This approach, however, is not currently practical. It is too expensive for each CASE vendor to create their own modeling/analysis component. Therefore, we seek a near-term capability to interface CASE tools to existing modeling tools. A previous paper defined the SPE information that CASE tools must collect [Williams and Smith, 1995]. This paper illustrates the translation from Object-oriented design models into performance models, and the use of the tool, *SPE•ED*™,[1] for early life cycle performance evaluation of object-oriented systems. *SPE•ED* is a performance modeling tool that supports the SPE process described in [Smith, 1990]. *SPE•ED*s software processing focus and automatic model generation make it easy to evaluate OOD architecture and design alternatives. Other features, such as the SPE project database and presentation and reporting features, support aspects of the SPE process other than modeling.

The paper begins by reviewing related work. This is followed by an overview of *SPE•ED*. We then present an overview of the process of software performance engineering for object-oriented systems. A simple example illustrates the process.

2.0 Related Work

Object-oriented methods typically defer consideration of performance issues until detailed design or implementation (see e.g., [Rumbaugh, et al., 1991], [Booch, 1994]). Even then, the approach tends to be very general. There is no attempt to integrate performance engineering into the development process.

Some work specifically targeted at object-oriented systems has emerged from the performance community. Smith and Williams [Smith and Williams, 1993] describe performance engineering of an object-oriented design for a real-time system. However, this approach applies general SPE techniques and only addresses the specific problems of object-oriented systems in an ad hoc way.

---

[1] *SPE•ED*™ is a trademark of Performance Engineering Services.

Hrischuk et. al. [Hrischuk, et al., 1995] describe an approach based on constructing an early prototype which is then executed to produce *angio traces*. These angio traces are then used to construct *workthreads* (also known as *timethreads* or *use case maps* [Buhr and Casselman, 1992],[Buhr and Casselman, 1994], [Buhr and Casselman, 1996]), which are analogous to execution graphs. Workthreads provide empirical information about traversal frequencies for data-dependent choices and loops. Service times are estimated. This differs from the approach described here in that scenarios are derived from prototype execution rather than from the design and the system execution model is then generated automatically from the angio traces.

Baldassari et.al. propose an integrated object-oriented CASE tool for software design that includes a simulation capability for performance assessment [Baldassari, et al., 1989, Baldassari and Bruno, 1988]. The CASE tool uses petri nets for the design description language rather than the general methods described above, thus the design specification and the performance model are equivalent and no translation is necessary. Using these capabilities requires developers to use both the PROTOB method and CASE tool.

This paper uses the SPE tool *SPE•ED* to conduct the performance analysis. Other software modeling tools are available, such as [Beilner, et al., 1988, Beilner, et al., 1995, Goettge, 1990, Grummitt, 1991, Rolia, 1992, Turner, et al., 1992]. The approach described here could be adapted to other tools. Adaptation is necessary for these other tools that do not use execution graphs as their model paradigm.

3.0 *SPE•ED* Overview
This section gives a brief overview of the features of the SPE tool that make it appropriate for OOD (and other) evaluations throughout their development life cycle.

3.1 Focus
SPE•ED's focus is the software performance model. Users create graphical models of envisioned software processing and provide performance specifications. Queueing network models are automatically generated from the software model specifications. A combination of analytic and simulation model solutions identify potential performance problems and software processing steps that may cause the problems. *SPE•ED* facilitates the creation of (deliberately) simple models of software processing with the goal of using the simplest possible model that identifies problems with the software architecture, design, or implementation plans. Simple models are desired because in the early life cycle phase in which they are created:

- developers seldom have exact data that justifies a more sophisticated model,
- they need quick feedback to influence development decisions,
- they need to comprehend the model results, especially the correlation of the software decisions to the computer resource impacts.

3.2 Model description
Users create the model with a graphical user interface streamlined to quickly define the software processing steps. The user's view of the model is a *scenario,* an execution graph of the software processing steps [Smith, 1990]. Software scenarios are assigned to the facilities that execute the processing steps. Models of distributed processing systems may have many scenarios and many facilities. Users specify *software resource requirements* for each processing step. Software resources may be the number of messages transmitted, the number of SQL queries, the number of SQL updates, etc. depending on the type of system to be studied and the key performance drivers for that system. A performance specialist provides *overhead specifications* that specify an estimate of the computer resource requirements for each software resource request. These are specified once and re-used for all software analysis that executes in that environment. This step is described in more detail later.

3.3 Model solution
SPE•ED produces analytic results for the software models, and an approximate, analytic MVA solution of the generated queueing network model. A simulation solution is used for generated queueing network models with multiple software scenarios executing on one or more computer system facilities.[2] Thus *SPE•ED* supports hybrid solutions - the user selects the type of solution appropriate for the development life cycle stage and thus the precision of the data that feeds the model. There is no need for a detailed, lengthy simulation when only rough guesses of resource requirements are specified.

3.4 Model results
The results reported by *SPE•ED* are the end-to-end response time, the elapsed time for each processing step, the device utilization, and the amount of time spent at each computer device for each processing step. This identifies both the potential computer device bottlenecks, and the portions of the device usage by processing step (thus the potential software processing bottlenecks).

Model results are presented both with numeric values and color coding that uses cool colors to represent relatively low values and hot colors (yellow and red) calling attention to relatively high values. Up to 4 sets of results may be viewed together on a screen. This lets users view any combination of performance metrics for chosen levels in the software model hierarchy, and even compare performance metrics for design or implementation choices. An export feature lets users copy model results and paste them into word processing documents and presentation packages, or write out results for charting packages to create custom charts for reports.

3.5 Application areas
SPE•ED is intended to model software systems under development. It may be any type of software: operating systems, database management systems, or custom

---

[2]   *SPE•ED* uses the CSIM modeling engine to solve the models [Schwetman, 1994].

applications. The software may execute on any hardware/software platform combination. The software may execute on a uniprocessor or in a distributed or client/server environment.

4.0 SPE Process Steps for OOD

The process for performing SPE for an object-oriented design begins with a set of *scenarios*. A scenario is a description of the interactions between the system and its environment or between the internal objects involved in a particular use of the system under development. The scenario shows the objects that participate and the messages that flow between them. A message may represent either an event or invocation of one of the receiving object's operations.

The use of scenarios has become popular in many current approaches to object-oriented development. Scenarios, known as "use cases," are an important component of Jacobson's Objectory Method [Jacobson, et al., 1992]. Scenarios are also used in OMT [Rumbaugh, et al., 1991], Booch [Booch, 1994], Fusion [Coleman, et al., 1994], and the new Unified Modeling Language [Booch and Rumbaugh, 1995]. In object-oriented methods, scenarios are used to:
- describe the externally visible behavior of the system,
- involve users in the requirements analysis process,
- support prototyping,
- help validate the requirements specification,
- understand interactions between objects, and
- support requirements-based testing.

Once the major functional scenarios have been identified, those that are important from a performance perspective are selected for performance modeling. Scenarios that are important to performance can be identified by a variety of techniques, including experience with similar systems and performance walkthroughs [Smith, 1990].

The scenarios are then translated to execution graphs (see below) which serve as input to *SPE•ED*. Currently, this translation is manual. However, the close correspondence between the way scenarios are expressed in object-oriented methods and execution graphs suggests that an automated translation should be possible.

The next SPE steps are conducted after the translated model is entered into *SPE•ED*. Performance engineers enter data for the processing steps in the execution graphs, ensure that correct overhead specifications are in the SPE database, and evaluate model solutions for alternatives. These steps are illustrated with the following example.

5.0 Example
To illustrate the use of SPE•ED for modeling and evaluating the performance of object-oriented systems, we present an example based on a simple automated teller machine (ATM).

The ATM accepts a bank card and requests a personal identification number (PIN) for user authentication. Customers can perform any of three transactions at the ATM: deposit cash to an account, withdraw cash from an account, or request the available balance in an account. A customer may perform several transactions during a single ATM session. The ATM communicates with a computer at the host bank which verifies the account and processes the transaction. When the customer is finished using the ATM, a receipt is printed for all transactions and the customer's card is returned.

Here, we focus on scenarios that describe the use of the ATM. A full specification would include additional models, such as a class diagram and behavior descriptions for each class. However, our interest here is primarily in the use of scenarios as a bridge between Object-Oriented Development and Software Performance Engineering. Thus, these additional models are omitted.

5.1 Example Scenarios
As described in [Williams and Smith, 1995], scenarios represent a common point of departure between object-oriented requirements or design models and SPE models. Scenarios may be represented in a variety of ways [Williams, 1994]. Here, we use Message Sequence Charts (MSCs) to describe scenarios in object-oriented models. The MSC notation is specified in ITU standard Z.120 [ITU, 1996]. Several other notations used to represent scenarios are based on MSCs (examples include: Event Flow Diagrams [Rumbaugh, et al., 1991]; Interaction Diagrams [Jacobson, et al., 1992], [Booch, 1994]; and Message Trace Diagrams [Booch and Rumbaugh, 1995]). However, none of these incorporates all of the features of MSCs needed to establish the correspondence between object-oriented scenarios and SPE scenarios.

Figure 1 illustrates a high-level MSC for the ATM example. Each object that participates in the scenario is represented by a vertical line or axis. The axis is labeled with the object name (e.g., anATM). The vertical axis represents relative time which increases from top to bottom; an axis does not include an absolute time scale. Interactions between objects (events or operation invocations) are represented by horizontal arrows.

Figure 1 describes a general scenario for user interaction with the ATM. The rectangular areas labeled "loop" and "alt" are known as "inline expressions" and denote repetition and alternation. This Message Sequence Chart indicates that the user may repeatedly select a transaction which may be a deposit, a withdrawal, or a balance inquiry. The rounded rectangles are "MSC references" which refer to other MSCs. The use of MSC references allows horizontal expansion of Message Sequence

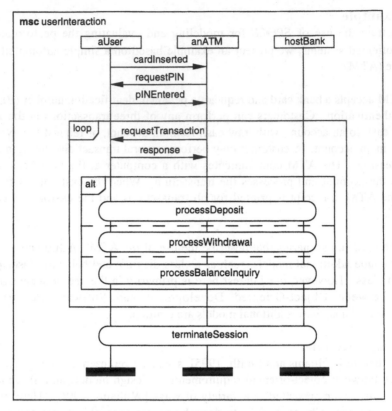

Figure 1. Message Sequence Chart for User Interaction with the ATM

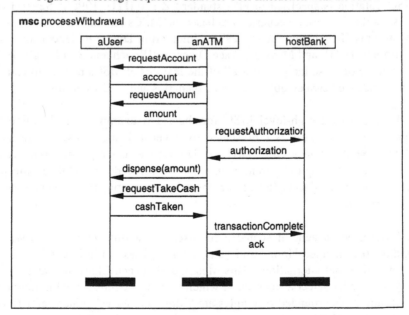

Figure 2. Message Sequence Chart processWithdrawal

Charts. The MSC that corresponds to ProcessWithdrawal is shown in Figure 2.

A Message Sequence Chart may also be decomposed vertically, i.e., a refining MSC may be attached to an instance axis. Figure 3 shows a part of the decomposition of the anATM instance axis. The dashed arrows represent object instance creation or destruction.

5.2 Mapping Scenarios to Performance Models

Models for evaluating the performance characteristics of the proposed ATM system are based on performance scenarios for the major uses of the system. These performance scenarios are the same as the functional scenarios illustrated in the message sequence charts (Figures 1 through 3). However, they are represented using Execution Graphs. Note that not all functional scenarios are necessarily significant

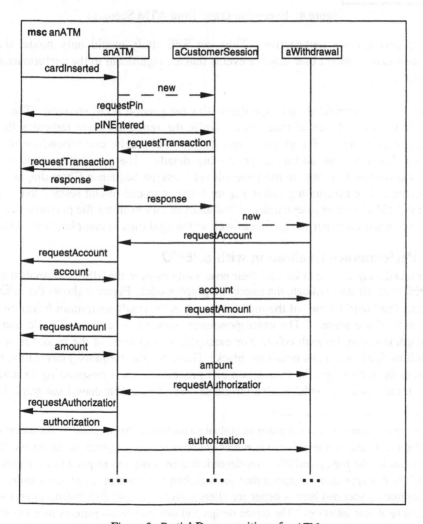

Figure 3. Partial Decomposition of anATM

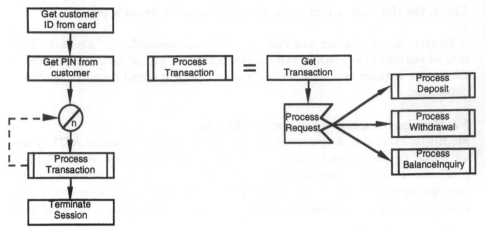

Figure 4. Execution graph from ATM Scenario

from a performance perspective. Thus, an SPE study would only model those scenarios that represent user tasks or events that are significant to the performance of the system.

Figure 4 shows an Execution Graph illustrating the general ATM scenario. The *case node* indicates a choice of transactions while the *repetition node* indicates that a session may consist of multiple transactions. Subgraphs corresponding to the *expanded nodes* show additional processing details. The processing steps *(basic nodes)* correspond to steps in the lowest-level Message Sequence Chart diagram for the scenario. The execution graph in Figure 4 shows an end-to-end session that spans several ATM customer interactions. Thus analysts can evaluate the performance for each individual customer interaction as well as the total time to complete a session. [3]

5.3 Performance Evaluation with *SPE•ED*

After identifying the scenarios and their processing steps in the MSC, the analyst uses *SPE•ED* to create and evaluate the execution graph model. Figure 5 shows the *SPE•ED* screen. The "world view" of the model appears in the small *navigation boxes* on the right side of the screen. The correspondence between an expanded node and its subgraph is shown through color. For example, the top level of the model is in the top-left navigation box; its nodes are black. The top-right (turquoise) navigation box contains the loop to get the transaction and process it. Its corresponding expanded node in the top-level model is also turquoise. The ProcessWithdrawal subgraph is in

---

3 Some performance analysts prefer to evaluate a traditional "transaction" -- the processing that occurs after a user presses the enter key until a response appears on the screen. This eliminates the highly variable, user-dependent time it takes to respond to each prompt. While that approach was appropriate for mainframe transaction based applications, the approach prescribed here is better for client/server and other distributed systems with graphical user interfaces. The screen design and user interaction patterns may introduce end-to-end response time problems even though computer resource utilization is low.

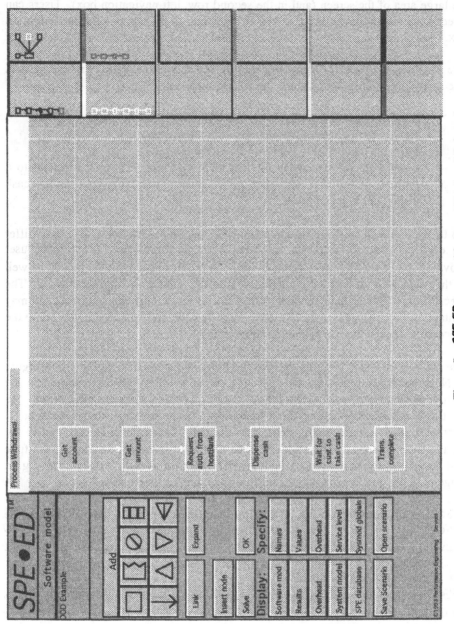

Figure 5. *SPE•ED* Screen with processWithdrawal Subgraph

the large area of the screen (and in the second row, left navigation box). Users can directly access any level in the model by clicking on the corresponding navigation box.

The next step is to specify *software resource requirements* for each processing step. The software resources we examine for this example are:

- *Screens* - the number of screens displayed to the ATM customer (aUser)
- *Home* - the number of interactions with the hostBank
- *Log* - the number of log entries on anATM machine
- *Delay* - the relative delay for the ATM customer (aUser) to respond to a prompt, or the time for other ATM device processing such as the cash dispenser or receipt printer.

Up to five types of software resources may be specified. The set of five may differ for each subgraph if necessary to characterize performance. The *SPE•ED* user provides values for these requirements for each processing step in the model, as well as the probability of each case alternative and the number of loop repetitions. The specifications may include parameters that can be varied between solutions, and may contain arithmetic expressions. Resource requirements for expanded nodes are in the processing steps in the corresponding subgraph.

The software resource requirements for the ProcessWithdrawal subgraph are in Figure 5. Note that the DispenseCash step displays a screen to inform the customer to take the cash, logs the action to the ATM's disk, and has a delay for the cash dispenser. We arbitrarily assume this delay to be 5 time units. In the software model the delay is relative to the other processing steps; e.g., the delay for the customer to remove the cash is twice as long as DispenseCash. The user may specify the duration of a time unit (in the overhead matrix) to evaluate the effect on overall performance; e.g., a range of .1 sec. to 2 sec. per time unit. In this example a time unit is 1 sec.

The ATM scenario focuses on processing that occurs on the ATM. However, the performance of anATM unit is seldom a performance problem. The *SPE•ED* evaluation will examine the performance at a hostBank that supports many ATM units.

5.4 Processing Overhead

SPE•ED supports the SPE process defined in [Smith, 1990]. Analysts specify values for the software resource requirements for processing steps. The *computer resource requirements* for each software resource request are specified in an overhead matrix stored in the SPE database. This matrix is used for all software models that execute in that hardware/software environment. Figure 6 shows the overhead matrix for this case study. The matrix connects the values specified in the "ATM Spec Template" software specification template with the device usage in the "Host Bank" computer facility. The software resources in the template are in the left column of the matrix; the devices in the facility are in the other columns. The values in the matrix describe the device characteristics.

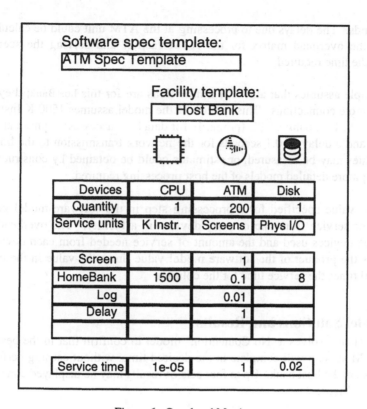

Figure 6. Overhead Matrix

The pictures of the devices in the facility are across the top of the matrix, and the device name is in the first row. The second row specifies how many devices of each type are in the facility. For example, if the facility has 20 disk devices, there is one disk device column with 20 in its quantity row. *SPE•EDs* (deliberately) simple models will assume that disk accesses can be evenly spread across these devices. The third row is a comment that describes the service units for the values specified for the software processing steps. The next five rows are the software resources in the specification template. This example uses only four of them. The last row specifies the service time for the devices in the computer facility.

The values in the center section of the matrix define the connection between software resource requests and computer device usage. The screen display occurs on anATM unit; its only affect on the hostBank is a delay. The 1 in the ATM column for the 'Screen' row means that each *screen* specified in the software model causes one visit to the ATM delay server. We arbitrarily assume this delay to be one second (in the service time row). Similarly, each *log* and *delay* specification in the software model result in a delay between hostBank processing requests. We assume the log delay is

0.01 seconds. The delays due to processing at the ATM unit could be calculated by defining the overhead matrix for the ATM facility and solving the scenario to calculate the time required.

This example assumes that all ATM transactions are for this hostBank; they do not require remote connections. This version of the model assumes 1500 K Instructions execute on the host bank's CPU (primarily for data base accesses), 8 physical I/Os are required, and a delay of 0.1 seconds for the network transmission to the host bank. These values may be measured, or estimates could be obtained by constructing and evaluating more detailed models of the host processing required.

Thus each value specified for a processing step in the software model generates demand for service from one or more devices in a facility. The overhead matrix defines the devices used and the amount of service needed from each device. The demand is the product of the software model value times the value in the overhead matrix cell times the service time for the column.

5.5 Model Solutions and Results

The analyst first solves a 'No Contention' model to confirm that in the best case, a single ATM session will complete in the desired time, without causing performance bottlenecks at the host bank. Up to four sets of results may be displayed concurrently, as shown in Figure 7.

The elapsed time result for the 'No Contention' model is in the top-left quadrant. The overall time is at the top, and the time for each processing step is next to the step. The color bar legend in the upper right corner of the quadrant shows the values associated with each color; the upper bound is set by defining an overall performance objective. Values higher than the performance objective will be red, lower values are respectively cooler colors. The 'Resource usage' values below the color bar legend show the time spent at each computer device. Of the 35.6 total seconds for the end-to-end scenario, 35.25 is due to the delays at the ATM unit for customer interactions and processing. Thus, no performance problems are apparent with this result.

The SPE tool evaluates the results of device contention delays by automatically creating and solving an analytic queueing network model. The utilization result for the 'Contention solution' of the ATM sessions with an arrival rate of 5 withdrawal transactions per second is in the top-right quadrant of Figure 7. The total utilization of each server is shown under the color bar, and the utilization of each device by each processing step is next to the step. The total CPU utilization is 15%, and the disk device is 100%. Even though the customer data base would fit on one disk device, more are needed to relieve the contention delays. In general, options for correcting bottlenecks are to reduce the number of I/Os to the disk, reduce the number of ATM units that share a host bank server, or add disks to the server. The options are evaluated by changing software processing steps, or values in the overhead matrix.

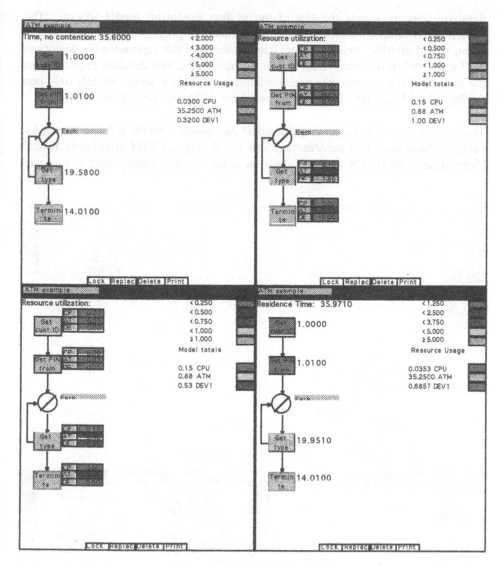

Figure 7. SPE Model Results

The results in the lower quadrants of Figure 7 show the utilization and response time results for 3 disk devices. The quadrants let the analyst easily compare performance metrics for alternatives.

5.6 System Execution Model

The 'System model solution' creates a queueing network model with all the scenarios defined in a project executing on all their respective facilities. The system execution model picture is in Figure 8. This example models one workload scenario: a session with one withdrawal transaction. The host bank may have other workloads such as teller transactions, bank analyst inquiries, etc. Each performance scenario in the SPE database appears across the top of the system execution model screen. The specification template beside the scenario name displays the current workload intensity and priority. Below the scenario is a template that represents the devices in the facility assigned to the scenario. The facilities in the SPE database appear across the bottom of the system execution model screen. This example models only one facility for the host bank. It could also model the ATM unit, other home banks, etc.

The model is solved by calculating the model parameters from the software model for each scenario and then constructing and evaluating a CSIM simulation model [Schwetman, 1994]. CSIM is a simulation product that is widely used to evaluate

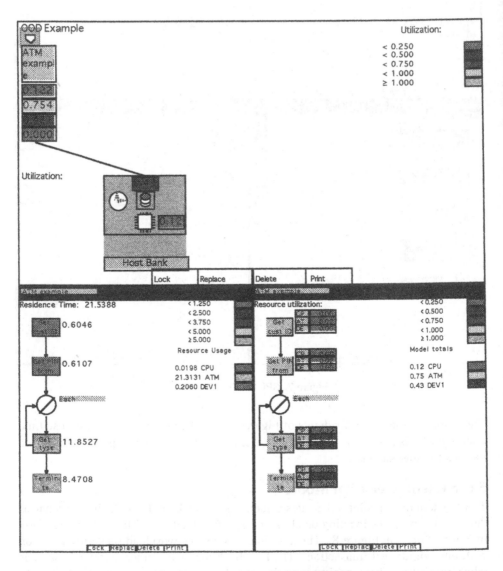

Figure 8. System Execution Model Results

distributed and parallel processing systems. By automatically creating the models, *SPE•ED* eliminates the need to code CSIM models in the C programming language. The model results show:

- the response time for the scenario and its corresponding color (inside the scenario name rectangle),
- the amount of the total response time spent at each computer device (the values and colors in the template below the scenario name)
- the average utilization of each device in each facility and its corresponding color.

One of the model scenarios may be a *focus scenario*, usually a scenario that is vital to the system development project. Users may view various system model results for processing steps in the focus scenario in 2 quadrants below the system model.

One of the difficult problems in simulation is determining the length of the simulation run. *SPE•ED* solves this problem with the performance results meter shown in Figure 9. It is based on work by [Raatikainen, 1993] adapted for SPE evaluations. The approach is adapted because results depend on the precision of the model parameters, and in early life cycle stages only rough estimates are available. Users may monitor simulation progress and stop the simulation to view results at any point. They may also set a confidence value or simulated run time to automatically terminate the

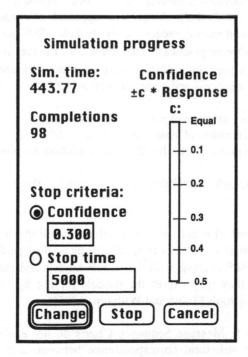

Figure 9. Interactive Simulation Control

simulation. The meter shows the progress of the current confidence; it is calculated with a batch-mean method. *SPE•ED* uses a default value of 70% probability that the reported response is within 30% of the actual mean. This bound is much looser than typically used for computer system models. We selected this value empirically by studying the length of time required for various models, versus the analytic performance metrics, versus the precision of the specifications that determine the model parameters. Users may increase the confidence value, but not the probability. It would be easy to add other controls, but experience with our users shows that this approach is sufficient for their evaluations and requires little expert knowledge of simulation controls.

6.0 Summary and Conclusions

This paper describes the SPE performance modeling tool, *SPE•ED*, and its use for performance engineering of object-oriented software. It describes how to use scenarios to determine the processing steps to be modeled, and illustrates the process with a simple ATM example defined with Message Sequence Charts. It then illustrates the SPE evaluation steps supported by *SPE•ED*.

Object-oriented methods will likely be the preferred design approach of the future. SPE techniques are vital to ensure that these systems meet performance requirements. SPE for OOD is especially difficult since functions may require collaboration among many different objects from many classes. These interactions may be obscured by polymorphism and inheritance, making them difficult to trace. Distributing objects over a network compounds the problem. Our approach of connecting performance models and designs with message sequence charts makes SPE performance modeling of object-oriented software practical. The *SPE•ED* tool makes it easier for software designers to conduct their own performance studies. Features that de-skill the performance modeling process and make this viable are:

- quick and easy creation of performance scenarios
- automatic generation of system execution models
- visual perception of results that call attention to potential performance problems
- simulation length control that can be adapted to the precision of the model input data.

Other features support SPE activities other than modeling such as SPE database archives, and presentation and reporting of results. Once performance engineers complete the initial SPE analysis with the simple models and ensure that the design approach is viable, they may export the models for use by "industrial strength" performance modeling tools [Smith and Williams, 1995].

As noted in section 5, Message Sequence Charts do not explicitly capture time. However, the close structural correspondence between scenarios expressed in Message Sequence Charts and those using Execution Graphs suggests the possibility of a straightforward translation from analysis/design models to performance scenarios. Standard SPE techniques, such as performance walkthroughs, best-and-worst-case analysis, and others, can then be used to obtain resource requirements or time estimates for processing steps.

Providing specifications for the overhead matrix still requires expert knowledge of the hardware/software processing environments and performance measurement techniques. Some performance modeling tools provide libraries with default values for the path lengths. If the benchmark studies that led to the library values closely match the new software being modeled, the default values are adequate. Someone must validate the default values with measurements to ensure that they apply to the new software. Thus the expert knowledge is necessary for both tool approaches. It would be relatively easy to build a feature to automatically populate *SPE•EDs* overhead matrix from customized measurement tool output, but it is not currently a high priority feature.

This paper demonstrates the feasibility of applying SPE to object-oriented systems. Future research is aimed at providing a smooth transition between CASE tools for OOD and SPE evaluation tools.

7.0 References

[Baldassari, et al., 1989] M. Baldassari, B. Bruno, V. Russi, and R. Zompi, "PROTOB: A Hierarchical Object-Oriented CASE Tool for Distributed Systems," Proceedings European Software Engineering Conference - 1989, Coventry, England, 1989.

[Baldassari and Bruno, 1988] M. Baldassari and G. Bruno, "An Environment for Object-Oriented Conceptual Programming Based on PROT Nets," in Advances in Petri Nets, Lectures in Computer Science No. 340, Berlin, Springer-Verlag, 1988, pp. 1-19.

[Beilner, et al., 1988] H. Beilner, J. Mäter, and N. Weissenburg, "Towards a Performance Modeling Environment: News on HIT," Proceedings 4th International Conference on Modeling Techniques and Tools for Computer Performance Evaluation, Plenum Publishing, 1988.

[Beilner, et al., 1995] H. Beilner, J. Mäter, and C. Wysocki, "The Hierarchical Evaluation Tool HIT," in Performance Tools & Model Interchange Formats, vol. 581/1995, F. Bause and H. Beilner, ed., D-44221 Dortmund, Germany, Universität Dortmund, Fachbereich Informatik, 1995, pp. 6-9.

[Booch, 1994] G. Booch, Object-Oriented Analysis and Design with Applications, Redwood City, CA, Benjamin/Cummings, 1994.

[Booch and Rumbaugh, 1995] G. Booch and J. Rumbaugh, "Unified Method for Object-Oriented Development," Rational Software Corporation, Santa Clara, CA, 1995.

[Buhr and Casselman, 1996] R. J. A. Buhr and R. S. Casselman, Use Case Maps for Object-Oriented Systems, Upper Saddle River, NJ, Prentice Hall, 1996.

[Buhr and Casselman, 1994] R. J. A. Buhr and R. S. Casselman, "Timethread-Role Maps for Object-Oriented Design of Real-Time and Distributed Systems," Proceedings of OOPSLA '94: Object-Oriented Programming Systems, Languages and Applications, Portland, OR, October, 1994, pp. 301-316.

[Buhr and Casselman, 1992] R. J. A. Buhr and R. S. Casselman, "Architectures with Pictures," Proceedings of OOPSLA '92: Object-Oriented Programming Systems, Languages and Applications, Vancouver, BC, October, 1992, pp. 466-483.

[Coleman, et al., 1994] D. Coleman, P. Arnold, S. Bodoff, C. Dollin, H. Gilchrist, F. Hayes, and P. Jeremaes, Object-Oriented Development: The Fusion Method, Englewood Cliffs, NJ, Prentice Hall, 1994.

[Goettge, 1990] R. T. Goettge, "An Expert System for Performance Engineering of Time-Critical Software," Proceedings Computer Measurement Group Conference, Orlando FL, 1990, pp. 313-320.

[Grummitt, 1991] A. Grummitt, "A Performance Engineer's View of Systems Development and Trials," Proceedings Computer Measurement Group Conference, Nashville, TN, 1991, pp. 455-463.

[Hrischuk, et al., 1995] C. Hrischuk, J. Rolia, and C. M. Woodside, "Automatic Generation of a Software Performance Model Using an Object-Oriented Prototype," Proceedings of the Third International Workshop on Modeling, Analysis, and Simulation of Computer and Telecommunication Systems, Durham, NC, January, 1995, pp. 399-409.

[ITU, 1996] ITU, "Criteria for the Use and Applicability of Formal Description Techniques, Message Sequence Chart (MSC)," International Telecommunication Union, 1996.

[Jacobson, et al., 1992] I. Jacobson, M. Christerson, P. Jonsson, and G. Overgaard, Object-Oriented Software Engineering, Reading, MA, Addison-Wesley, 1992.

[Raatikainen, 1993] K. E. E. Raatikainen, "Accuracy of Estimates for Dynamic Properties of Queueing Systems in Interactive Simulation," University of Helsinki, Dept. of Computer Science Teollisuuskatu 23, SF-00510 Helsinki, Finland, 1993.

[Rolia, 1992] J. A. Rolia, "Predicting the Performance of Software Systems," University of Toronto, 1992.

[Rumbaugh, et al., 1991] J. Rumbaugh, M. Blaha, W. Premerlani, F. Eddy, and W. Lorensen, Object-Oriented Modeling and Design, Englewood Cliffs, NJ, Prentice Hall, 1991.

[Schwetman, 1994] H. Schwetman, "CSIM17: A Simulation Model-Building Toolkit," Proceedings Winter Simulation Conference, Orlando, 1994.

[Smith, 1990] C. U. Smith, Performance Engineering of Software Systems, Reading, MA, Addison-Wesley, 1990.

[Smith and Williams, 1993] C. U. Smith and L. G. Williams, "Software Performance Engineering: A Case Study Including Performance Comparison with Design Alternatives," IEEE Transactions on Software Engineering, vol. 19, no. 7, pp. 720-741, 1993.

[Smith and Williams, 1995] C. U. Smith and L. G. Williams, "A Performance Model Interchange Format," in Performance Tools and Model Interchange Formats, vol. 581/1995, F. Bause and H. Beilner, ed., D-44221 Dortmund, Germany, Universität Dortmund, Informatik IV, 1995, pp. 67-85.

[Turner, et al., 1992] M. Turner, D. Neuse, and R. Goldgar, "Simulating Optimizes Move to Client/Server Applications," Proceedings Computer Measurement Group Conference, Reno, NV, 1992, pp. 805-814.

[Williams, 1994] L. G. Williams, "Definition of Information Requirements for Software Performance Engineering," Technical Report No. SERM-021-94, Software Engineering Research, Boulder, CO, October, 1994.

[Williams and Smith, 1995] L. G. Williams and C. U. Smith, "Information Requirements for Software Performance Engineering," in Quantitative Evaluation of Computing and Communication Systems, Lecture Notes in Computer Science, vol. 977, H. Beilner and F. Bause, ed., Heidelberg, Germany, Springer-Verlag, 1995, pp. 86-101.

Measurement Tools and Modeling Techniques for Evaluating Web Server Performance

John Dilley[1], Rich Friedrich[1], Tai Jin[1], Jerome Rolia[2]

1) Hewlett-Packard Laboratories, 1501 Page Mill Road
Palo Alto, CA 94304, USA

2) Carleton University, 1125 Colonel By Drive
Ottawa, Canada K1S 5B6

ABSTRACT

The past few years have seen a rapid growth in the popularity of the Internet and the World Wide Web. Many companies are deploying Web servers and seeing their usage rates climb rapidly over time. Our research focused on analyzing and evaluating the performance of Internet and intranet Web servers with a goal of creating a Layered Queueing Model to allow capacity planning and performance prediction of next generation server designs. To achieve this we built a tool framework that enables us to collect and analyze empirical data necessary to accomplish our goals.

This paper describes custom instrumentation we developed and deployed to collect workload metrics and model parameters from several large-scale, commercial Internet and intranet Web servers over a time interval of many months. We describe an object-oriented tool framework that significantly improves the productivity of analyzing the nearly 100 GBs of collected measurements. Finally, we describe the layered queueing model we developed to estimate client response time at a Web server. The model predicts the impact on server and client response times as a function of network topology and Web server pool size.

1.0 Introduction

The World Wide Web [1] is a phenomenon which needs little introduction. The primary driving factors for the rapid growth of the WWW include rich content types, ease of use, prevalence of TCP/IP, and ease of publishing. Network administrators and webmasters at professionally managed business sites need to understand the ongoing behavior of their systems. They must assess the operation of their site in terms of the request traffic patterns, analyze the server's response to those requests, identify popular content, understand user behavior, and so on. A powerful set of analysis tools working in tandem with good modeling techniques are an invaluable assistance in this task.

Results from a two month period at one of our commercial Internet measurement sites [2] is illustrated in Figure 1. It shows the periodicity of requests with the day of week, and documents a dramatic increase in the number of hits per week—a linear regression shows traffic increasing at a rate of 7000 hits per week and 37MB per week (the graph also illustrates Web traffic periodicity with day of week). This is a powerful motivator for capacity planning of these services.

1.1 Related Work

Previous studies of World Wide Web performance have provided many useful insights into the behavior of the Web. At the University of Saskatchewan, Arlitt and Williamson [4] examined Web Server workloads through an in-depth study of the performance characteristics of six web server data sets with a range of time periods, from one week to one year. In addition that group has studied and modeled the workload from the client perspective by instrumenting the Mosaic browser [5]. One result of their work is a proposed set of workload invariants for Web traffic. We have corroborated several of these findings with our own data.

Kwan, McGrath, and Reed at NCSA studied user access patterns to NCSA's Web server complex [6]. This paper presents an in-depth study of the traffic at their web server over a five month period. The NCSA site was the busiest of the early sites (since most Mosaic browsers when they started made a request to the site), although traffic has declined. Their findings illustrate the growth of traffic on the WWW, and describe the request patterns at their server.

Our study has examined logs from very busy, large-scale, Internet and private intranet commercial sites over a period of several months. We have focused on understanding the fundamental workload characteristics and capacity planning techniques for these large intranet (10,000+ users) and Internet sites (100,000+ hits per day). In particular we have developed new techniques to visualize workload parameters from extremely busy sites, and to model traffic at these sites.

1.2 Web Server System Modeling

The architecture of a typical WWW service environment is depicted by the model in Figure 4. Our focus is on the Web server system (hardware and software). The Web server receives requests for its content from one or more client browser applications. Requests arrive at the httpd Listener process on the server and are dispatched to one of a pool of httpd Server processes. The number of servers in the pool can vary between a fixed lower and an elastic upper bound; each process can serve one request at a time. If the request is for HTML (HyperText Markup Language) or image content the httpd Server retrieves the content and returns it directly to the client. If the request is for dynamic (Common Gateway Interface or CGI) content the httpd Server creates a child process which runs a CGI script to compute the requested information and

Figure 1   Daily Traffic Trends

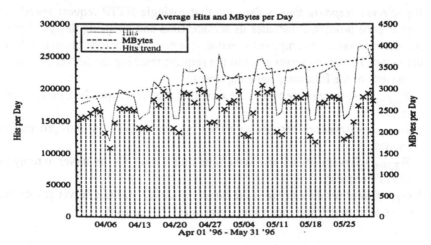

return output for the server to send back to the client. All of these processes execute in user space on the Web server.

Our research goal was to construct a model of commercial Web servers with parameters that could be measured from a real system, allowing us then to apply the model to help understand the relationships between Web servers, clients, and the Internets and intranets that connect them.

Layered Queueing Models (LQM) have been proposed to study distributed application systems [7][8][9] and we extend and apply them in this paper to address Web servers. They are extended Queueing Network Models (QNM) [10] that consider contention for processes as well as physical resources such as processors and disks. An LQM can be used to answer the same kinds of capacity planning questions as QNMs, but also estimate client queueing delays at servers. Figure 4 models clients competing for access to a Web server. When the number of clients is large client queueing delays at the server can increase much more quickly than server response times and are a better measure of end-user quality of service.

This paper documents our methodology for World Wide Web performance evaluation and is structured as follows.

- Section 2.0 discusses the metrics and instrumentation required to capture response time and service demand at WWW server sites.
- Section 3.0 presents the performance analysis toolkit that supports rapid data reduction and visualization for large measurement logs.
- Section 4.0 describes Layered Network Queueing Models and presents an LQM for one of the sites we measured. The model defines the relationship between the number of httpd processes, the number of CPUs, network delays, and client response times.
- Section 5.0 summarizes our contributions and outlines areas of future research.

2.0 Metrics and Instrumentation

Our study focused on the following metrics: server response and service demand, and client residence time at the server.

- R_S—*Server response time* is the time that a single HTTP request spends at the Server pool process. It includes its service time and queueing delays at physical resources in order to complete the request; it does not include queueing delays in the network or at the server prior to the request reaching the Server pool process. It consists of the following sub-components.
    - $R_{S,Parse}$—*Server parse time* is the time that the server spends reading the client request.
    - $R_{S,Proc}$—*Server processing time* is the time that the server spends processing the request.
    - $R_{S,Net}$—*Server network time* is the time that it takes for the server to reply to the client's request.
- Res_C—*Client residence time* is the queueing delay plus the Server response time for one visit to the web server (i.e. a single HTTP request).

- **R_C**—*Client response time* is the network communication latency plus the client residence time (i.e., end-to-end or last byte latency for one request).
- **D_S**—*Server service demand* is the amount of system resources consumed by each client HTTP request. It consists of the following sub-components.
  - ❏ **$D_{s,CPU}$** is the average CPU time for the request.
  - ❏ **$D_{s,Disk}$** is the average disk demand for the request.
  - ❏ **$D_{s,Net}$** is the average network delay for the request.

R_S is distinct from the classical "response time" metric in several ways.

- Server response time does not include all of the network time of the request. It does not capture the time between the user's initial click at the client browser, the latency in the network, or the server time to dispatch the request to the httpd; nor does it record the time between when the server writes the last byte to the network stack and the time the last byte actually arrives at the client. Even if the end-to-end network delay is accurately measured, there may be additional time for the client browser to display the information to the user.
- The server response time metric is recorded for each *hit* at the server, i.e. for a single browser HTTP request and not for the end user's request, which may require several hits (i.e. HTTP requests) in the case of an HTML page or CGI request that contains inline images. When a browser receives a request with inline images (HTML IMG SRC directives) it usually attempts to retrieve and display each of those images as part of the page the user selected. A more precise response time metric must take into account the aggregate latency of retrieval for all of the images visible to the user.

R_S is important for understanding server utilization and hence for capacity planning. R_S underestimates Res_C because R_S does not include client queueing delays at the server. R_C on the other hand includes latencies beyond the control of the Web server so it is not a good measure of client quality of service at the server (R_C overestimates Res_C). Res_C is a better measure of end user quality of service for a Web server. Since this value cannot be measured directly with server-side instrumentation we use LQMs and analytic performance evaluation techniques to estimate it based upon the measured values R_S.

The commercial sites we studied used a variety of Web server implementations from NCSA, OpenMarket, and Netscape. All of these systems record incoming requests but for varying metrics and with various precision. Two of our most important sites were running the NCSA implementation during the period of our study. Since the source code was available we added custom instrumentation to measure the R_S and $D_{s,CPU}$ values for each request at the server. This data was written in extra fields in the httpd logs. The following section describes this in more detail.

2.1 Measurement Issues

Our choice of metrics leads to some measurement issues due to the instrumentation being in the application and not on the network or in the server host's network stack. The measurement intervals are identified in Figure 2, and show that R_S does not measure the network and queueing delays from the time the client made the request (the click of the hypertext link) and arrival of the request at the httpd process ($Q_{Net,Client}$ and Q_S in Figure 2). R_S also does not measure the network queueing and transmission delay for the last window of TCP data, which is queued in the server's network buffers after the final write system call completes ($Q_{Net,Server}$ in the figure). Our technique does measure the delay due to network congestion for all packets except for those in the last window, since they must be received and acknowledged before the last window can be queued for delivery to the server's network stack.

While this metric does not provide an accurate indication of client response time at the server, it does measure the time a Server pool process spends servicing each request. This is the data we use to construct our analytic models, from which we estimate server queueing delay and client residence time.

2.2 NCSA httpd Instrumentation

The NCSA 1.5 httpd was instrumented to provide server response time (R_S) and CPU service demand ($D_{s,CPU}$). R_S is measured as the real or wall-clock time spent processing the request using the gettimeofday(2) system call rounded to millisecond precision. We distinguish between different HTTP request types (e.g. HTML, Image, CGI, etc.) and further subdivide the metrics.

$D_{s,CPU}$ is measured using the times(2) system call, which indicates the user and system CPU time consumed by the process and its children with millisecond precision (the accuracy is system dependent but is typically 10 milliseconds).

The instrumentation captures the three separate R_S intervals which when combined comprise the overall server response time, R_S. $R_{S,Parse}$ measures the length of time from the client connection to the httpd server process to the reading of the first line of the HTTP request. $R_{S,Proc}$ measures the time spent by the server in processing the request, including reading in the rest of the request and internal processing up to the point of sending the response. $R_{S,Net}$ begins with the sending of the response and ends with the final send of data from the httpd Server pool process. $D_{s,CPU}$ is measured over the same time period as R_S.

R_S and D_S are logged as two additional fields appended to the end of the common log format entries in the access logfile. Both fields have the format msec/msec/msec. For R_S each millisecond value represents each of the three intervals of the server response time. For D_S the first and second values represent the CPU time spent by the server process in the kernel and in user spaces, respectively; the third value represents the CPU time spent by any child processes in both kernel and user spaces (child processes satisfy CGI requests).

Figure 2   HTTP Request Timeline with Instrumentation Intervals

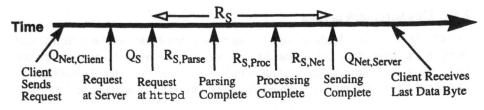

When used in analysis the three intervals of R_S are typically combined to obtain a single server response time value since the individual intervals are not precise measures (the point at which the three intervals end is imprecise due to the structure of the code where processing and sending data overlap).

The overall impact of the code changes was slight; only a few lines were changed in the daemon and the performance impact of these additional system calls was insignificant when compared with the amount of work done by an HTTP connection request. The additional information allowed us to develop predictive models for the system with minor perturbation on the running system.

3.0 Log Analysis Framework and Tools

The process of analyzing HTTP server performance begins with the collection of log files spanning some analysis time period. To understand traffic trends we collected logs over a period of two to twelve months at our instrumented sites. All of our sites compressed their log files with gzip prior to retrieval. At our busiest site the *compressed* logs were on the order of 30-40 MB per day (240+ MB per day uncompressed); our second busiest Internet site's logs were 6-8 MB per day (30 MB per day uncompressed). The logs are kept compressed on an HP 9000/755 workstation with a modest disk farm.

By converting the raw ASCII log files into a record-oriented binary format and mapping them into system memory our tools are able to operate with a 50x speedup as compared with previous perl tools while saving 70-80% of the disk space required by the ASCII logs. Plus, common library facilities make writing new tools almost trivial.

3.1 Data Conversion

The first step in the process is to convert the compressed or uncompressed httpd log files into a reduced binary representation in which the request timestamp is stored as a UNIX time_t or timeval structure, the number of bytes returned is stored as an unsigned int, the URL (Uniform Resource Locator, or content location) is stored as an index into a string symbol table, and so on. The conversion utility creates two output files for each log file: the binary compressed data (with fixed size log records) and a symbol table containing the variable-length strings from the original log file (client addresses, URLs, user IDs). One symbol table can be used by multiple log files since there tend to be relatively few unique URLs requested many times, and few clients making repeated requests.

3.2 Data Reduction

Once the files are compressed into their binary format a set of tools reduce the data by extracting various data fields from the logs. The Log Analysis Framework provides access to the log data as an array of fixed-length records in memory. By mapping the converted data files into memory the framework saves IO overhead at application start-up time and uses the operating system to manage data access; furthermore use of memory mapping avoids a copy of data onto the heap.

Application access this data using the C++ Standard Template Library (STL [11][12]) *generic programming* paradigm. Each log record is viewed as an element in a *container* (log file) with an associated *iterator* type; an instance of the iterator points to each record in turn, starting with the element returned by the container's `begin` method, incrementing using the iterator's `operator++` method until reaching the container's end iterator position. At each record the iterator is *dereferenced* via its opera-tor* method; the application can access each of the elements of the log record (i.e., `(*iterator).requestUrl`).

Using Framework capabilities an application can visit each log record in all log files specified on the command line using about a dozen lines of boilerplate code (including exception handling); this leaves the developer to focus on the custom logic to analyze the data in the log files rather than writing more parsing code.

3.3 Uniform Filtering Capability

When analyzing a response size distribution some questions can arise of the form, "What traffic is responsible for the peak at 4KB?", or, "What is the server response time of requests from the AOL domain?" To answer these questions requires examina-tion of a subset of the data in the log files that match some criteria, or pass some *filter*. Due to the size of the data, extracting each subset and placing it in a separate file is impractical (because of both size and time concerns). In addition, reuse of existing software is essential to maximize developer and user productivity.

The uniform filtering capability allows logs to be filtered transparently to the accessing code; therefore a single tool can operate on entire logs or, with a set of predefined com-mand line arguments, only on the subset of the log entries matching the user-specified filter criteria. The standard filters include client host ID, timestamp (day of week, or month and day), size (range or exact value), and many more. Figure 3 shows the file size distribution after applying a filter that selected only HTML requests over a two month period (computed from 60 individual `access_log` data files).

Figure 3   Example Filtered Distribution

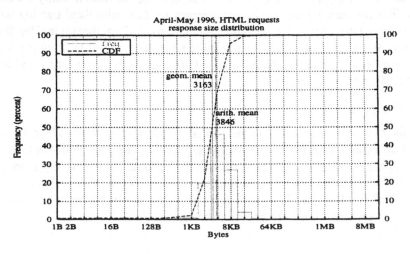

3.4   Statistical Analysis

Now that the response size for each request is known, how should the data be visualized? There are several possibilities, but the most concise way to view the data distribution is through a histogram and Cumulative Distribution Function (CDF) plot. A histogram displays the data summarized into *buckets*; each bucket contains the proportion of observed values that fell into the range of that bucket. The *CDF* plot indicates the proportion of the observed values whose value was less than that bucket's value. The point at which the CDF plot crosses the 50% mark indicates the median of the observed sample. We also typically indicate the arithmetic and geometric means using vertical lines in the distribution.

Most data from Web servers tends to have a very wide dynamic range, and approximates a log-normal distribution. Therefore we usually apply a logarithmic transformation to the data prior to placing it into buckets. Since this is such a prevalent component of data analysis we created the class Distribution to assist with the collection and reporting of data. Each observed data value is added to a Distribution class instance; after all files have been processed the distribution is printed to a file. The distribution provides a concise representation of the data population, including its arithmetic mean and geometric mean (which can be useful with a log-normal distribution), standard deviation, minimum and maximum values, and the bucket populations. Visualization tools read the distribution output and create the charts and graphs used for our analysis.

4.0   Layered Queueing Models for Capacity Planning

Measurement tools are essential for characterizing the current and past behavior of a system. However it is also important to be able to anticipate future behavior with different hardware and software configurations or under different workloads. For this reason we develop an analytic queueing model for the system. Analysis is chosen over simulation because of its speed and the easier interpretation of results. We rely on Mean Value Analysis (MVA [10][13]) based techniques and Queueing Network Models (QNMs) for our analysis. In this section we describe Layered Queueing Models (LQMs) and briefly outline the Method of Layers solution algorithm for LQMs. We then give an LQM for the Web server and identify its parameters. These parameters are gathered using the instrumentation and tools described in Section 2.0 and Section 3.0. Last, we use the model to predict client response times under different Web server and network configurations.

LQMs are QNMs extended to reflect interactions between client and server processes. The processes may share devices and server processes may also request services from one another. LQMs are appropriate for describing distributed application systems such as OMG CORBA [14], OSF DCE [15], and Web server applications. In these applications a process can suffer queueing delays both at its node's devices and at its software servers. If these software delays are ignored, response time and utilization estimates for the system will be incorrect.

The Method of Layers (MOL) [7] is an iterative technique that decomposes an LQM into a series of QNMs. Performance estimates for each of the QNMs are found and used as input parameters of the other QNMs. The purpose of the MOL is to find a fixed point where the predicted values for mean process response times and utilizations are consistent with respect to all of the submodels. At that point the results of the MVA calculations approximate the performance measures for the system under consideration. Intuitively, this is the point at which predicted process response times and utilizations are balanced so that each process in the model has the same throughput whether it is considered as a customer in a QNM or as a server: the rate of completions of the server equals the rate of requests for its service according to the flow balance assumption, and the average service time required by callers of a process equals its average response time. The following are the parameters for an LQM:

- process classes and their populations or threading levels
- devices and their scheduling policies
- for each service s of each process class c:
  - the average number of visits $V_{c,s,k}$ to each device k
  - the average service time $S_{c,s,k}$ per request at each device k
  - and the average number of visits $V_{c,s,d,s2}$ to each service $s2$ of each of server process class d

Note that the client's service times at the services it visits are not specified. These values must be estimated by performance evaluation techniques.

Services identify separate visit ratio specifications that characterize the types of work supported by a server pool. A visit ratio specification describes the physical resource demands required by a type of work within a server and its requests for service from other servers. With this extra degree of detail client and server service response times, and response times for specific client/server interactions can be estimated.

In addition to the results from MVA for QNMs, LQM output values include for each process class c:

- the average response time $R_{c,s}$ of each service s
- the average response time $R_{c,s1,d,s2}$ of each client of service $s1$ at each service $s2$ of its serving process class d
- its utilization $U_{c,s}$ of each serving process class
- the total average queue length Q_c of this process class c and its services $Q_{c,s}$
- the total utilization U_c of this process and its services $U_{c,s}$

4.1   An LQM for a Web Server

An LQM for the Web server is shown in Figure 4. The client class generates the workload for the server. We give it a single service with the name *request*. It is used to generate the visits to all of the Web server's services. The Listener process has a single service named *accept* that accepts client requests and forwards them to the server pool. This is reflected in the LQM as a visit by the client class to the Listener process and then a visit to the server pool. With this approach we maintain the visit ratio and blocking relationships present in the real system.

The server pool offers three services that require significantly different resource demands. These are *Image*, *Html*, and *CGI*. The *Image* and *Html* requests use processor and disk resources of the server process. The *CGI* service spawns another process to execute a corresponding CGI program. The server pool process waits for the CGI program to complete so it can return results to the client. In general, these CGI programs could exploit middleware platforms such as DCE or CORBA to interact with other layers of servers. However this was not the case for this application. For this reason we included the spawned processes CPU demand in the *CGI* service. To complete the request using the HTTP protocol, the server process must wait for all but the last TCP/IP window to be forwarded to the client over the network and acknowledged. The time to send results was measured as $R_{s,Net}$. Since it includes relatively little CPU demand it gives a good estimate for the network delay; we use this value as an input parameter for our model.

The measurement tools were used to estimate the following LQM model parameters:

- for the *request* service of the client class *c*:
  - the arrival rate of requests λ_{Client}
  - the average number of visits to Listener per request $V_{c,request,Listener,accept} = 1$
  - the average number of visits to each Web service per request
    - $V_{c,request,Pool,Image} = 57\%$
    - $V_{c,request,Pool,Html} = 30\%$
    - $V_{c,request,Pool,Cgi} = 13\%$
- N_{Pool} the number of processes in the server pool
- for each service *s* of the server pool class of processes:
  - $D_{s,CPU}$ the average CPU time of each service
  - $D_{s,Disk}$ the average disk demand of each service
  - $D_{s,Net}$ the average network delay

For clients, the arrival rate of requests was estimated as the measured number of hits per measurement period. This is a low estimate, because requests will be dropped when it is not possible for a client to establish a connection. To emulate an open class we set the client population to a very large value with think time equal to the population size divided by the hit rate. For each request, the client visits the Listener once to get forwarded to a server pool process. The measured fraction of each type of hit gives the probability and hence average number of visits to each service.

The $D_{s,CPU}$ values were captured for each request then aggregated by service type. The $D_{s,Disk}$ could not be captured on a per service basis so they had to be estimated.

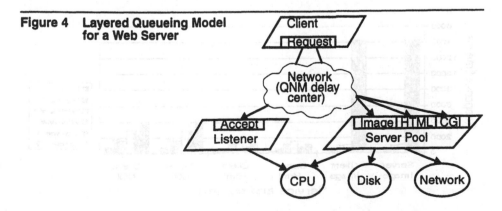

Figure 4   Layered Queueing Model for a Web Server

Because of caching, the $D_{s,Disk}$ quantities were quite small compared to the measured response times for the services. As a result we believe our analysis is not sensitive to these estimates. The $R_{s,Net}$ were captured for each request and were also aggregated by service type to estimate $D_{s,Net}$. They are large compared to CPU and disk times and have a significant impact on server behavior.

4.2 Server Capacity Planning

We now use the LQM to consider the performance impact of the server and network configuration on client response times at the server. The results of this modeling are shown in Figure 5. Client response times include queueing for access to a server in the server pool, the time needed for the service, and the time up to the point the last portion of the request's results are submitted to TCP/IP. We consider:

- Three types of network delay characteristics:
  - Internet: using data from our measurement site
  - wide area intranet (labeled in the figure as *Wintranet*): using a delay value of 1000 msec.
  - local area intranet (labeled as *Lintranet*): using a delay value of 10 msec.
- Server pool sizes of between 1 and 60.
- Either one or two CPUs on the server node, (labeled in the figure with the suffix of 1 or 2).

The client and server response times for the Image, HTML, and CGI workload classes are outputs of the model.

The wide area intranet and local area intranet examples make use of the same measured data as the Internet case for their workload characterization but use estimated network delay times for $D_{s,Net}$.

In Figure 5 the response time is plotted as a function of the network type, workload class, and whether measured on the client or server. From these results we deduce that:

- Network delay has a dramatic impact on both server and client response times with the Internet having the worst response time characteristics.

Figure 5   Estimated Client and Server Response Times With Pool Size of 60

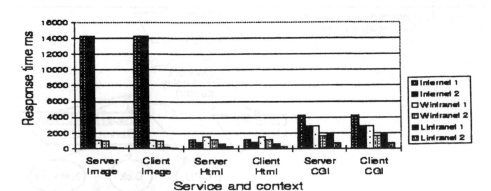

- The addition of a second CPU on the server significantly improves the response time for the CGI workload but has less of an effect for the HTML case and very little for the Image case.

In Figure 6 the response time is plotted for the Internet case as a function of the workload class and varying server pool size. From the results from the model we deduce that:

- Client response times can be much larger than server response times if the pool size is not sufficient.
- Increasing the size of the server pool significantly decreases client response times.
- Larger network delays require more servers in the server pool.

These results assume a very large population of clients with each arriving client completing its requests for service. In a real system calls will simply be lost from the socket queue when the server becomes too busy. However, when the system is well behaved then few calls will be lost. For these cases we believe the model captures the trend in client residence times at the server.

When the servers in the server pool approach full utilization, the estimated client response times increase very quickly. This is the case in Figure 6. The CPU and Disk utilizations were approximately 60% and 3%, yet with low pool size the server processes were nearly fully utilized. This is because the Internet acts as a delay center that holds a server process until the last TCP/IP window worth of data is submitted. This causes the server pool to become a software bottleneck. In Figure 6, the network delays were between 625ms and 14000ms for the different types of services (and hence result sizes). If result sizes were smaller, for example on the order of 1KB, we would not expect to see such a large impact on system behavior.

This model and analysis describes a server with a fixed upper limit on the number of server pool processes. Some server implementations allow additional processes to be spawned when their configured upper limit is reached. However there is an eventual upper limit (e.g., the size of the process table or amount of physical memory). We can increase the workload and encounter this same effect at that limit. The key point is that the number of available processes in the pool must be sized based upon the expected workload and network delay.

Figure 6   Internet Case With Measured Delay and Pool Sizes of 29, 30, and 35

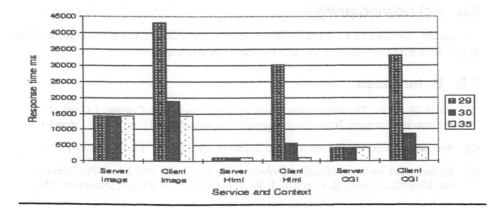

We validated the model using the measurements collected and described in Section 2.0. The model used as input data from six hours of data early in the two month investigation period. Using the full two month time period we computed the following average response times:

- $R_{S,Image}$ = 13.0 sec
- $R_{S,Html}$ = 1.0 sec
- $R_{S,CGI}$ = 3.1 sec.

These values agree closely with those predicted by the model as illustrated in Figure 6 (compare these values with the corresponding 35-process server columns in the figure). This is not a full validation of the model, but does indicate that the model is able to predict server performance with a limited amount of parameterization.

5.0 Contributions and Future Work

This paper describes our contributions in measurement tools and modeling techniques for evaluating Web server performance. Specifically, we created custom instrumentation and collected representative workload data from several large-scale, commercial Internet and intranet Web servers over a time interval of many months. We developed an object-oriented tool framework that significantly improved the productivity of analyzing the 100s of GBs of measurement data. The framework's binary data format allows a common set of tools to analyze data from diverse HTTP server implementations.

Metrics were chosen that allowed us to construct a Layered Queueing Model. We used the model to predict client response times at the server, a value which could not be measured directly but is a good measure of client quality of service at the Web server. We show that client response times are quite sensitive to the number of servers in the server pool and are more sensitive in environments with high network latency such as the Internet.

Our future research will focus on validating and extending this model beyond a single Web server and using the model to explore Web server performance in the new broadband networks being deployed to the home via cable modem and Digital Subscriber Line (ADSL, HDSL, XDSL) technologies.

6.0 Acknowledgments

The authors would like to thank Sailesh Chutani, Gita Gopal, Gary Herman, and Jim Salehi for their review comments and feedback on this paper.

7.0 References

[1] *World-Wide Web: The Information Universe*. T. Berners-Lee, R. Cailliau, J. Groff, B. Pollermann. Electronic Networking: Research, Applications and Policy, v2n1. Spring 1992.

[2] *Web Server Workload Characterization*. J. Dilley. HPL TR 96-160, December 1996.

[3] *Measurement Tools and Modeling Techniques for Evaluating Web Server Performance* (unabridged). J. Dilley, R. Friedrich, T. Jin, J. Rolia. HPL TR 96-161, December 1996.

[4] *Web Server Workload Characterization: The Search for Invariants*. M. Arlitt, C. Williamson, University of Saskatchewan. In ACM SIGMETRICS, Philadelphia, May 1996.

[5] *A Synthetic Workload Model for Internet Mosaic Traffic*. M. Arlitt, C. Williamson, Discus Working Paper 95-8, University of Saskatchewan.

[6] *User Access Patterns to NCSA's World Wide Web Server*. T. Kwan, R. McGrath, D. Reed, University of Illinois. IEEE Computer, Vol 28, No. 11, November 1995.

[7] *The Method of Layers*, J. Rolia and K. Sevcik, IEEE Transactions on Software Engineering, Vol 21, No. 8, pp 689-700, August 1995.

[8] *A Toolset for Performance Engineering and Software Design of Client-Server Systems*, G. Franks, A. Hubbard, S. Majumdar, D. Petriu, J. Rolia, C.M. Woodside, Special Issue of the Performance Evaluation Journal, Volume 24, Number 1-2, Pages 117-135.

[9] *The Stochastic Rendezvous Network Model for Performance of Synchronous Client-Server-like Distributed Software*. IEEE Transactions on Computers, C.M. Woodside, J.E. Neilson, D.C. Petriu, and S. Majumdar, Volume 44, Number 1, pages 20-34, January 1995.

[10] *Quantitative System Performance: Computer System Analysis Using Queueing Network Models*. E.D. Lazowska, J. Zahorjan, G.S. Graham, K.C. Sevcik, Prentice-Hall, 1984.

[11] *The Standard Template Library*. A. Stepanov, M. Lee, Hewlett Packard. ANSI Document No. X3J16/94-0030 WG21/N0417. March 1994.

[12] *STL<ToolKit> Users Guide*. ObjectSpace, Inc. C++ Component Series. Version 1.1, May 1995.

[13] *A Queueing Network Analysis of Computer Communication Networks with Window Flow Control*. M. Reiser. IEEE Transactions On Communications, August 1979, pp. 1201-1209.

[14] *Common Object Request Broker Architecture and Specification (CORBA)*. Object Management Group Document Number 91.12.1, Revision 1.1.

[15] *OSF DCE*. H. Lockhart. McGraw Hill, 1994. ISBN 0-07-911481-4.

Workload Characterization of Input/Output Intensive Parallel Applications *

Evgenia Smirni and Daniel A. Reed

Department of Computer Science
University of Illinois
Urbana, Illinois 61801, USA
{esmirni,reed}@cs.uiuc.edu

Abstract. The broadening disparity in the performance of input/output (I/O) devices and the performance of processors and communication links on parallel systems is a major obstacle to achieving high performance for a wide range of parallel applications. I/O hardware and file system parallelism are the keys to bridging this performance gap. A prerequisite to the development of efficient parallel file systems is detailed characterization of the I/O demands of parallel applications. In this paper, we present a comparative study of the I/O access patterns commonly found in I/O intensive parallel applications. Using the Pablo performance analysis environment and its I/O extensions we captured application I/O access patterns and analyzed their interactions with current parallel I/O systems. This analysis has proven instrumental in guiding the development of new application programming interfaces (APIs) for parallel file systems and in developing effective file system policies that can adaptively respond to complex application I/O requirements.

1 Introduction

The broadening disparity in the performance of input/output (I/O) devices and the performance of processors and communication links on parallel platforms is the primary obstacle to achieving high performance in parallel application domains that require manipulation of vast amounts of data. Understanding the interactions between application I/O request patterns and parallel I/O system hardware and software is necessary for the design of more effective I/O management policies. The primary objectives of the Scalable I/O initiative (SIO) [11] are (a) to assemble a suite of I/O intensive, national challenge applications, (b) to collect detailed performance data on application characteristics and access patterns, and (c) use this information to design and evaluate parallel file system

* This work was supported in part by the Defense Advanced Research Projects Agency under DARPA contracts DABT63-94-C0049 (SIO Initiative), DAVT63-91-C-0029, DABT63-93-C-0040, F30602-96-C-0161, DABT63-96-C-0027, and F30602-96-2-0264, by the National Science Foundation under grant NSF ASC 92-12369, and by the Aeronautics and Space Administration under NASA contracts NGT-51023, USRA 5555-22, and NAG-1-613.

management policies and parallel file system application programming interfaces (APIs).

In this paper, we present the I/O behavior of three representative scientific applications from the SIO code suite. Using the Pablo performance analysis environment and its I/O extensions, we captured and analyzed the access patterns of the SIO applications and their interactions with Intel's parallel file system (PFS) on the Paragon XP/S. This analysis proved instrumental in guiding the development of new file system application programming interfaces (APIs) and adaptive file system policies. We demonstrate why API controls for efficient data distribution, collective I/O, and data caching are necessary to maximize I/O throughput.

The remainder of this paper is organized as follows. In §2, we present related work. This is followed in §3 by an overview of the Pablo performance environment and its I/O extensions, and a high level description of the selected SIO applications. In §4–§5, we describe the applications' detailed I/O access patterns. This is followed in §6 by a discussion of the proposed SIO API and the design issues that are important for parallel I/O performance. Finally, §7 summarizes our observations.

2 Related Work

The first I/O characterization efforts of scientific applications on vector supercomputers concluded that I/O behavior is regular, recurrent, and predictable [8, 10], characteristics that were attributed to the iterative nature of such applications. In contrast to the results on vector systems, recent analyses on the Intel Paragon XP/S [4], the Intel iPSC/860 [6], and the CM-5 [12], showed greater irregularity in I/O access patterns, with the majority of file requests being small but with the greatest data volume generated by a few large requests.

To accommodate the variability of parallel I/O, a growing number of parallel system vendors provide extended I/O APIs that describe, at a higher semantic level, the access patterns that have been observed in practice. Early experience with these APIs has shown major I/O performance improvements — with high-level descriptions of I/O request patterns, file system policies can more intelligently prefetch and cache I/O data.

The desire for intuitive APIs with high expressive power has led to a host of experimental I/O libraries [9, 2, 1] that support specific problem domains and access pattern classes. For example, such domain-specific libraries have emerged for computational chemistry [5] and out-of-core linear algebra computations [16].

Despite the demonstrated performance rewards from use of more expressive APIs, several studies have shown that users frequently opt to continue using UNIX I/O primitives on parallel systems. The rationale for this lies in the desire to maximize code portability across diverse parallel platforms and to minimize software restructuring [15]. Simply put, many scientific application developers are unwilling to sacrifice portability for performance. Only when a standard parallel I/O API is widely deployed, these developers will restructure their codes.

3 Experimental Infrastructure

To illustrate the variability and complexity of the observed I/O behavior in the
SIO application suite, we selected three representative applications. Below, we
present the Pablo performance environment and its I/O analysis mechanisms,
followed by a brief description of the selected applications.

3.1 Pablo Performance Environment

Pablo [13] is a portable performance environment that supports performance
data capture and analysis. The Pablo instrumentation software captures dynamic
performance data via instrumented source code that is linked with a data capture
library. During program execution, the instrumented code generates dynamic
performance data that can be directly recorded by the data capture library
for off-line analysis, processed by one or more data analysis extensions prior to
recording, or directly processed and displayed in real time [14].

Via the Pablo I/O extensions, one can capture detailed traces of I/O events
during application program execution. These I/O event traces include the time,
duration, size, file name, the processor identifier that initiated the I/O call, and
other parameters particular to each I/O operation.

The Pablo environment's off-line analysis tools provide a wide variety of I/O
statistical characterizations, including file lifetime summaries, time window summaries, and file region summaries. File lifetime summaries include the number
and total duration of file related operations (e.g., reads, writes, seeks, opens,
closes) as well as the number of bytes accessed for each file, and the total time
each file had been open. Time window summaries contain similar data, but for
a specified window of time. File region summaries describe I/O accesses to each
range of file byte offsets.

Finally, using Pablo's dynamic graphics displays, one can visualize I/O activity using either workstation graphics or immersive virtual environments. Collec-
tively, the event traces, the statistical summaries, and the visualization toolkit
provide a powerful set of I/O analysis and display options.

3.2 SIO Application Suite

Space precludes a complete description of the I/O behavior of all SIO applications. In this study, we selected a representative subset from the SIO application
suite that highlights the access patterns commonly found in parallel codes.[2] A
high level description of the selected applications follows.

QCRD This quantum chemical reaction dynamics (QCRD) application is used
to understand the nature of elementary chemical reactions. The code is written in C and uses symmetric hyperspherical coordinates and local hyperspherical surface functions to solve the Schrödinger equation for the cross-
sections of the scattering of an atom by a diatomic molecule. Parallelism is
achieved by data decomposition (i.e., all processors execute the same code

---

[2] For a detailed analysis of the SIO application access patterns see
http://www-pablo.cs.uiuc.edu/Projects/IO

on different data portions of the global matrices, with data elements equally distributed among processors).

PRISM The PRISM code is a parallel implementation of a three-dimensional numerical simulation of the Navier-Stokes equations written in C and models high speed turbulent flow that is periodic in one direction. Slices of the periodic domain are proportionally distributed among processors, and a combination of spectral elements and Fourier modes is used to investigate the dynamics and transport properties of turbulent flow. The input data provide an initial velocity field, and the solution is integrated forward in time from the fluid's current state to its new state by numerically solving the equations that describe advection and diffusion of momentum in the fluid.

NWChem The NWChem code is a Fortran implementation of the Hartree-Fock self-consistent field (SCF) method that calculates the electron density around a molecule by considering each electron in the molecule in the collective field of the others. The calculation iterates until the field felt by each electron is consistent with that of the other electrons. This "semi-empirical" computational chemistry method predicts molecular structures, reaction energetics, and other chemical properties of interest.

Below, we describe the I/O attributes of the three application codes, with emphasis on request sizes, temporal and spatial patterns, and observed performance on the Intel Paragon XP/S.

4 I/O Requirements

Our experiments were conducted on the Caltech 512 node Intel Paragon XP/S at the Caltech Center for Advanced Computing Research. The system, which is configured for high-performance I/O research, supports multiple I/O hardware configurations. The experiments presented in this paper were conducted using two of the possible I/O configurations: (a) 12 I/O nodes, each controlling a relatively slow 2 GB RAID-3 disk array and (b) 64 4 GB Seagate disks, each attached to a computation node. For all experiments, files were striped across the disks in units of 64 KB, the default configuration for the Intel Paragon XP/S Parallel File System (PFS).

All experiments were conducted on 64 computation nodes in dedicated mode, using representative application data sets. The NWChem application used the 12 RAID-3 disk arrays, whereas the QCRD and PRISM codes used the 64 Seagate disks.[3] The NWChem, QCRD, and PRISM execution times were 5,439 seconds, 16,356 seconds, and 7,394 seconds, respectively.

---

[3] As we shall see, the older, slower RAID-3 disk arrays give the illusion that NWChem is more I/O intensive than QCRD or PRISM. Via other experiments using different hardware configurations, we have verified that the fraction of application execution time devoted to I/O is sensitive to hardware configuration but that the application I/O behavior is qualitatively unchanged.

4.1 I/O Overview

Table 1 summarizes the I/O activity for the three codes. Based on the fraction of execution time spend performing I/O operations, NWChem and QCRD are significantly more I/O intensive than PRISM. This is despite the fact that PRISM's total I/O operation count is twice that of NWChem and QCRD. Intuitively, most of the PRISM read operations are small and are efficiently satisfied from local I/O buffers.

Looking more closely at individual codes shows that NWChem is dominated by read operations. During NWChem's execution, all processors repeatedly read integrals from secondary storage to construct the Fock matrix and then solve the SCF equations. Because this integral database is computed and written to storage once, but then reread many times, the NWChem code is heavily read limited.

In contrast to the NWChem code, the QCRD code's behavior is dominated by file seeks, both in number and cost. The large number of seeks is a direct effect of the code's data decomposition and storage scheme — each processor must repeatedly seek to its designated portion of the global matrices before each access. In §5 we will return to this issue, showing how much higher application I/O performance could be achieved with minimal code change.

4.2 I/O Request Sizes

The distribution of I/O request sizes is a key determinant of possible file system optimizations. For example, the overhead for small reads can decrease by aggressive prefetching, and small writes are best served by conservative write behind. Conversely, large I/O requests require different approaches like direct streaming to/from storage devices.

Figure 1 shows the cumulative distribution function (CDF) of the percentage of reads and writes versus the request size for the three SIO codes, as well as the fraction of data transferred by each size request. For PRISM, about eighty percent of read and write requests are small (less than 40 bytes), though a few large requests (greater than 150 KB) constitute the majority of I/O data volume. These small requests are excellent candidates for data aggregation.

QCRD shows much less variability in read and write request sizes. For this code, 99 percent of requests are of a single size (2400 bytes) and represent almost all the data volume. Like QCRD, about 90 percent of NWChem's operations are of a single size, in this case 64 KB.

Although these three SIO applications are each dominated by a few request sizes, the range of sizes across the applications is quite large, ranging from a few bytes to several megabytes. In short, parallel I/O file systems must efficiently support a variety of request sizes, both small and large, with policies appropriate to each. In §6, we will return to this issue.

5 Temporal and Spatial Access Patterns

Like request sizes, the temporal and spatial attributes of requests have profound implications for file system policies. Most workstation file systems are

Operation	Operation Count	Percentage Count	I/O Time (seconds)	I/O Time Percentage	Exec. Time Percentage
open	92	0.02	317.25	0.12	0.09
read	465,154	93.05	251,105.84	92.53	72.13
seek	2,115	0.42	36.87	0.01	0.01
write	32,398	6.48	18,746.65	6.91	5.39
close	153	0.03	1,158.43	0.43	0.33
All I/O	499,910	100.00	271,365.03	100.00	77.95

(a) NWChem (12 RAIDs)

Operation	Operation Count	Percentage Count	I/O Time (seconds)	I/O Time Percentage	Exec. Time Percentage
open	6,592	1.29	3,618.32	1.4	0.45
read	176,228	34.52	8,027.68	3.12	0.99
seek	258,648	50.66	238,770.16	92.73	29.5
write	61,904	12.13	6,148.96	2.4	0.75
close	7,168	1.4	975.17	0.35	0.08
All I/O	510,670	100.00	257,493.07	100.00	31.77

(b) QCRD

Operation	Operation Count	Percentage Count	I/O Time (seconds)	I/O Time Percentage	Exec. Time Percentage
open	415	0.04	203.12	12.51	0.04
read	1,037,568	93.70	950.11	58.50	0.20
seek	704	0.06	293.17	18.05	0.06
write	68,273	6.17	42.93	2.64	0.01
close	414	0.04	134.82	8.30	0.03
All I/O	1,107,374	100.00	1,624.16	100.00	0.34

(c) PRISM

Table 1. Basic I/O summary table

optimized for sequential file access. Burstiness and non-sequentiality necessitate new and different file system approaches (e.g., aggressive prefetch or write behind or skewed data storage formats). Below, we consider the implications of these temporal and spatial patterns based on the SIO code suite.

Because in the NWChem and the PRISM codes logical processor (node) zero executes more operations and consistently transfers more data than the the other processors, we focus on two representative processors, zero and sixty. In the QCRD code there is no such behavior – all nodes execute the same operations and we demonstrate the activity of a representative node only.

5.1 Sequential Access Patterns

Figure 2 illustrates the operation durations of nodes zero and sixty of NWChem as a function of the program execution time.[4] The three NWChem code phases

---

[4] To increase legibility, we plot only the first 2500 seconds of NWChem's execution.

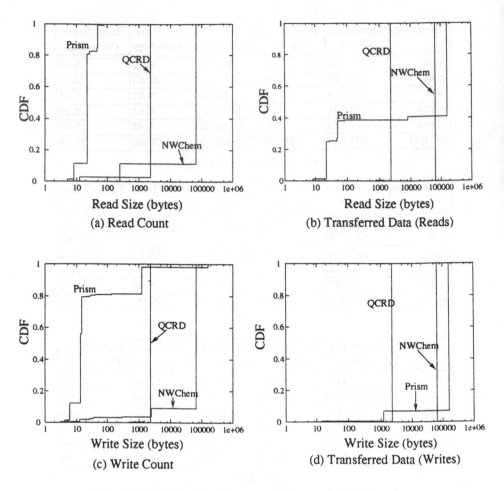

Fig. 1. CDF of read/write request sizes and data transfers.

are clearly distinguished in the figure. First, node zero loads the problem definition from the various input files, the basis sets are calculated, and the results are written to the disks.

In the second phase all nodes participate in I/O: they evaluate the integrals and write them to secondary storage. The work is distributed across all nodes, with each node accessing a *private* file that stores the locally computed integrals. Because NWChem's designers opted to store the integral data such that each node could read independently, the quadrature data write pattern is predominately sequential. Each processor first seeks to rewind the file, then sequentially writes the quadrature data.

In the third phase, all nodes concurrently open their private integral files, repeatedly read integral data, construct the Fock matrix, compute, synchronize, and solve the SCF equations. Node zero periodically collects the results and writes them to disk; these are the short, bursty writes in Figure 2(a). Again, the read access pattern is sequential, with a single seek preceding bursts of intense read activity on the file.

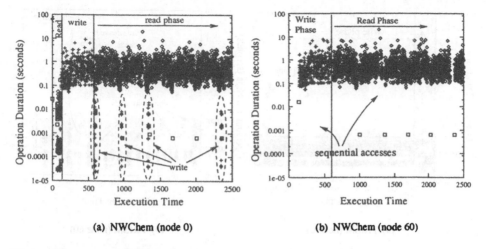

(a) NWChem (node 0)   (b) NWChem (node 60)

Fig. 2. Operation durations for NWChem. Rectangles represent seeks, diamonds represent reads, and crosses represent writes.

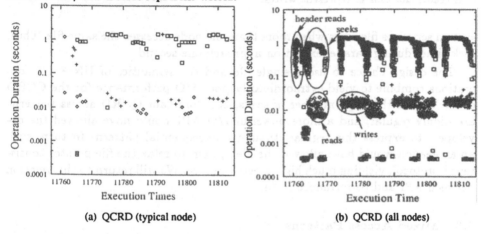

(a) QCRD (typical node)   (b) QCRD (all nodes)

Fig. 3. Operation durations for QCRD. Rectangles represent seeks, diamonds represent reads, and crosses represent writes.

5.2 Interleaved Access Patterns

Rather than using private files to store the portion of the global matrix apportioned to each node, QCRD's developers opted to use a single file for the matrix. As Figure 3 shows, this leads to a strikingly different I/O access pattern.

Because all nodes in QCRD must contend for access to the single, shared file, each read or write operation is preceded by a seek to position the file pointer. The pattern is clearly visible in Figure 3(a), a snapshot of one node's activity near the end of its execution.

As a comparison, Figure 3(b) shows the combined effects of I/O operations by all nodes during the same time period. The Intel Paragon XP/S OSF/1 file

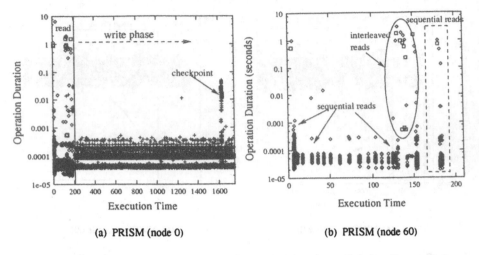

(a) PRISM (node 0) (b) PRISM (node 60)

Fig. 4. Operation durations for PRISM. Rectangles represent seeks, diamonds represent reads, and crosses represent writes.

system serializes file seeks when more than one node accesses the same file. Thus, seek times during parallel execution approach one second.

The design choice to use a single file and the semantics of UNIX I/O operations combine to yield extraordinarily poor I/O performance for the QCRD code. Despite the large number of seeks, the dominant QCRD access patterns are highly regular, and a more powerful I/O API would have allowed the developers to express this regular, though non-sequential pattern. In turn, such an expression would have allowed the file system to relax the file pointer consistency protocol, yielding much higher performance. We will return to this relation between API and performance in §6.

5.3 Mixed Access Patterns

Figure 4 illustrates the duration and spacing of I/O operations for the PRISM code. Figure 4(a) depicts the I/O activity of node zero for the first 1,700 seconds of application execution time. During the first 200 seconds, all nodes access the initialization files. During the subsequent, write intensive phase, results are written to disk and these writes are administered through node zero only.

The mixed sequential and interleaved access patterns used to access the initialization files are clearly demonstrated in Figure 4(b). During the read phase, three files are accessed. The first file and the third files are accessed sequentially by all nodes. The second file is a restart file that contains the initial conditions for the simulation; each node first reads the file header sequentially and then accesses its own portion in an interleaved fashion. The code demonstrates a case commonly found in the SIO applications: file headers that contain metadata information are accessed sequentially by all nodes while the rest of the file body is accessed in an interleaved fashion.

6 Discussion

Characterization studies are by their nature inductive, covering a subset of the possibilities. Although the three SIO applications in this study differ dramatically in their algorithmic approaches, they share certain common features and are amenable to some general observations about I/O characteristics.

- Parallel I/O is bursty, with computation intervals of little or no I/O activity interleaved with time periods of intense, concurrent I/O operations. In such situations, I/O can be effectively overlapped with computation via caching, prefetching, and write-behind mechanisms.
- The size of requests can differ dramatically, even within the same application, ranging from a few bytes to several kilobytes each. Different optimization mechanisms are required for such transfers (i.e., aggregating small requests into large data chunks in cache before initiating a transfer or disabling all caching and bypassing the cache for large request sizes). Understanding when and how to aggregate requests is essential for high performance.
- Access patterns range from simple sequential to interleaved. Furthermore, there are combinations of sequential and interleaved accesses even within the same file. Due to the high concurrency of such operations, efficient file pointer consistency protocols are necessary to deliver high performance. Alternatively, expressive APIs are needed to describe internal file structure and expected access patterns, enabling the file system to relax the consistency protocol.
- Request parallelism ranges from little or none (i.e., all I/O is administered through a single node) to full parallelism (i.e., all nodes concurrently send independent requests to disks). Channeling all requests through a single node is often an alternative solution chosen by application developers to avoid inefficient parallel file systems. Collective I/O is a desirable alternative for high-performance concurrent accesses.
- Files can be either shared across processors or can be simply private per processor. Different file system policy optimization approaches should be used if files are shared or private.

6.1 Current I/O APIs

One of the most striking observations of our characterization study was that despite the existence of several parallel I/O APIs and clear performance advantages, most computational scientists eschew their use. Discussions with these researchers revealed that the restricted, often inefficient, but highly portable UNIX API was preferable to vendor provided, extended I/O interfaces.

Comparisons of vendor proprietary I/O interfaces (e.g., IBM's PIOFS and Intel's PFS) show that they have few shared features, mainly due to different design philosophies. Therefore, the design and implementation of a standard parallel I/O API that is expressive, compact, intuitively appealing, and at the same time offers high performance [3] is one of the goals of the SIO effort.

6.2   Emerging I/O APIs

Even within our small application sample, the diversity of I/O request sizes and patterns suggests that achieving high performance is unlikely with a single file system policy. Instead, one needs a file system API via which users can "inform" the file system of expected access patterns. Using such hints or an automatic access pattern classification scheme [7], an adaptive file system could then choose those file policies and policy parameters best matched to the access pattern.

For example, via user controls and hints one might advise the file system that the file access pattern is read only, write only, mixed read/write sequential, or strided. For small, read only requests, the file system would aggressively prefetch large blocks of data, satisfying future requests for previously cached data. Similarly, for small strided writes, the file system might first cache the data then write large blocks using a log-structured file model.

Similarly, with knowledge of request concurrency and real-time measurements of I/O device performance, a flexible file system might dynamically choose the number of disks across which data is striped and the size of the stripes. When there are few competing requests, striping data in large blocks across all disks reduces write time by trading inter-request parallelism for reduced intra-request latency.

Finally, with knowledge of the evolution of access patterns, a file system might choose a file striping that optimizes globally across multiple patterns. Thus, a system could balance the cost of efficiently writing a file against the cost of repeatedly reading the file using an access pattern not well matched to the storage format.

All these examples share a common theme — they presume higher level knowledge of current and future I/O access patterns. Rather than composing complex access patterns from read, write, and seek "atoms," with expressive I/O APIs users can describe temporal and spatial access patterns directly. Alternatively, file systems must glean this information automatically (e.g., by classifying access patterns using trained neural networks or hidden Markov models). In either case, only with such knowledge can flexible file systems maximize performance by matching policies to access patterns

7   Conclusions

Even with the restricted application subset that we investigated here, we demonstrated that there is much variation in temporal and spatial I/O patterns across applications, with both very small and very large request sizes, sequential and interleaved accesses, shared and non-shared files, and access time scales ranging from microseconds to minutes. We conclude that there are many opportunities for improving the performance of parallel file system and parallel I/O standardization is an important step towards this process. The analysis of the parallel I/O workload characteristics of the SIO suite has contributed towards this effort. From this analysis, various design issues related to parallel I/O application programming interfaces have emerged. An API that is compact, expressive, and provides the access pattern information to the file system, can exploit alternative data management policies that better match these patterns. Controls for efficient data distribution, collective I/O, and data caching are necessary to provide high I/O throughput.

References

1. BENNETT, R., BRYANT, K., SUSSMAN, A., DAS, R., AND SALTZ, J. Jovian: A framework for optimizing parallel I/O. In *Proceedings of the Scalable Parallel Libraries Conference* (October 1994), IEEE Computer Society Press, pp. 10–20.
2. BORDAWEKAR, R., THAKUR, R., AND CHOUDHARY, A. Efficient compilation of out-of-core data parallel programs. Tech. Rep. SCCS-622, NPAC, April 1994.
3. CORBETT, P. F., PROST, J.-P., DEMETRIOU, C., GIBSON, G., RIEDEL, E., ZE-LENKA, J., CHEN, Y., FELTEN, E., LI, K., HARTMAN, J., PETERSON, L., BER-SHAD, B., WOLMAN, A., AND AYDT, R. Proposal for a common parallel file system programming interface version 1.0, September 1996.
4. CRANDALL, P., AYDT, R. A., CHIEN, A. A., AND REED, D. A. Input/Output characterization of scalable parallel applications. In *Supercomputing 1995* (1996).
5. FOSTER, I., AND NIEPLOCHA, J. ChemIO: High-performance I/O for computational chemistry applications. http://www.mcs.anl.gov/chemio/, February 1996.
6. KOTZ, D., AND NIEUWEJAAR, N. Dynamic file-access characteristics of a production parallel scientific workload. In *Supercomputing '94* (November 1994).
7. MADHYASTHA, T., AND REED, D. A. Intelligent, adaptive file system policy selection. In *Proceedings of Frontiers'96* (1996).
8. MILLER, E. L., AND KATZ, R. H. Input/Output behavior of supercomputer applications. In *Supercomputing '91* (November 1991), pp. 567–576.
9. NIEUWEJAAR, N., AND KOTZ, D. The Galley parallel file system. In *Proceedings of the 10th ACM International Conference on Supercomputing* (May 1996).
10. PASQUALE, B. K., AND POLYZOS, G. C. Dynamic I/O characterization of I/O intensive scientific applications. In *Proceedings of Supercomputing '94* (November 1994), pp. 660–669.
11. POOLE, J. T. Scalable I/O Initiative. California Institute of Technology, Available at http://www.ccsf.caltech.edu/SIO/, 1996.
12. PURAKAYASTHA, A., ELLIS, C. S., KOTZ, D., NIEUWEJAAR, N., AND BEST, M. Characterizing parallel file-access patterns on a large-scale multiprocessor. In *Proceedings of the Ninth International Parallel Processing Symposium* (April 1995), pp. 165–172.
13. REED, D. A., AYDT, R. A., NOE, R. J., ROTH, P. C., SHIELDS, K. A., SCHWARTZ, B. W., AND TAVERA, L. F. Scalable performance analysis: The Pablo performance analysis environment. In *Proceedings of the Scalable Parallel Libraries Conference*, A. Skjellum, Ed. IEEE Computer Society, 1993, pp. 104–113.
14. REED, D. A., ELFORD, C. L., MADHYASTHA, T., SCULLIN, W. H., AYDT, R. A., AND SMIRNI, E. I/O, performance analysis, and performance data immersion. In *Proceedings of MASCOTS '96* (Feb. 1996), pp. 1–12.
15. SMIRNI, E., AYDT, R. A., CHIEN, A. A., AND REED, D. A. I/O requirements of scientific applications: An evolutionary view. In *High Performance Distributed Computing* (1996), pp. 49–59.
16. TOLEDO, S., AND GUSTAVSON, F. G. The design and implementation of SO-LAR, a portable library for scalable out-of-core linear algebra computations. In *Fourth Workshop on Input/Output in Parallel and Distributed Systems* (May 1996), pp. 28–40.

Interval Based Workload Characterization for Distributed Systems*

M. Braun, G. Kotsis

Institut für Angewandte Informatik und Informationssysteme
Universität Wien, Lenaugasse 2/8, A-1080 Vienna, Austria
Email [braun,kotsis]@ani.univie.ac.at

Abstract. In this paper we analyze a graph model representing the coarse grain dependency and communication structure of a distributed application. The model is called Timed Structural Parallelism Graph (TSPG). Nodes represent program components, arcs represent dependencies among components. This workload model differs from well known task graphs in two ways: (1) arcs can either have dependence or activation semantics and (2) timing parameters associated to arcs and nodes are given as intervals. Besides describing this new workload model, we sketch the issues and problems in corresponding evaluation techniques. In particular, we investigate techniques for estimating the total execution time and for deriving potential parallelism profiles. The proposed techniques are illustrated by example.

1 Introduction

To analyze and predict the performance of computer systems and networks, it is necessary to characterize the load of the system in terms of a workload model (see e.g. [CS93] for a survey). In this paper we propose a graph model representing the (typically coarse grain) dependency and communication structure of a distributed application. In contrast to well known graph models characterizing parallel applications (e.g. task graphs), our approach tries to model applications at a higher granularity. In previous work [CHK+95], a Structural Parallelism Graph (SPG) was proposed, where nodes represent program components and arcs represent either dependencies (e.g. the preceding component must have finished before its successor) or activation (the preceding component activates its successor, but continues its own execution).

We extend this SPG model to Timed Structural Parallelism Graphs (TSPGs). Timing information is associated to both, arcs and nodes in the graph. The timing parameters are specified as intervals with an associated probability. Intervals associated to a node represent possible durations of the component's execution time. Timing parameters associated to arcs represent the possible timing interval during which the successive component will be activated.

Both, the concept of activation arcs and the concept of associating timing intervals instead of average values or distributions contribute to the suitability of the model for the characterization of distributed applications. The components of a distributed application are typically coarse grain and it is much likely, that

---

* This work is supported by the Austrian National Science Foundation (FWF).

a component will activate another component during its execution. Furtheron, it might be difficult to give an accurate estimate of the execution time of a component in terms of a mean value or a distribution, but the analyst might have a good guess for the approximate duration specified as an interval. Variabilities and uncertainties in the execution time motivate the specification of timing information by means of intervals.

The idea of using intervals as timing parameters has also been applied to other models. In [vdA94] interval timed colored Petri nets are investigated. Solution techniques for queuing network models with interval-based input parameters are for example presented in [MR95] or in [LKMH96]. Client-Server Architectures are analyzed using interval arithmetic in [WMN91].

In this work, we present three techniques for estimating the total execution time and for deriving potential parallelism profiles from TSPGs. The first analysis technique is based on determining all possible "states" of a timed SPG, where a state is defined by the state of its components (not started, active or terminated). This information can be transformed into a parallelism profile by aggregating the number of active components at a certain instance in time. Using this approach, the most detailed results can be obtained but the computational complexity limits the practical use. The second approach derives parallelism profiles under minimum or maximum execution time assumption. The profiles are easy to compute, but only give a rough estimate on system behavior. In the third approach, a technique similar to networking techniques is applied. For each component, the possible start and end times are calculated. By comparing the start and end times for the components, the parallelism profiles can be derived. The techniques are demonstrated on simple examples. The computational complexity of the proposed algorithms is investigated and techniques for reducing the complexity are discussed. A set of tools supporting the analysis is currently under development.

2 Description of the Workload Model

2.1 Definition of an SPG

The Structural Parallelism Graph (SPG) has been proposed as part of a hierarchical approach for workload characterization of parallel applications:

Definition 1 *A **Structural Parallelism Graph** is an acyclic directed graph $SPG = (V, D, W)$, where V is a set of vertices corresponding to the components (parts of the application defined at the desired granularity level) and $D = (D^p \cup D^a)$ is a set of directed arcs defining two different types of relations between the components.*

$d_{i,j} \in D^p$ *denotes a precedence relation between vertices (components) i and j such that j is activated (starts execution) after i has finished. This activation can also involve sending of data (communication). i and j may never run in parallel, but are strictly sequential. We will call this type of arc a precedence arc. Graphically such an arc is depicted as a thin arrow.*

$d_{i.j} \in D^a$ denotes an activation relation between vertices (components) i and j such that j is activated (starts execution) somewhen during the execution of i. This activation can also involve sending of data (communication). Thus i and j may run in parallel, but j must not start before i. We will call this type of arc an activation arc. The graphical representation is a thick arrow.

W is a set of weights assigned to outgoing arcs, which represent branching probabilities.

Figure 1 shows two very simple examples. Both examples consist only of three nodes. Nodes 1 and 3 are connected via a precedence arc $(d_{1.3} \in D^p)$, nodes 1 and 2 are connected via an activation arc $(d_{1.2} \in D^a)$. In example (a) the semantic of the outgoing arcs is AND, in example (b) either one OR the other branch is taken. Incoming arcs can also have either AND or (exclusive) OR semantics (not shown in this example, as each node has only 0 or 1 incoming arcs).

The components of an SPG can be specified at different levels of detail. In a fine grain representation, each statement constitutes a component, thus the graph model will have a large number of nodes. In this work, we assume a coarse grain representation, i.e. a large number of statements is grouped together in a single component. The grouping is defined by the structure of the application. A component could therefor be seen as a part of the application, e.g. a certain (sub)function or procedure, which will be executed on a particular computer in the distributed system. We assume, that no parallelism within a component will be exploited, but that a component may activate other components which can then be executed in parallel

The SPG in Figure 1 (b) could for example represent a distributed application, where component 1 performs some initial computations. During its execution, either a second component can be activated resulting in two components being executed in parallel (e.g. with probability 0,4 component 1 distributes some of its load to another processing element). But it is more likely (prob=0,6), that component 1 terminates and component 3 will finish the computation.

2.2 Histogram Based Timing Parameters

For a quantitative analysis, it is necessary to associate timing information to the nodes in the SPG. We define a timed SPG (see Figure 1 (c)) as follows:

Definition 2 A **Timed Structural Parallelism Graph** is an acyclic directed graph $TSPG = (V, D, W, T)$, where V, D, and W are defined as in an SPG and $T = \{T^V \cup T^{D^a}\}$ is a set of timing parameters. A timing parameter $t_i^v \in T^V$ is associated to a node and is given by a histogram which specifies the duration of the corresponding program component. A timing parameter $t_{i.j}^{D^a} \in T^{D^a}$ is associated to an activation arc connecting nodes i and j and is given by a histogram. It defines the moment (or interval) within the duration of the activating node when activation of node j will happen.

Communication and contention costs are assumed to be either incorporated in the task execution time or are neglected.

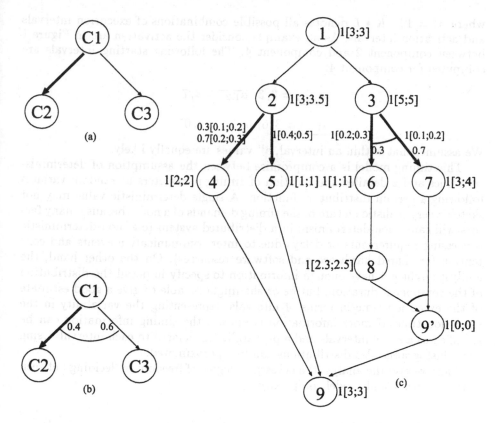

Fig. 1. Examples of a SPGs (a,b) and a Timed SPG (c)

Mathematically the timing parameter t_i^v which is associated to a node is defined as follows:

$$t_i^v : p_{i,k}^v[\underline{t_{i,k}^v}, \overline{t_{i,k}^v}], \quad k = 1 \dots K$$

where $\underline{t_{i,k}^v}$ is the lower and $\overline{t_{i,k}^v}$ the upper bound of the execution time interval and $p_{i,k}$ represents the probability that the execution time of component i is within the interval k. The timing parameter $t_{i.j}^{D^a}$ is defined as

$$t_{i.j}^{D^a} : p_{i.j,l}^{D^a}[\underline{x_{i.j,l}^{D^a}}, \overline{x_{i.j,l}^{D^a}}]$$

where $\underline{x_{i.j,l}^{D^a}}$ denotes a percentage and is the lower bound of the relative part in the execution time of component i where i can activate component j, $\overline{x_{i.j,l}^{D^a}}$ represents the corresponding upper bound and $p_{i.j,l}^{D^a}$ represents the probability that component j is activated by component i in the interval l. To transform these relative activation intervals into starting intervals for component j the following computation has to take place:

$$\underline{a_{i.j,m}} = \underline{t_{i,k}^v} * \underline{x_{i.j,l}^v} \tag{1}$$

$$\overline{a_{i.j,m}} = \overline{t_{i,k}^v} * \overline{x_{i.j,l}^v} \tag{2}$$

where $M = 1 \ldots K * L$ denotes all possible combinations of execution intervals and activation intervals. As an example consider the activation arc in Figure 1 between component 2 and component 4. The following starting intervals are computed for component 4:

$$a_{1.2,1} = 3, 3; \quad \overline{a_{1.2,l}} = 3, 7$$

$$a_{1.2,2} = 3, 6; \quad \overline{a_{1.2,2}} = 4, 05$$

We assume, that within an interval, all values are equally likely.

This timing model is a compromise between the assumption of deterministic values and a detailed specification of timing parameters as random variates following a certain distribution function. A single deterministic value may not sketch a very realistic picture of the timing demands of a node, because many factors will cause non-determinism in a distributed system (e.g. non-deterministic processing requirements or delays due to inter communication events and contention for shared hardware and software resources). On the other hand, the analyst might not have enough information to specify in detail the distribution of the component duration, but he or she might be able to give a good estimate of the execution time in terms of intervals, representing the variability in the execution time. If more information is known, the timing information can be specified as a set of intervals and a probability associated to each interval. Using these histograms, also distributions can be approximated.

Thus we give the analyst the necessary degree of freedom in deciding between model accuracy and model complexity.

3   Analysis Techniques

3.1   General Idea

Although efficient solution techniques and tool implementations exist for conventional task graphs (e.g. SHARPE [ST86] or PEPP [HM92]), these approaches cannot be applied in the analysis of TSPGs, because of the new concept of activation arcs. As an initial approach, a set of analysis tools has been presented in [BHK96] for the analysis of SPGs (without considering timing information). Based on the SPG representation, a state graph (SG) of the program is generated. A state in the SG is characterized by a vector containing the state of each of the components of an SPG (not started=0, active=1, or terminated=2). A state transition ($0 \rightarrow 1$ or $1 \rightarrow 2$) is characterized by the change of the state of one of the components. The state transitions are discretized, i.e. there is a hypothetical time axis and at each clock tick a transition may occur. A sequence of state transitions from an initial state to a final state is a possible path in the execution. Such a path can be represented in a Gantt Chart from which both, the execution time as well as potential parallelism profiles can be derived. At this level of abstraction, only the number of active components at a given instant in time is of importance, no matter which components they are exactly. This information may be helpful in the initial design phase of the application and might provide information for scheduling decisions.

When considering timing information, state transitions will occur with a certain probability in a certain time interval. Thus, changes in the parallelism profile occur with a certain probability in a certain time interval. The problem is now, how to derive the state transition times and probabilities.

We propose three different techniques for deriving parallelism profiles:

1. The SG model can be extended to a timed SG model. But this approach wouldn't be very efficient, because of its computational complexity. It can be shown, that the transition probabilities and the transition times depend on the history, i.e. on the previous nodes on the path in the TSG. This approach would give the most detailed information on potential parallelism profiles. However, it can already be seen for the simple example, that the number of possible intervals grows rapidly, thus resulting in a large number of different parallelism profiles.

2. To obtain a more general view of the potential parallelism profile, either the minimum or the maximum execution times can be considered for each node. Thus, each node has only a single value timing parameter and the computation of the potential parallelism profile is comparatively fast and simple.

3. The Activity Interval Approach (discussed in detail in Section 3.2) is a technique similar to techniques used in project planning. For each component, the possible start and end times are calculated and by comparing the start and end times for the components, the parallelism profiles can be derived.

3.2 The Activity-Interval Approach

The Activity Interval Approach is a four step procedure which determines potential parallelism profiles at a more detailed level than the MIN/MAX approach, but is of less computational complexity than the TSG approach. It will be explained on the example graph in Figure 1 (c). This graph represents a distributed application, where component 1 performs some initial computations. After its termination it activates component 2 and 3. During its execution component 2 activates components 4 and 5 (e.g. two subfunctions or subprocedures of component 2) at the specified activation intervals. Component 3 also activates its successor components during it's execution. It either activates component 6 (with probability 0.3) or component 7 (with probability 0.7). Component 9' is just a dummy node to reunite the OR branches in the TSPG. The execution of component 9 starts after the execution of component 4, 5, 8 or 4, 5, 7 has finished.

The four steps of the Activity-Interval approach are:

Step 1 Firstly all alternative paths through the TSPG are determined. The number of paths depends on the number of outgoing arcs with OR semantic. The following paths are identified in the TSPG in Figure 1 (c).

```
path 1:   1;2;3;4;5;6;8;9';9
path 2:   1;2;3;4;5;7;9';9
```

Step 2 For all nodes the possible starting and terminating time intervals and the corresponding probabilities have to be determined. The input to this step is the specification of the TSPG (its structure and the timing parameters). The output is a set of interval pairs for each node i

$$p_{i,j}([\underline{s_{i,j}}; \overline{s_{i,j}}], [\underline{e_{i,j}}; \overline{e_{i,j}}])$$

giving the earliest possible starting time $\underline{s_{i,j}}$, the latest possible starting time $\overline{s_{i,j}}$ and the earliest possible end time $\underline{e_{i,j}}$ and the lates possible end time $\overline{e_{i,j}}$ where $p_{i,j}$ represents the probability that the execution takes place in the denoted interval.

Figure 2 shows the generated starting and terminating time intervals for path 1 of the TSPG in Figure 1.

Node	Starting	Terminating	Probability
1	[0.0;0.0]	[3.0;3.0]	1.0
2	[3.0;3.0]	[6.0;5.5]	1.0
3	[3.0;3.0]	[8.0;8.0]	1.0
4	[3.3;3.7]	[5.3;5.7]	0.3
4	[3.6;4.05]	[5.6;6.05]	0.7
5	[4.2;4.75]	[5.2;5.75]	1.0
6	[4.0;4.5]	[5.0;5.5]	1.0
8	[5.0;5.5]	[7.3;8.0]	1.0
9'	[7.3;8.0]	[7.3;8.0]	1.0
9	[7.3;8.0]	[10.3;11]	1.0

Fig. 2. Starting and Terminating Intervals

Step 3 After determining starting and terminating time intervals for each node, these intervals have to be aggregated in order to derive parallelism profiles. Each combination of a starting and a terminating interval is reduced to one interval taking the mean value of the starting interval as the lower bound and the mean value of the terminating interval as the upper bound of the possible execution time. Formally this transformation step can be described in the following way:

$$p_{i,j}([\underline{s_{i,j}}; \overline{s_{i,j}}], [\underline{e_{i,j}}; \overline{e_{i,j}}]) \Rightarrow p_{i,k}([\underline{q_{i,k}}; \overline{q_{i,k}}])$$

with

$$\underline{q_{i,k}} = \underline{s_{i,j}} + \frac{\overline{s_{i,j}} - \underline{s_{i,j}}}{2}$$

$$\overline{q_{i,k}} = \underline{e_{i,j}} + \frac{\overline{e_{i,j}} - \underline{e_{i,j}}}{2}$$

Step 4 Finally parallelism profiles are generated for all possible combinations of component execution times and the corresponding probabilities for the combination are calculated. By interval splitting it is determined how many components are active at a given time.

We will now discuss in detail the computations involved in these steps and give closed expressions for calculating the corresponding values.

First, we will show, how the starting and terminating time intervals and the associated probabilities are computed. We assume without loss of generality, that there is a single component which starts the execution[2]. For this single component (node 0), the following equations hold:

$$\underline{s_0} = \overline{s_0} = 0$$

and

$$\underline{e_{0,j}} = \underline{s_{0,j}} + \underline{t_{0,j}}^v \tag{3}$$

$$\overline{e_{0,j}} = \overline{s_{0,j}} + \overline{t_{0,j}}^v \tag{4}$$

for $j = 1 \ldots J$, where J denotes the number of timing intervals associated to node 0. The probabilities associated to the J different intervals are given by the probabilities associated to the terminating time intervals in the TSPG specification $p_{0,j}^v$

For all other nodes, the end times are calculated analogously:

$$\underline{e_{i,m}} = \underline{s_{i,k}} + \underline{t_{i,l}}^v$$

$$\overline{e_{i,m}} = \overline{s_{i,k}} + \overline{t_{i,l}}^v$$

For each of the K possible starting times, L different time intervals are associated, thus $M = K * L$ possible end times are obtained.

For computing the starting times and the interval probabilities, we have to distinguish four cases:

1. node j has exactly one predecessor i and
   (a) i and j are connected via a dependence arc
   (b) i and j are connected via an activation arc
2. node j has more that one predecessor i
   (a) its input has OR semantic
   (b) its input has AND semantic

If component j has just one predecessor i and is connected with this predecessor by a

"dependence" -arc the starting time correspond to the terminating time of the predecessor node i:

$$\underline{s_{j,k}} = \underline{e_{i,k}}$$

$$\overline{s_{j,k}} = \overline{e_{i,k}}$$

The terminating times are determined using equations 3 and 4. For each of the K starting time, there are L different terminating times. The corresponding probabilities for each of the $M = K * L$ combinations of starting time and terminating time is computed by multiplying the probability of the

---

[2] If there is more than one starting component, a dummy component with execution time 0 can be introduced.

starting time (which corresponds to the probability of the terminating time of the predecessor node) with the probability of the execution time of the node itself:

$$p_{j,m} = p_{i,k}^v * p_{j,l}^v$$

"activating" -arc the starting times correspond to all possible activating times and are given by

$$s_{j,o} = s_{i,k} + a_{i.j,l}$$

$$\overline{s_{j,o}} = \overline{s_{i,k}} + \overline{a_{i.j,l}}$$

where $a_{i.j,l}$ and $\overline{a_{i.j,l}}$ are computed as shown in equations 2 and 2. The end time intervals are computed using equations 3 and 4. The probabilities for each start/end combination are computing by multiplying the probability of the starting time with the probability of the activating time and of the execution time of the node itself:

$$p_{j,o} = p_{i,k}^v * p_{i.j,m}^{D^a} * p_{j,l}^v$$

resulting in $O = K * L * M$ combinations.

If component j has more than one predecessor and is connected with its predecessors by

"OR"-semantic the execution times and probabilities are computed analogously to the case of just one predecessor since we assume an exclusive OR-semantic. Depending on the previous decision in branching at the outgoing OR-node, the corresponding incoming OR branch will be considered.

"AND"-semantic to cases can be distinguished:

1. If there exists one predecessor whose terminating time dominates (i.e. is larger than) the intervals of all other predecessor components, the starting times of the successor component correspond to the terminating times of this predecessor. The terminating times and probabilities are computed as if the component would have only one predecessor.

2. If the starting time of a component is determined by more than one predecessor an interval splitting has to take place to determine the latest possible end times of all predecessors (see Figure 3).

Node	Start.	Term.	Prob
A	[0.0;0.0]	[4.0;6.0]	0.4
A	[0.0;0.0]	[6.0;8.0]	0.6
B	[0.0;0.0]	[5.0;7.0]	1.0
C	[5.0;6.0]	[6.0;8.0]	0.2
C	[6.0;7.0]	[7.0;9.0]	0.5
C	[7.0;8.0]	[8.0;10.0]	0.3

Fig. 3. Example for a TSPG with an AND connection

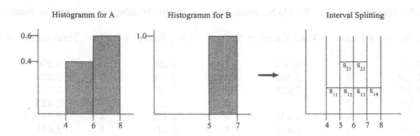

Fig. 4. Histograms and Interval Splitting for Node 1 and Node 2

The terminating times can be depicted as histograms (the values on the x-axes correspond to the terminating time intervals and the values on the y-axes correspond to the probabilities of the interval) (see Figure 4). To compute the respective probabilities for all possible combinations of execution times, the interval parameters $(e_{i,j}, \overline{e_{i,j}})$, are transformed into subintervals $(S_{i1}, \ldots, S_{im}; \ldots; S_{k1}, \ldots, S_{kn})$ such that for each two S_{im}, S_{kn} of these subintervals it holds that either $S_{im} = S_{kn}$ or $S_{im} \cap S_{kn} = 0$.

This allows for a total ordering of the subintervals. To these subintervals corresponding probabilities are assigned, representing the share of subinterval of its original interval. Then all possible combinations of subintervals together with their probabilities of occurrence are analyzed and for each possible combination the probabilities are aggregated. These probabilities correspond to the probability that the starting time of the successor component is determined by a specific time interval.

3.3   Results

Figure 5 shows the parallelism profiles for the TSPG of Figure 1.

Figure 5 shows the parallelism profiles for the TSPG of Figure 1. The shapes of all profiles are similar, but they differ slightly in terms of execution times. When calculating hypothetical execution times for 1, 2, ... 5 processing elements, speed up curves can be derived as shown in Figure 6. To determine the optimum number of processing elements, further metrics (e.g. efficacy) can be derived easily.

The presented analysis techniques thus provide a convenient method for doing rough estimates on execution time and for deriving parallelism profiles. The execution time of the analysis technique presented depends on the number of nodes, the number and size of the timing intervals, but mostly on the number of OR branches as each OR branch causes the generation of a different path through the TSPG. But since step two to four of the Activity Interval Approach are applied to each path independently the processing of these procedure steps could be distributed to different processing elements and therefor run in parallel.

Profile Number: 1		Profile Number: 2		Profile Number: 3		Profile Number: 4	
Time Stamp	# Tasks	Time Stamp	# Tasks	Time Stamp	# Tasks	Time Stamp	# Tasks
0.000	0	0.000	0	0.000	0	0.000	0
3.000	1	3.000	1	3.000	1	3.000	1
3.500	2	3.825	2	3.500	2	3.750	2
4.250	3	4.250	3	3.750	3	3.825	3
4.475	4	4.475	4	4.475	4	4.475	4
5.475	5	5.475	5	5.475	5	5.475	5
5.500	4	5.825	4	5.500	4	5.825	4
6.250	3	6.250	3	6.250	3	6.250	3
8.000	2	8.000	2	8.000	2	8.000	2
10.650	1	10.650	1	10.250	1	10.250	1
Profile Prob.: 0.09		Profile Prob.: 0.21		Profile Prob.: 0.21		Profile Prob.: 0.49	

Fig. 5. Parallelism Profiles

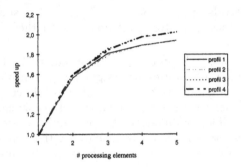

Fig. 6. Speed-up Profile

4   Conclusions and Future Work

In this work, we have addressed the problem of workload modeling for distributed systems. A graph model – the Timed Structural Parallelism Graph – has been proposed. This model provides the appropriate level of detail for modeling the typically coarse grain parallelism in distributed applications. In addition, component's execution times can be given as intervals, thus supporting flexibility in model parametrization.

We have discussed three approaches for deriving estimates on the total execution time and for deriving potential parallelism profiles. The first approach offers a very detailed result at the cost of prohibitively high computational complexity. The MIN/MAX approach can be computed easily, but the resulting parallelism profile is only a rough estimate of the actual profile. As a compromise, we have developed an activation-interval approach. The algorithm is sketched in the paper. Also this approach can become rather complex if the number of components connected via activation arcs is large. Therefore, future work will focus on optimization techniques. Currently, the aggregation of "similar" intervals is investigated: When generating starting or terminating intervals, some intervals are rather close to each other or even overlapping. Others may only have a very small probability of occurrence. In these cases, it might be helpful to combine similar intervals into a single interval or to omit intervals, if the probability is very small. Ideally, the analyst should have the possibility to specify the degree up to which aggregation should be allowed. The actual influence of this optimization is subject to future research.

References

[BHK96]   Markus Braun, Guenter Haring, and Gabriele Kotsis. Deriving parallelism profiles from structural parallelism graphs. In *Proc. of the TDP'96*, 1996.

[CHK+95] Maria Calzarossa, Guenter Haring, Gabriele Kotsis, Alessandro Merlo, and Daniele Tessera. A hierarchical approach to workload characterization for parallel systems. In B. Hertzberger and G. Serazzi, Ed., *High Performance Computing and Networking, LNCS vol. 919*, pages 102–109, 1995.

[CS93]   Maria Calzarossa and Guiseppe Serazzi. Workload characterization: A survey. *Proc. of the IEEE*, 81(8):1136–1150, August 1993.

[HM92]   Franz Hartleb and Vassilis Mertsiotakis. Bounds for the mean runtime of parallel programs. In Rob Pooley and Jane Hillston, Eds., *Proc. of the 6th Int. Conf. on Modelling Techniques and Tools for Computer Performance Evaluation*, pages 197–210, 1992.

[LKMH96] Johannes Lüthi, Gabriele Kotsis, Shikharesh Majumdar, and Günter Haring. Bounds-based performance analysis for distributed systems with variabilities and uncertainties in workload. In *Proc. of DAPSYS'96*, pages 51–58, Hungarian Academy of Sciences Report KFKI-1996-09/M,N, October 1996.

[MR95]   Shikharesh Majumdar and Revathy Ramadoss. Interval-based performance analysis of computing systems. In Patrick Dowd and Erol Gelenbe, Eds. *Proc. MASCOTS 95*, pages 345–351. IEEE CS Press, Jan. 1995.

[ST86]   Robin A. Sahner and Kishor S. Trivedi. *SHARPE: Symbolic Hierarchical Automated Reliability and Performance Evaluator – Introduction and Guide for Users*. Gould CSD, Urbana, 1101 E. University, Urbana, IL 61801, Sep. 1986.

[vdA94]   W. M. P. van der Aalst. Using interval timed coloured petri nets to calculate performance bounds. available upon request from wsinwa@win.tue.nl, 1994.

[WMN91]   C. Murray Woodside, Shikharesh Majumdar, and J. E. Neilson. Interval arithmetic for computing performance guarantees in client-server software. In F. Dehne, F. Fiala, and W. W. Koczkodaj, Eds. *LNCS 497: Proc. ICCI '91*, pages 535–546, Berlin, et al., 1991. Springer-Verlag.

Bounding the Loss Rates in a Multistage ATM Switch [*]

J.-M. FOURNEAU[1] & L. MOKDAD[1] & N. PEKERGIN[1,2]

[1] PRiSM,

Université de Versailles Saint-Quentin

45 av. des Etats Unis, 78 035 Versailles Cedex, FRANCE

[2] CERMSEM,

Université de Paris I Sorbonne

90, rue de Tolbiac, Paris, FRANCE

email : {jmf,mokdad,nih}@prism.uvsq.fr

Abstract

We study the cell loss rates in a multistage ATM switch. We present some numerical computations for small configurations which prove that first order approximation may not be accurate. We present stochastic bounds for these loss rates using simple arguments which lead to models easier to solve. For ill-balanced configurations these models give good estimates of loss rates.

1   Introduction

We study the cell loss rates in a multistage ATM switch. Such a switch is decomposed into several queues with feed-forward routing; and external arrivals always take place at the first stage. We assume a discrete-time switching as the ATM cells have a constant size. All the queues are finite. Thus losses occur in all queues due to the variability of the input processes. Loss rates are very important as they may be part of the contract on the quality of service (QoS) between the user and the network provider. Unfortunately such a network of discrete-time queues with losses does not have a known analytical solution. However, the topology suggests to use a decomposition to find loss rates stage by stage.

The analysis of the first stage is not very difficult. Several solutions may be considered according to the arrival process. If we assume i.i.d batch arrivals or Markov modulated batch arrivals (MMBP), we can easily build a Markov chain of one buffer. Let B be the size of the buffer, if we consider i.i.d. batch process, the chain has $B + 1$ states. For a MMBP with n states for the modulation,

---

[*]This work is partially supported by CNRS, Gdr PRS and a grant from CNET.

the size of the chain is $n * (B + 1)$. Thus, the numerical computation is always possible. If we restrict ourselves to less general processes, analytical solutions may also be obtained (see Beylot's Phd thesis for some results on Clos networks [1]).

However, the second stage is much more difficult to analyze. Indeed, it is quite impossible to know exactly the arrival process into a buffer in the second stage even if we assume a simple i.i.d batch arrival process at the first stage. The output process of the first stage is usually unknown due to the losses at the first stage and the superposition of such processes is unknown even if we assume independence. It may be possible that under some restricted assumptions, some asymptotic results may be established. We do not try to prove such a result here, but we hope that we will be able to combine asymptotic results and bounds in the near future.

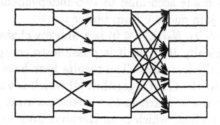

Figure 1: A multistage ATM switch

Usually such a decomposition method based on the routing uses an approximation for the arrival process into the queues. A first order approximation means that the approximate arrival process is chosen according to one parameter: in general, the expected number of arrivals per slot (in discrete time) or the interarrival time (in continuous time). The process is selected among a family of well known processes (for instance Poisson or Geometric processes). We have used such an approximation to analyze a simple model of three buffers. The results may be quite inaccurate as the relative errors on the loss rates may be as large as 10^5 as it could be seen in section II.

We advocate that stochastic bounds may lead to better estimates of the loss rates. In this paper, we develop an idea proposed by Truffet in his thesis [8] to model such a switch: replace the buffers by sources or by buffers easier to model. We define two families of models which give upper and lower bounds for the loss rates. Our method applies to the other stages of the buffer as well. Thus, it may be possible to warrant a quality of service in terms of loss rates in the switch and the network.

The paper is organized as follows. Section II presents a simple first order approximation and shows that the results are inaccurate. In section III, we propose two models which provide stochastic bounds for the loss rates, while in section IV, we present numerical results which show that for ill-balanced loads the results may be quite good.

2 A Simple but Inaccurate First Order Approximation

We consider a simpler system with only two buffers in the first stage. For the sake of keeping the chain size as small as possible, we only consider one buffer of the second stage. This buffer receives cells from both buffers of the first stage. The service times are constant (i.e. 1), the arrivals follow an i.i.d batch process built as the superposition of two independent Bernoulli processes. Let p be the rate of both Bernoulli processes. The arrivals take place just after the end of services. The buffer of the second stage is denoted as buffer 0 while the buffers in the first stage are numbered 1 and 2. Let N_i ($i = 0, 1, 2$) be the number of cells in buffer i and let B_i be the size of buffer i. Let S denotes the state space. The routing is made according to two independent Bernoulli processes with probability β_i to join queue 0 from buffer i.

Obviously $(N_0(t), N_1(t), N_2(t), t \leq 0)$ is a Markov chain of size $(B+1)^3$. For small values of B (typically $B < 50$) it is possible to compute the steady-state distribution to obtain the loss rates. The results here have been obtained using two numerical methods: the GTH algorithm [4] which is an adaptation of Gaussian elimination to stochastic matrices to warrant accurate numerical results [5], and the Gauss-Seidel method which is an iterative and accurate method whose convergence rate is unknown (see [6] for more details on the numerical computation of the steady-state distribution). The loss rate R is the expected number of lost cells in queue 0 per unit of time. It is defined as a reward function on the steady-state distribution.

$$R = \sum_{s \in S} \pi(s) \sum_{j=1}^{m} p[j, s]((n_0 - 1)^+ + j - B_0)^+ \tag{1}$$

where $p[j, s]$ is the probability that j arrivals take place into buffer 0, and n_0 is the cell number in this buffer, when the chain is in state s. As usual x^+ denotes $max(0, x)$.

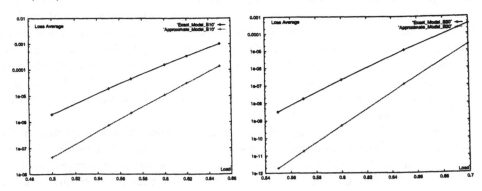

Figure 2: Buffers of size 10 and 20 with hot spot

We study this problem of small size to compare first order approximation to the exact values of the loss rates. We check an usual approximation: buffers of the first stage are analyzed first and we find $\pi_i(0)$ the probability that queue i is empty. Then the output process of queue i is approximated by a Bernoulli processes with probability $(1-\pi_i(0))$. After routing, the input process into queue 0 is approximated by the superposition of two independent Bernoulli process with probability $\beta_i(1 - \pi_i(0))$. Basically, we always have to solve numerically very small chains with the same structure. We use GTH algorithm to perform these computations.

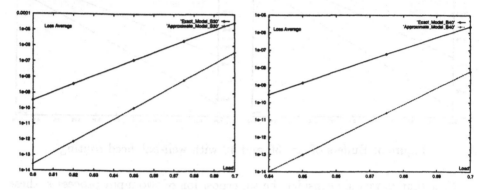

Figure 3: Buffers of size 30 and 40 with hot spot

We present here typical results for two configurations: a well-balanced load with an uniform routing and an ill-balanced configuration with a large difference between the intensity of the two processes which are superposed at buffer 0. In both cases, we have computed the numerical results for buffer sizes between 10 and 40 and a load between 0.5 and 0.9. Some results for the loss rates are depicted in figures 2 and 3 for the ill-balanced routing and in figures 4 et 5 for the well-balanced configuration.

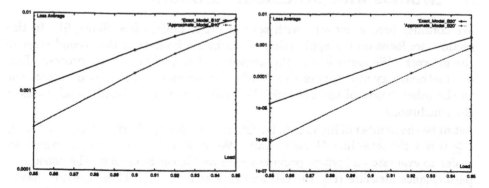

Figure 4: Buffers of size 10 and 20 with well-balanced routing

Clearly, the first order approximation provides inaccurate results. The error is typically between 1 and 5 order of magnitude. It is quite impossible to use such an approximation to optimize the buffer size subject to some QoS requirements on the loss rates. Furthermore, the exact results are always larger than the approximation, even if we have not yet proved such a relation between the processes. It seems that this approximation is too optimistic and leads to very bad results.

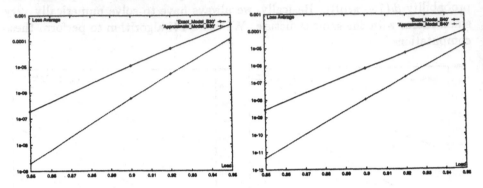

Figure 5: Buffers of size 30 and 40 with well-balanced routing

Note that as we only consider the superposition of two input processes, these conclusions do not apply to networks with a large number of inputs such as the Clos network studied in [1]. For such networks, it may be possible that the superposition of several real output processes of the input queues will asymptotically behaves like the superposition of independent Bernoulli processes. Such a conjecture has not been proved yet, to the best of our knowledge.

Finally, it could be worthy to remark that the bounding technique we develop in the next section is mostly independent of the network topology.

3   Models and Stochastic Bounds

We consider here a network with several input buffers (see figure 6). In this section, we focus on the application of stochastic bounds to the second stage of the network. We assume that the arrivals follow an i.i.d. batch process. But, our methodology also applies to a Markov modulated batch arrival process and to the other stages of the network. We will show how to handle such cases in the conclusions.

Let m be the number of input buffers. Obviously, $(N_0(t), N_1(t), N_2(t), ..., N_m(t))$, $t \geq 0$ is a discrete-time Markov chain. We now define two systems which are easier to evaluate and which provide upper and lower bounds on the considered performance measure (i.e. the cell loss rate at buffer 0). These systems have a smaller size, then it is not possible to compare directly the steady-state distribution on the same state space. This is a major difference with Truffet's approach which is based on the comparison on the same space with distributions which

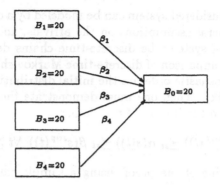

Figure 6: Exact Model

are obtained analytically. We first define the state space of comparison ε, and the preorder $\preceq$ defined on this space.

We will use a limited representation for the input buffers in the space ε, while we represent explicitly the evolution in buffer 0. Let $s = (N_0, X_1, X_2, \cdots, X_m) \in \varepsilon$, where

- N_0 is the exact number of cells at buffer 0.
- for the buffers of the first stage i.e., $1 \leq i \leq m$:
  - $X_i = 1$, if there are some cells at buffer i,
  - $X_i = 0$, if there are no cells.

Since $N_0 \in \{0, B_0\}$ and $X_i \in \{0, 1\}$ $1 \leq i \leq m$, the comparison state space is $\varepsilon = \{0 \cdots B_0\} \times \{0, 1\} \times \cdots \times \{0, 1\}$ where $\times$ is the cartesian product. We now define the preorder $\preceq$ on ε: Let $x = (x_0, x_1, \cdots x_m)$, $y = (y_0, y_1, \cdots y_m) \in \varepsilon$.

$$\begin{cases} x \preceq y & if \quad x_0 \leq y_0 \text{ and } x_1 = y_1 \cdots x_m = y_m \text{ and} \\ x = y & if \quad x_i = y_i, \ 0 \leq i \leq m \end{cases}$$

It may be worthy to remark that this preorder is chosen in order to compare the cell loss rates at buffer 0 (equation 1). Intuitively, when we compare the systems with the same capacity for buffer 0 if x, $y \in \varepsilon$ are two states such that $x \preceq y$, then the number of lost cells at state x will be less or equal to the number of lost cells at state y, since the arrival probabilities $p[i, j]$ depend on the binary functions $1\!\!1 x_i > 0$, $1 \leq i \leq m$, and x_0 and y_0 represent the cell number at buffer 0.

We compare the images of the considered systems on the state space ε in the sense of the stochastic order $\preceq_{st}$. The basic definitions and theorems for stochastic bounds are given in the appendix, and more detailed information can be found in [2], [7], [8]. First, we define the following many-to-one mappings in order to project the state spaces of the compared systems into ε. Let S^{inf} be the state space of the system which provides the lower bound, while S^{sup} be the state space of the one associated to the upper bound.

$$\varphi : S^{inf} \to \varepsilon \qquad \alpha : S \to \varepsilon \qquad \beta : S^{sup} \to \varepsilon$$

Remember that the considered system can be modeled by a discrete-time Markov chain with rather general assumptions on the arrivals, and will be denoted by $\{s(t)\}_t$. Let bounding systems be discrete-time chains denoted by $\{s(t)^{inf}\}_t$ and $\{s(t)^{sup}\}_t$. The comparison of discrete-time Markov chains is defined as the conservation of the stochastic order on the initial distributions at each step (see def. 1 in the appendix). Then one must demonstrate the following stochastic order relations between the images of the chains:

$$\varphi(s^{inf}(t)) \preceq_{st} \alpha(s(t)) \preceq_{st} \beta(s^{sup}(t)) \quad \forall t \geq 0 \tag{2}$$

We now give an outline of the proof, using a sample-path approach (see appendix):

1. In the first step we prove the existence of realizations verifying the following inequalities:

$$\varphi(s^{inf}(t)) \preceq \alpha(s(t)) \preceq \beta(s^{sup}(t)) \quad \forall t \geq 0$$

Because of the preorder $\preceq$, one must build the realizations such that:
for the lower bound:

- for all input buffers, $1 \leq i \leq m$:
  if $X_i(t) = 0$, then $X_i^{inf}(t) = 0$, $\forall t \geq 0$.
  This condition means that when no arrival may occur from buffer i to buffer 0 in the original system, then no arrival may occur in the lower bounding system.
- and $N_0(t) \geq N_0^{inf}(t)$, $\forall t \geq 0$

for the upper bound:

- for all input buffers, $1 \leq i \leq m$:
  if $X_i(t) = 1$, then $X_i^{sup}(t) = 1$, $\forall t \geq 0$.
  This condition means that when an arrival may occur from buffer i to buffer 0 in the upper bounding system then an arrival may occur in the original one.
- and $N_0(t) \leq N_0^{sup}(t)$, $\forall t \geq 0$

2. Then, the stochastic ordering $\preceq_{st}$ between the images (equation 2) follows from the first step as a consequence of the sample-path property (equation1). Moreover, if there are steady-state distributions of the chains, then

$$\varphi(\Pi^{inf}) \preceq_{st} \alpha(\Pi) \preceq_{st} \beta(\Pi^{sup}) \tag{3}$$

where Π denotes the steady-state distribution.

3. The last step consists of the proof of the inequalities between the rewards on the steady-state distributions of the chains:

$$R^{inf} \leq R \leq R^{sup} \tag{4}$$

First we rewrite the reward function on the steady-state distribution defining cell loss rate (equation 1) :

$$R = \sum_{s \in S} \pi(s) f(s) \quad \text{where} f(s) = \sum_{j=1}^{m} p[j, s]((n_0 - 1)^+ + j - B_0)^+$$

Remember that the arrival probabilities $p[j, s]$ for a state $s = (n_0, x_1, x_2, \cdots x_m)$, are computed from the values of x_i, $1 \leq i \leq m$. Then it is easy to see that if $s_1 \leq s_2$, then $f(s_1) \leq f(s_2)$, so $f(s)$ is a $\preceq$-increasing function. Since the stochastic order has been proved between steady-state distributions (3), and the preorder is chosen such that the functions defining the performance measure are $\preceq$-increasing, then the inequalities (equation 4) are the direct consequence of the stochastic order $\preceq_{st}$ (see definition with class of functions in the appendix).

3.1 Lower Bound

We now propose systems providing lower bounds by considering the same topology for the network with smaller input buffers (see figure 7). Recall that the bounding system must be easier to evaluate than the original one. So, one must consider sufficiently small capacities to get a tractable numerical solution. Hence

$$B_i^{inf} \leq B_i, \quad 1 \leq i \leq m \quad \text{and} \quad B_0^{inf} = B_0$$

Obviously, at least one of these inequalities must be strict.

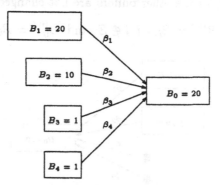

Figure 7: A Model for Lower Bound

We only give the demonstration of the first step.

- If $N_i^{inf}(0) \leq N_i(0)$, since the external arrivals to the input buffers are the same, we have :

$$N_i^{inf}(t) \leq N_i(t), \quad 1 \leq i \leq m \quad \forall t \geq 0$$

Then the first condition is established :

$$\text{if } X_i(t) = 0, \quad \text{then } X_i^{inf}(t) = 0, \quad \forall t \geq 0$$

- We now consider the evolution of the cell number at buffer 0. A cell arrival to this buffer may occur if a service has been completed in the input buffers. As a result of the former step, one may build realizations of compared systems such that if there is an arrival in the bounding system then there is also an arrival in the original one. Therefore if $N_0^{inf}(0) \leq N_0(0)$, we may have

$$N_0^{inf}(t) \leq N_0(t) \quad \forall t > 0$$

We do not prove the other steps, since the stochastic order relation between the images of the steady-state distributions exist and the preorder $\preceq$ is chosen such that the reward functions on these distributions are $\preceq -increasing$, we have the inequality (equation 4).

3.2 Upper Bound

We simplify the original system by deleting some of the input buffers and we replace them by sources (see figure 8). An equivalent view is that these buffers are never empty. The resolution of the bounding system will be easier since we do not consider the evolution of the cell numbers at these input buffers. Let E be the set of the deleted input buffers, then

$$X_j(t) = 1, \quad \forall t \geq 0 \ j \in E$$

The buffer capacities for the other buffers are not changed :

$$B_i^{sup} = B_i, \ \text{if} \ i \notin E \ \text{and} \ B_0^{inf} = B_0$$

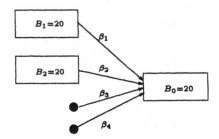

Figure 8: Model for Upper Bound

Again, we only prove here the first step for the upper bound.

- Obviously, the cell numbers at the input buffers which are not deleted change in the same manner. Then if $N_i(0) \leq N_i^{sup}(0)$, we have :

$$N_i(t) \leq N_i^{sup}(t), \quad \forall t > 0 \ i \notin E$$

Then the first condition is established for all input buffers, $1 \leq i \leq m$:

$$\text{if} \ X_i(t) = 1 \ \text{then} \ X_i^{sup}(t) = 1 \ \forall t \geq 0$$

- Now we consider the evolution at buffer 0. Since if one cell arrival may occur in the original system then it may also occur in the upper bounding one, then if $N_0(0) \leq N_0^{sup}(0)$, we may have :

$$N_0(t) \leq N_0^{sup}(t) \quad \forall t > 0$$

So we prove the stochastic comparison between the images of the considered Markov chains. Since the same stochastic order relation exist between the steady-state distributions and the reward functions are $\preceq -increasing$, we have the inequality (equation 4).

4 Numerical Computations

We apply this method to several topologies, several batch distributions of arrivals and several routing probabilities. We present here some typical results. We consider a system with 4 input buffers with the same size. Two cases are presented: buffers of size 10 and 20. The exact model is associated to a Markov chain of size $(B+1)^5$.

The upper bound is obtained with a model of two input buffers and two sources. Thus the chain size is only $(B+1)^3$. To compute the lower bounds, we keep two buffers unchanged and we change the size of the two others to only 2 cells. This leads to a chain of size $9(B+1)^3$. Clearly the upper bound is much easier to compute than the lower bound.

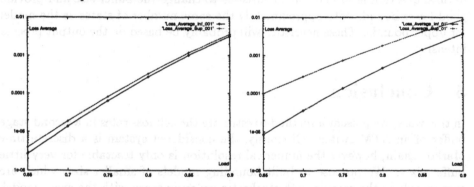

Figure 9: Buffer of size 10, q=0.01 and q=0.1

The best results are obtained when the flows of arrivals from the input buffers are unbalanced. For instance, in figure 9 and 10, we present the bounds for buffer of sizes 10 and 20. We assume that the external arrivals batch is the superposition of 2 independent Bernoulli processes with probability p. So, the load in queues of the first stage is $2p$. The probabilities β_i are defined as $(0.4 - q, 0.6 - q, q, q)$.

The second example is a system with buffers of size 20. The lower bound is computed using the following sizes for the 4 input buffers $(20, 10, 1, 1)$. More accurate lower bounds may be found with more computation times.

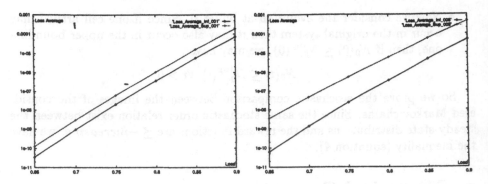

Figure 10: Buffer of size 20, q=0.01 and q=0.05

We can compute several bounds using our results. For the upper bounds the number of buffers replaced by sources is arbitrary. For the lower bounds, all buffers may be shortened. Clearly, this gives a hierarchy of bounds with a tradeoff between accuracy and computation times.

Furthermore, even if we keep constant the state space, the lower bounds can be obtained by several strategies. For instance, we may consider a model with two buffers of size $\sqrt{A}$ or a model with a buffer of size $A/3 - 1$ and a buffer of size 2. These two configurations have roughly the same number of states. A natural question is to find some heuristics to change the buffer size and provide good lower bounds with approximately the same number of states as the model for upper bounds. These heuristics will probably be based on the output process intensity.

5 Conclusion

In this work, we present a method to estimate the cell loss rates in a second stage buffer of an ATM switch. Obviously, the considered system is a discrete time Markov chain, however the numerical resolution is only tractable for very little buffer sizes. We propose to built bounding models of smaller sizes which are comparable in the sample-path stochastic ordering sense with the exact model. We obtain accurate results with these bounding models which are scarcely more difficult than the first order approximation models.

Our method could be used to analyze rewards which are not decreasing functions of the steady-state distribution such as the losses or the delay. And it may be applied to all systems where the routing allows the decomposition and the analysis stage by stage for networks with independent flows of cells as feedforward networks. Indeed, the same argument gives upper bound for the third stage (see figure 11). Some buffers are replaced by deterministic sources of cells with rate equal to 1. Then, these output processes follows the independent Bernoulli routing and are superposed with the others output processes which join at the third stage queue.

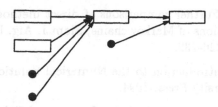

Figure 11: Upper Bound for the third stage

Similarly, this method can be applied to networks with Markov modulated batch processes for the external arrivals. Deterministic sources will replace buffers to obtain the upper bound, while the model for lower bound will include the modulating chain to describe the external arrivals. Some interconnection networks exhibit dependence between the flows of cells after some stage. For instance, in the third stage of Clos networks, input process are correlated because arrival processes into queues of the second stage are negatively correlated. It may be possible that upper bound may be obtained using our technique even with such a negative correlation of input processes.

It seems from realized experiences that first order model provides a lower bound. Intuitively, this approximation can not provide a stochastic order relation in the sense of sample-path ordering, but rather in the sense of variability orderings. We are working to find lower bounds related to this approximation by applying the variability ordering.

Acknowledgement : We thank Laurent Truffet for discussions during his Phd. We gracefully acknowledge is help and his imagination.

References

[1] A.L. Beylot, Modèles de Trafics et de Commutateurs pour l'Evaluation de la Perte et du Délai dans les Réseaux ATM, Phd thesis, Université Paris 6, 1993.

[2] M. Doisy, Comparison de Processus Markoviens, Ph-D thesis, Univ. de Pau et des Pays de l'Adour, 1992.

[3] J.-M.Fourneau, N. Pekergin, and H. Taleb, An Application of Stochastic Ordering to the Analysis of the Push-Out mechanism, in "Performance Modelling and Evaluation of ATM Networks", Chapman-Hall, London, 1995, (Ed. D. Kouvatsos).

[4] W.K. Grassman, M.I. Taksar et D.P. Heyman, Regenerative analysis and steady state distributions for Markov chains, Oper. Res., 1985, V13, P1107-1116.

[5] D.P. Heymann, Further comparisons of direct methods for computing stationary distributions of Markov chains, Siam J. Alg. Disc. Meth., Vol. 8, N 2, (April 1987) 226-232.

[6] W.J. Stewart, Introduction to the Numerical Solution of Markov Chains, Princeton University Press, 1994.

[7] D. Stoyan, Comparison Methods for Queues and Other Stochastic Models, Wiley, New York, 1983.

[8] L. Truffet, Méthodes de Calcul de Bornes Stochastiques sur des Modèles de Systèmes et de Réseaux, Phd thesis, Université Paris 6, 1995.

Appendix

Let $\preceq$ be a preorder (reflexive, transitive but not necessarily anti-symmetric) on a discrete, countable space ε. We consider two random variables X and Y defined respectively on discrete, countable spaces E and F, and their probability measures are given respectively by the probability vectors p and q where $p[i] = Prob(X = i)$, $\forall i \in E$ (resp. $q[i] = Prob(Y = i)$, $\forall i \in F$).

We define two many-to-one mappings $\alpha : E \to \varepsilon$ and $\beta : F \to \varepsilon$ to project the states of E and F into ε. First, we give the following proposition for the comparison of the images of X and Y on the space ε in the sense of $\preceq_{st}$ ($\alpha(X) \preceq_{st} \beta(Y)$) :

Proposition 1 *The following propositions are equivalent:*
- $\alpha(X) \preceq_{st} \beta(Y)$
- *definition with class of functions :*
$\sum_{s \in \varepsilon} f(s) \sum_{n \in E | \alpha(n) = s} p[n] \leq \sum_{s \in \varepsilon} f(s) \sum_{m \in F | \beta(m) = s} q[m]$ $\forall f \preceq -increasing$
f *is* $\preceq -increasing$ *iff* $\forall x, y \in \varepsilon$, $x \preceq y \to f(x) \leq f(y)$
- *definition with increasing sets :*
$\sum_{n \in E | \alpha(n) \in \Gamma} p[n] \leq \sum_{m \in F | \beta(m) \in \Gamma} q[m]$ *for all increasing set* Γ
Γ *is an increasing set iff* $\forall x, y \in \varepsilon$, $x \preceq y$ *and* $x \in \Gamma$ $\to y \in \Gamma$
- *sample-path property :*
There exist random variables $\tilde{X}$ *and* $\tilde{Y}$ *defined respectively on* E *and* F, *having the same probability measure as* X *and* Y *such that:*

$$\alpha(\tilde{X}) \preceq \beta(\tilde{Y}) \text{ almost surely}$$

We now give the definition of the stochastic ordering between the images of discrete-time Markov chains.

Definition 1 *Let* $\{X(i)\}_i$ *(resp.* $\{Y(i)\}_i$*) be discrete-time Markov chain in* E *(resp.* F*), we say the image of* $\{X(i)\}_i$ *on* ε *(*$\{\alpha(X(i))\}_i$*) is less than the image of the* $\{Y(i)\}_i$ *on* ε *(*$\{\beta(Y(i))\}_i$*) in the sense of* $\preceq_{st}$ *if*

$$\alpha(X(0)) \preceq_{st} \beta(Y(0)) \longrightarrow \alpha(X(i)) \preceq_{st} \beta(Y(i)) \quad \forall i > 0$$

Simple Bounds for Queues Fed by Markovian Sources: A Tool for Performance Evaluation

Brian McGurk[1], Raymond Russell[1]

Dublin Institute for Advanced Studies, 10 Burlington Road, Dublin 4, Ireland.

Abstract. ATM traffic is complex but only simple statistical models are amenable to mathematical analysis. We discuss a class of queuing models which is wide enough to provide models which can reflect the features of real traffic, but which is simple enough to be analytically tractable, and review the bounds on the queue-length distribution that have been obtained. We use them to obtain bounds on QoS parameters and to give approximations to the effective bandwidth of such sources. We present some numerical techniques for calculating the bounds efficiently and describe an implementation of them in a computer package which can serve as a tool for qualitative investigations of performance in queuing systems.

1 Introduction

The nature of VBR and other classes of ATM traffic is complex; different classes of traffic have very different characteristics, and the impact of the traffic on the networks designed to carry it is poorly understood. On the other hand, the behaviour of queues fed by probabilistic traffic models has been examined and analysed in some detail and a lot of results have been obtained for some simple classes of model. In this paper, we consider the case of Markov Additive Processes (MAP's), a class of traffic model which is wide enough to provide models which can capture qualitatively the features of real traffic but which is simple enough to be analytically tractable. We can construct models which reflect a particular characteristic observed in ATM traffic, such as burstiness, and apply the analytic results to them; by doing this, we can develop intuition about how the characteristic in question affects queuing systems in general.

In Section 2, we review some results from the probability literature which show that, when fed by MAP's, the distribution of the queue-length has exponential tails. This can be exploited by constructing a simple bound of the form

$$\mathbb{P}\left[Q > b\right] \leq \varphi e^{-\delta b},$$

where δ is the asymptotic decay-rate of the tail of the distribution, and φ is a constant chosen to make the bound valid for all values of b. We show how this simple bound on the queue-length distribution can be used to put bounds on different Quality of Service (QoS) parameters for the queue and how this leads naturally to the concept of *effective bandwidth* of a source. This is the the minimum bandwidth that must be allocated to a source in order to guarantee a given QoS requirement.

It is important to know how easily these bounds can be computed; in Section 3, we show how to calculate φ and δ for MAP's. One attraction of the method is that the complexity of the calculation is independent of the number of sources present in the traffic stream arriving at the queue. This gives a great advantage over estimates derived from a complete solution of the model queuing problem: these generally require the analysis of matrices whose dimension is proportional to the number of sources. We present some numerical techniques for evaluating the analytical expressions efficiently, with particular emphasis on the expression for δ. Finally, we illustrate these techniques by calculating the bound for a simple two-state Markov chain in Section 4 and outline how they are implemented in an interactive computer package. Although the models we analyse may not be useful as detailed models of real ATM traffic, and we certainly do not propose them as such, this package can serve as a useful tool in the qualitative evaluation of performance of queuing systems. It is also useful as a pedagogical tool, helping to illustrate some examples of simple queues and allowing the user to visualise the general behaviour of queues, thereby building valuable intuition.

2 Theoretical background

In order to develop some intuition for the behaviour of queues in the buffers of ATM switches and multiplexors, we analyse a simple situation: the buffer is of infinite size, the service rate is a constant s per unit time and the arrivals to the buffer have a simple (Markovian) statistical nature. The arrivals of ATM cells are not independent: if a cell arrives in one tick of the clock, it is highly likely that another cell will arrive in the next tick, or after some fixed delay. For data traffic, this is because large packets from higher level protocols must be segmented, each generating a burst of cells; for voice traffic, this is due to regular digital sampling. The simplest class of traffic models which exhibit correlations is that of Markovian arrivals. These models are flexible enough to capture the general features of ATM traffic, and yet are tractable enough to allow us calculate accurate bounds quickly.

2.1 The two-state model

Buffet and Duffield [1] considered a two-state Markov model: at time T, an input line connected to a buffer can be in one of two states. One ($X_T = 1$) corresponds to the arrival of a cell in the present clock-cycle, and the other ($X_T = 0$) to no cell arrival. The bursty nature of the arrivals is captured in the dependence of the distribution of the arrivals in the present clock-cycle on what happened in the previous clock-cycle. If a cell arrived just previously, then the probability of another cell arriving is high, close to 1; if, however, no cell arrived, then the probability of a cell arrival is small. We express this dependence precisely in the transition matrix:

$$P = \begin{pmatrix} 1-a & a \\ d & 1-d \end{pmatrix}, \qquad \text{where} \qquad \begin{aligned} a &= \mathbb{P}[X_T = 1 \mid X_{T-1} = 0] \\ d &= \mathbb{P}[X_T = 0 \mid X_{T-1} = 1] \end{aligned}$$

The closer a and d are to zero, the burstier the model is. Buffet and Duffield analysed the queue formed when a superposition of these arrivals at a buffer is served at a constant rate s. Using martingale techniques, they obtained a simple upper bound on the queue-length distribution:

$$\mathbb{P}[Q > b] \leq \varphi e^{-\delta b}.$$

Fig. 1 shows the typical form of the logarithm of the queue-length distribution, and the corresponding Duffield-Buffet bound.

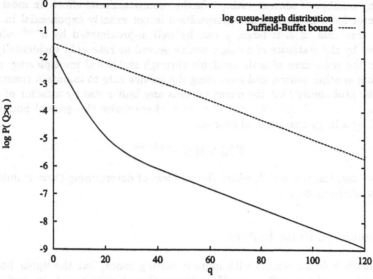

Fig. 1. The Duffield-Buffet bound

φ and δ are determined by the parameters a, d and s through a single transcendental equation. The equation is simple to solve numerically in a few iterations, yielding a fast bound on the probability of the queue exceeding any given length.

2.2 General Markov models

Duffield [2] extended these results to any queue driven by a Markov Additive Process (MAP). The workload W_T of the queue is defined to be the total arrivals up to time T less the total service available up to time T. With a MAP there is some controlling Markov process X_T and the activity of the source in time-slot T is $a(X_T)$, so

$$W_T = \sum_{t=1}^{T} a(X_t) - sT$$

Duffield again uses martingale techniques to derive an upper bound of the form

$$\mathbb{P}[Q > b] \leq \varphi e^{-\delta b}, \tag{1}$$

and shows that the decay constant δ is optimal in that it also provides an asymptotic lower bound:

$$\lim_{b \to \infty} \frac{1}{b} \log \mathbb{P}[Q > b] \geq -\delta.$$

In the case of L independent, identically distributed sources, the structure of the prefactor can be used to derive our bounds quickly: for some models we have

$$\varphi = e^{-\mu L}$$

where μ is characterised by the prefactor for a queue fed by a single source and served at rate s/L. This allows us to extend the bounds derived in the simple single source case to any number of sources without further computational effort. In most models, the prefactor for a homogeneous superposition is not exactly exponential in L but it is always true that, if L is large, φ can be well approximated by $e^{-\mu L}$ where μ is determined by the statistics of a single source served at rate s/L. Incidentally, it also illustrates the economies of scale available through statistical multiplexing: if $\mu > 0$, then adding another source, and increasing the service rate to maintain constant load, reduces the probability that the queue exceeds any buffer size by a factor of $e^{-\mu}$. See [3] and [4] for more details. We can, therefore, characterise the general bound for the queue fed by a large number L of sources,

$$\mathbb{P}[Q > b] \leq e^{-\mu L - \delta b}$$

by just two constants, μ and δ, where the problem of determining them is independent of the size of the system.

2.3 Queues in finite buffers

These bounds hold for queues with infinite waiting space, but the upper bounds are also useful for the finite buffer case. If we denote the queue in an infinite buffer by Q_∞, and the queue in a finite buffer of size B by Q_B, then $\mathbb{P}[Q_B > b] \leq \mathbb{P}[Q_\infty > b]$, and so we can use any upper bounds on Q_∞ for Q_B too:

$$\mathbb{P}[Q_B > b] \leq \varphi e^{-\delta b}.$$

For large buffer size B, these bounds will obviously be as good as for the infinite buffer case; for small buffers, however, they may not be tight enough. Toomey [5] has studied the problem of MAP's queuing in finite buffers, and has shown that the distribution of a queue with integer arrivals and service has the general form

$$\mathbb{P}[\text{overflow}] = c_0 e^{-\delta_0 B} + c_1 e^{-\delta_1 B} + \cdots$$

Each of the decay constants δ_i is an eigenvalue of the *twisted transition matrix*, $\tilde{P}_\delta$ (see section 3.1); the coefficients may be determined by solving for the corresponding eigenvector. The smallest eigenvalue, δ_0, corresponds to the decay constant δ of the Duffield-Buffet formula (equation 1). This suggests a practical procedure : one could start with the smallest eigenvalue and solve for as many as are necessary to refine the bound to the desired degree.

2.4 The effective bandwidth approximation

In ATM networks, the buffer sizes are generally fixed and the service available is variable. It is natural, then, to ask questions about how much service we need to allocate to guarantee a certain quality of service. Since the size of the fixed buffer determines the maximum cell delay variation the problem is to ensure that the cell-loss ratio will be less than some target value. We can obtain bounds on the cell-loss ratio in a finite buffer using our bounds on the queue length distribution.

The probability that a queue in a finite buffer of size B overflows is bounded by the probability that the corresponding queue in an infinite buffer exceeds length B:

$$\mathbb{P}[Q_B \text{ overflows}] \leq \mathbb{P}[Q_\infty > B] \leq \varphi e^{-\delta B}.$$

The expected number of cells lost per clock-cycle due to buffer overflow is given by

$$\mathbb{E}[\text{no. of cells lost}] = \mathbb{E}[\text{no. of cells arriving while } Q_B \text{ overflows}] \, \mathbb{P}[Q_B \text{ overflows}].$$

The arrivals are approximately independent of the state of the queue, and so the expected number of cells arriving while Q_B overflows is approximately the mean activity of the sources. The cell-loss ratio is the ratio of the number of cells lost to the total number of cells arriving, or

$$\begin{aligned} \text{C.L.R.} &= \frac{\mathbb{E}[\text{no. of cells lost}]}{\mathbb{E}[\text{no. of cells arriving}]} \\ &= \frac{\mathbb{E}[\text{no. of cells lost}]}{\text{mean activity}} \end{aligned}$$

giving

$$\text{C.L.R.} \approx \mathbb{P}[Q_B \text{ overflows}] \leq \varphi e^{-\delta B}.$$

We want to try to bound the minimum service rate required to guarantee that the cell-loss ratio will be less than some acceptable target ratio.

$$\text{minimum required service} = \min\{s : \text{C.L.R.}(s) \leq t\}$$

We can approximate this minimum by using the bound on the C.L.R.; in the case where φ is close to 1, this yields the effective bandwidth function σ

$$\begin{aligned} \sigma(t) &= \min\{s : e^{-\delta B} \leq t\} \\ &= \min\{s : \delta(s) \geq -\log(t)/B\} \end{aligned}$$

If φ is significantly less than 1, we improve our approximation and define the refined effective bandwidth function by

$$\sigma_{\text{ref}}(t) = \min\{s : \log\varphi(s) - \delta(s)B \leq \log(t)\}$$

In either case, the effective bandwidth gives a conservative bound on the minimum required service.

3 Calculation techniques

3.1 Calculating δ

The queue process is completely determined by the arrivals process and the service rate, and therefore, not surprisingly, we calculate the asymptotic decay rate of the queue-length distribution, δ, from the asymptotics of the distribution of the arrivals. First, we define the scaled cumulant generating function λ of the arrival process, as

$$\lambda(\theta) := \lim_{T \to \infty} \frac{1}{T} \log \mathbb{E}\left[e^{\theta \sum_{t=1}^{T} a(X_t)}\right].$$

$\lambda(\theta)$ is, by construction, a convex function. It is easy to verify that the slope of λ at $\theta = 0$ is the mean arrival rate, and that the asymptotic slope is the maximum achievable arrival rate. For the queue to be stable, the service rate must be greater than the mean arrivals; furthermore, for the queue to be non-empty, the maximum arrivals must exceed the service rate. δ can be calculated from λ ([8],[9]) as

$$\delta = \sup\{\theta > 0 \, : \, \lambda(\theta) \leq s\theta\},$$

that it, by solving for the positive root of the equation

$$\lambda(\theta) = s\theta. \tag{2}$$

Since $\lambda(\theta)$ is a convex function, the stability conditions for the queue ensure that such a root will exist (see Fig. 2) and will be unique.

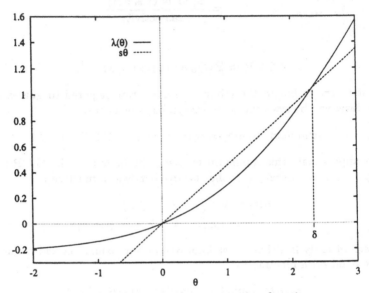

Fig. 2. The scaled cumulant generating function

We start solving this equation by examining the structure of the expectation for a finite state MAP. Let X_T be the controlling Markov chain, N be the number of states of X_T, and $a(x)$ be the increment to the arrivals at the queue when X_T is in state x. Consider $\mathbb{E}[e^{\theta \sum_{t=1}^{T} a(X_t)}]$: because of the Markovian property, we may write

$$\mathbb{E}\left[e^{\theta \sum_{t=1}^{T} a(X_t)}\right] = \sum_{x_1=1}^{N} \cdots \sum_{x_T=1}^{N} e^{\theta \sum_{t=1}^{T} a(x_t)} \times$$

$$\prod_{t=2}^{T} \mathbb{P}\left[X_t = x_t \mid X_{t-1} = x_{t-1}\right] \mathbb{P}\left[X_1 = x_1\right],$$

where x_t labels the state of the chain at time t. We now pair each of the exponential factors $e^{\theta a(x_t)}$ with the corresponding transition probability by defining

$$(\tilde{P}_\theta)_{x_t x_{t-1}} := e^{\theta a(x_t)} \mathbb{P}\left[X_t = x_t \mid X_{t-1} = x_{t-1}\right],$$

$$(\pi_\theta)_{x_1} := e^{\theta a(x_1)} \mathbb{P}\left[X_1 = x_1\right].$$

The T summations of the product of these factors is nothing other than $T-1$ matrix multiplications written out explicitly; the expectation may now be written in matrix notation as

$$\mathbb{E}\left[e^{\theta \sum_{t=1}^{T} a(X_t)}\right] = \pi_\theta \left(\tilde{P}_\theta\right)^{T-1} 1^\dagger,$$ (3)

where $1^\dagger$ is the transpose of a vector containing 1's in each column. The matrix $\tilde{P}_\theta$ is called the *twisted transition matrix* because it is the transition matrix P twisted by the exponential factors $e^{\theta a(x_t)}$. Thus we have that λ is given by

$$\lambda(\theta) = \lim_{T \to \infty} \frac{1}{T} \log \left[\pi_\theta \left(\tilde{P}_\theta\right)^{T-1} 1^\dagger\right]$$
$$= \log \rho \left(\tilde{P}_\theta\right),$$

where $\rho(\tilde{P}_\theta)$ is the spectral radius of $\tilde{P}_\theta$. If X_T is ergodic (stationary, recurrent and irreducible), then $\rho(\tilde{P}_\theta)$ is the maximum modulus of the eigenvalues of $\tilde{P}_\theta$ (see [10] for more details). The problem of determining δ is then the following: find the unique $\theta > 0$ such that

$$\log \rho \left(\tilde{P}_\theta\right) = s\theta$$

We have developed a number of different ways of solving this problem, outlined as follows.

The Powell method We may take a direct approach, using techniques from linear algebra to evaluate the largest eigenvalue of $\tilde{P}_\theta$ as a function of θ. The equation $\lambda(\theta) = s\theta$ is then readily solved using a simple bisection algorithm. It turns out that one competitive method for determining the spectral radius of a matrix is the Powell method. The spectral radius $\rho(A)$ of a matrix A is defined by $\rho(A) := \sup_v |Av|/|v|$, so that after a large number n of iterations of A, $|A^n v| \approx \rho(A)^n |v|$. To find $\rho(A)$, one starts with a random initial vector, v_0 say, and forms the iterates of A applied to it:

$$v_1 := Av_0, \quad v_2 := Av_1, \quad \ldots \quad v_k := Av_{k-1} = A^k v_0.$$

$\rho(A)$ is then estimated as the ratio of the moduli of successive vectors in the sequence: $\rho(A) = |v_k|/|v_{k-1}|$. If A has other eigenvalues close in modulus to $\rho(A)$, then this estimate will only converge poorly. In this case, a better estimate is $\rho(A) = \sqrt{|v_{k+1}|/|v_{k-1}|}$. The choice of v_0 can also strongly affect the convergence of this method. For example, if v_0 is a vector which contains no component in the direction of the eigenvector corresponding to $\rho(A)$, then the method will not converge to the eigenvector at all. For practical purposes, a good choice of initial vector is suggested by Equation 3: the vector π_0 is the stationary measure of the controlling chain X_t, and hence the eigenvector of $\tilde{P}_0$ corresponding to eigenvalue 1. By the Perron-Frobenius theorem, 1 is the largest eigenvalue of $\tilde{P}_0$ and so, for small values of θ, π_θ will be close to the eigenvector of $\tilde{P}_\theta$ of corresponding to eigenvalue $\rho(\tilde{P}_\theta)$. The Powell method will then converge rapidly, quickly yielding a good estimate of $\lambda(\theta)$.

The determinant method An alternative approach is to start with the eigenvalue equation for $\tilde{P}_\theta$: α is an eigenvalue of $\tilde{P}_\theta$ iff $\det(\tilde{P}_\theta - \alpha I) = 0$, where I is the identity matrix. We are looking for the value of θ which gives $\log \rho(\tilde{P}_\theta) = s\theta$, i.e. $\rho(\tilde{P}_\theta) = e^{s\theta}$. Since $\rho(\tilde{P}_\theta)$ is an eigenvalue of $\tilde{P}_\theta$, we could also look for solutions to

$$\det(\tilde{P}_\theta - e^{s\theta} I) = 0.$$ (4)

In general, there will be many values of θ such that $\tilde{P}_\theta$ has eigenvalue $e^{s\theta}$, but we know that δ will be the smallest positive such θ. In some situations, calculating determinants is easier than calculating eigenvalues; in these cases, it will be easier to find the roots of Equation 4 than those of Equation 2.

However, we have very little information about the form of $\det(\tilde{P}_\theta - e^{s\theta} I)$ as a function of θ. It is difficult to know precisely how many zeros it has, and whether or not any particular solution to Equation 4 is the smallest positive one. We can, however, test any solution θ_0 found by using a single evaluation of λ using the Powell method:

$$\delta = \theta_0 \quad \text{iff} \quad \lambda(\theta_0) = s\theta_0.$$

The root-tracking method This method is based on the observation that the eigenvalues of $\tilde{P}_\theta$ are smooth functions (continuous functions with continuous first derivatives) of θ, and the knowledge that, for Markov chains, the eigenvalue of largest modulus at $\theta = 0$ is the eigenvalue of largest modulus for all values of θ. Let us call this eigenvalue $\alpha(\theta)$. It satisfies the eigenvalue equation

$$f(\theta; \alpha(\theta)) = 0, \qquad \text{where} \qquad f(\theta; \alpha) = \det(\tilde{P}_\theta - \alpha I);$$

$f(\theta; \alpha)$ is a polynomial function of α and the coefficients are smooth functions of θ so that $\alpha(\theta)$ is also a smooth function of θ and hence

$$\frac{\partial f}{\partial \theta}(\theta; \alpha(\theta)) + \frac{\partial f}{\partial \alpha}(\theta; \alpha(\theta))\frac{d\alpha}{d\theta} = 0.$$

Noting also that $\alpha(0) = 1$, we may calculate $\alpha(\theta)$ by solving the first order O.D.E.

$$\frac{d\alpha}{d\theta} = -\frac{\partial f}{\partial \theta}(\theta; \alpha(\theta))/\frac{\partial f}{\partial \alpha}(\theta; \alpha(\theta))$$

starting with the initial value $\alpha(0) = 1$. The attraction of this method is that the numerical solution of O.D.E.'s is a subject which has attracted much attention. Because of this, there are a great many powerful and well-tested methods for solving them; see Press et al. [6] for an illuminating review and more references. In practice, the accuracy of the solution need not be that great; it is sufficient to track $\alpha(\theta)$ approximately as it initially decreases with increasing θ, until it exceeds $e^{s\theta}$. (Recall that $\log \alpha(\theta) = \lambda(\theta)$ and look again at Fig. 2.) The value of θ at which this occurs may then be used as an initial point in a Newton-Raphson solution to Equation 4 from the previous method. The expressions for the partial derivatives of f are, in general, quite cumbersome, and so this method is best suited to models in which the determinant in f may be explicitly evaluated.

3.2 Calculating the prefactor φ

We saw how the scaled cumulant generating function λ is the logarithm of the largest eigenvalue of the twisted transition matrix $\tilde{P}_\theta$. [2] shows that we can calculate the prefactor φ from the corresponding eigenvector of $\tilde{P}_\theta$ as follows.

Let $\mathbf{v}(s)$ be the eigenvector of $\tilde{P}_{\delta(s)}$ of eigenvalue $e^{s\delta(s)}$:

$$\mathbf{v}(s)\tilde{\mathbf{P}}_{\delta(s)} = e^{s\delta(s)}\mathbf{v}(s).$$

This is a vector with a real component $v_i(s)$ corresponding to each state i $(1 \leq i \leq N)$ of the controlling Markov chain; we take $\mathbf{v}(s)$ to be normalised so that $v_1(s) + \ldots + v_N(s) =$

1. We denote by E those states of the Markov chain such that the activity of the source while in those states exceeds the service rate s:

$$E = \{\, x_i \,:\, a(x_i) > s \,\}.$$

The prefactor φ is then simply

$$\varphi(s) = \max_{x_i \in E} \frac{1}{v_i(s)}.$$

3.3 Homogeneous superpositions

Suppose that the arrivals consist of a homogeneous superposition of sources, that is, the total arrivals in a time slot come from the sum of the activities of L independent and identically distributed Markov chains $X_T^{(1)}, \ldots X_T^{(L)}$:

$$a_{\text{total}}(X_T) = a(X_T^{(1)}) + \ldots + a(X_T^{(L)}).$$

In this case, the state space of the controlling Markov chain X_T is the product space $\{1, 2, \ldots N\}^L$ and the transition matrix is the L-fold tensor product of the common transition matrix of each source.

Calculating δ Consider the scaled cumulant generating function of the arrivals process. The arrivals can be written as the sum of the arrivals from each of the L sources:

$$\sum_{t=1}^{T} a(X_t) = \sum_{t=1}^{T} a(X_t^{(1)}) + \ldots + \sum_{t=1}^{T} a(X_t^{(L)}).$$

Since the L Markov chains are independent, the expectation in the scaled cumulant generating function breaks up into a product of L terms,

$$\mathbb{E}\left[e^{\theta \sum_{t=1}^{T} a(X_t)}\right] = \mathbb{E}\left[e^{\theta \sum_{t=1}^{T} a(X^{(1)})}\right] \ldots \mathbb{E}\left[e^{\theta \sum_{t=1}^{T} a(X^{(L)})}\right]$$

and, since they are identically distributed, we have

$$\mathbb{E}\left[e^{\theta \sum_{t=1}^{T} a(X_t)}\right] = \left(\mathbb{E}\left[e^{\theta \sum_{t=1}^{T} a(X^{(1)})}\right]\right)^L,$$

giving

$$\log \mathbb{E}\left[e^{\theta \sum_{t=1}^{T} a(X_t)}\right] = L \cdot \log \mathbb{E}\left[e^{\theta \sum_{t=1}^{T} a(X^{(1)})}\right].$$

Thus the scaled cumulant generating function for the total arrivals is

$$\lambda(\theta) = L\lambda^{(1)}(\theta),$$

where $\lambda^{(1)}$ is the common scaled cumulant generating function of all the sources. To find δ for the superposition, we need to solve Equation 2 which is, in this case, equivalent to solving

$$\lambda^{(1)}(\theta) = (s/L)\theta.$$

Calculating φ Since the transition matrix has a product structure, so do the twisted transition matrix and its eigenvector $\mathbf{v(s)}$ of maximal eigenvalue. We can exploit this structure to obtain a prefactor φ which is itself an L-fold product:

$$\varphi = e^{-L\mu},$$

where μ can be determined from $\mathbf{v}^{(1)}$, the eigenvector (of maximal eigenvalue) of the twisted transition matrix of a single source. Details are given in [2].

Thus, to calculate our simple two-parameter bound in the case of a homogeneous superposition of L sources, we need only solve Equation 2 and calculate the corresponding eigenvector for the case of one source.

3.4 Calculating effective bandwidths

As we have seen, $\delta(s)$ is the unique positive solution of the equation

$$\lambda(\theta) = s\theta \tag{5}$$

so that,

$$\frac{\lambda(\delta(s))}{\delta(s)} = s$$

Now, the effective bandwidth function is defined by

$$\sigma(t) = \min\{\, s \,:\, \delta(s) \geq -\log(t)/B \,\}$$

where t is the highest acceptable loss-ratio. If δ_t is the fraction on the right hand side of the inequality then $\sigma(\delta_t)$ is the value of s for which

$$\delta(s) = \delta_t$$

and so,

$$\sigma(\delta_t) = \lambda(\delta_t)/\delta_t. \tag{6}$$

In general, the refined effective bandwidth function is difficult to evaluate explicitly since both δ and μ are functions of s; however, it is still readily calculated numerically.

4   Implementation

4.1   Calculations for a 2-State Markov Model

For the case of a 2-state Markov model, calculating μ and δ reduces to a numerically solvable transcendental equation. We need to examine the maximum modulus of the eigenvalues of the twisted transition matrix. For the 2-state model this is a simple problem. Assuming the activity in state 1 be 0 and in state 2 to be 1, and the transition probabilities to be as defined in section 2.1 , the matrix in question is

$$\tilde{P}_\theta = \begin{pmatrix} (1-a) & e^\theta a \\ d & e^\theta(1-d) \end{pmatrix} \tag{7}$$

We can easily solve the eigenvalue equation for this matrix and determine the largest eigenvalue :

$$\begin{vmatrix} (1-a)-\alpha & e^\theta a \\ d & e^\theta(1-d)-\alpha \end{vmatrix} = 0$$

$$\alpha^2 - (1-a+e^\theta(1-d))\alpha + e^\theta(1-a-d) = 0$$

Solving this equation for α, we get

$$\alpha = \frac{1}{2}\left[1-a+(1-d)e^\theta \pm \sqrt{(1-a+(1-d)e^\theta)^2 - 4(1-a-d)e^\theta}\right]$$

$$\lambda(\theta) = \log(\alpha\text{max})$$

$$= \log\left[1-a+(1-d)e^\theta \pm \sqrt{(1-a+(1-d)e^\theta)^2 - 4(1-a-d)e^\theta}\right] - \log 2$$

The effective bandwidth is now easily calculated by using this expression for $\lambda(\theta)$ in equation 6. In order to find $\delta(s)$, we must solve Equation 5 numerically. As discussed in section 3.2, $\varphi(s)$ is found from the eigenvector, $\mathbf{v}(s)$, of the maximal eigenvalue of $\tilde{P}_{\delta(s)}$. Since we are dealing with a simple on-off model, we have that

$$\varphi(s) = \frac{1}{v_2(s)}.$$

We know from equation 5 that the maximal eigenvalue of $\tilde{P}_{\delta(s)}$ is $e^{s\delta(s)}$; thus we are looking for the value of v_2 in the equation

$$(v_1 \ \ v_2)\tilde{P}_{\delta(s)} = e^{s\delta(s)}(v_1 \ \ v_2).$$

Taking the equation corresponding to the first column of the matrix, we get

$$v_2 = \frac{e^{s\delta(s)}-1+a}{d}v_1,$$

and, using the normalisation that v_1 and v_2 sum to 1, we find that

$$\varphi(s) = \frac{e^{s\delta(s)}+a-1}{e^{s\delta(s)}+a+d-1}.$$

4.2 A proposal for an interactive tutorial package

The numerical techniques for evaluating δ and φ which we outlined in Section 3, and illustrated above for the two-state model, are very efficient. We have tested them by implementing them in C on a 66MHz Intel 486 for various different MAP's and, even for moderately large state-spaces (N=100), δ and φ can be evaluated in a negligible amount of time (less than 1s). This suggested that an interactive package could be built around these routines; such a package could exploit the excellent graphical capabilities which even modest PC's possess today. We have designed such a package: it allows the user choose from a range of Markov models, allows them to specify the parameters of the model (such as mean activity, burstiness and so on) and the service rate of the queue and displays the bound on the queue-length distribution and various QoS parameters. Since the calculations are effected almost instantaneously, the user can play around with many different scenarios, allowing them to develop intuition about what the impact of the different characteristics of the traffic is on its queuing behaviour. The package is licensed for free use and is available for ftp from `ftp://ftp.stp.dias.ie/DAPG/`

5 Conclusion

In this paper, we considered the queuing behaviour of arrivals processes called MAP's which have an underlying Markov structure. We reviewed some results from the probability literature which show that, when fed by MAP's, the distribution of the queue-length has exponential tails. We exploited this by constructing a simple bound of the form

$$\mathbb{P}\left[Q > b\right] \leq \varphi e^{-\delta b},$$

where δ is the asymptotic decay-rate of the tail of the distribution, and φ is a constant chosen to make the bound valid for all values of b. We showed how this simple bound on the queue-length distribution can be used to put bounds on different Quality of Service (QoS) parameters for the queue and how the concept of effective bandwidth arises naturally.

We showed how to calculate φ and δ for MAP's and presented some numerical techniques for evaluating the analytical expressions efficiently. We illustrated these techniques in the case of a two-state Markov chain and outlined how these techniques have been used to implement an interactive tutorial package.

References

1. E. Buffet and N.G. Duffield (1992) Exponential upper bounds via martingales for multiplexers with Markovian arrivals. *J. Appl. Prob.* **31** 1049–1061
2. N.G. Duffield (1994) Exponential bounds for queues with Markovian arrivals. *Queuing Systems* **17** 413–430
3. D.D. Botvich and N.G. Duffield Large deviations, the shape of the loss curve, and economies of scale in large multiplexers. Preprint DIAS-APG-94-12 Accepted for Queuing Systems subject to revision.
4. D.D.Botvich, T.J. Corcoran, N.G. Duffield, P.Farrell Economies of scale in long and short buffers of large multiplexers. Proceedings of 12th UK Teletraffic Symposium.
5. F. Toomey (1994) Queues in finite buffers with Markovian arrivals: an application to bursty traffic. Preprint.
6. W.H. Press, S.A. Teukolsky, W.T. Vetterling, B.P. Flannery *Numerical Recipes in C* Cambridge University Press, Cambridge (1992)
7. J. Y. Hui (1988) Resource allocation for broadband networks. *IEEE J. Selected Areas in Commun.* **SAC-6** 1598–1608
8. P. Glynn and W. Whitt (1994) Logarithmic asymptotics for steady-state tail probabilities in a single-server queue. *J. Appl. Prob.*, vol. 31A pp 131-159
9. N.G. Duffield and Neil O'Connell (1995) Large deviations and overflow probabilities for the general single-server queue, with applications *Proc. Cam. Phil. Soc.*, 118 (1995) pp 363-374
10. S. Karlin and H. M. Taylor (1975) *A First Course in Stochastic Processes*, Academic Press (London)

On Queue Length Moments in Fork and Join Queuing Networks with General Service Times

Simonetta Balsamo[1], Ivan Mura[2]

[1] Dept. of Mathematics and Computer Science, Via delle Scienze 206, 33100 Udine, Italy
[2] Dept. Information Engineering, University of Pisa, Via Diotisalvi 2, 56100 Pisa, Italy

Abstract. Fork and join queueing network models can be used to represent and analyse the performance of distributed and parallel processing computer systems with concurrence and synchronisation constraints and shared resources. Concurrence and synchronisation make the solution of such performance models more complex than classical queueing network analysis. We consider parallel processing systems where a set of independent tasks are executed simultaneously and can be represented by fork and join queueing networks. We present an approximate method to analyse open fork and join queueing networks with general service time distribution represented by Coxian distribution. Specifically, we derive two approximations of the joint queue length distribution and closed form expressions for all the moments of this distribution. We prove that the method provides lower and upper bounds on the queue length moments.

1 Introduction

Heterogeneous parallel processing systems are becoming increasingly important with the growing demand for system performance and reliability. We consider parallel processing systems where a set of independent tasks are executed simultaneously and can be represented by fork and join queueing networks. These performance models can be used to represent and analyse the performance of distributed and parallel processing computer systems with concurrence and synchronisation constraints along with shared resources. Concurrence and synchronisation make the solution of such performance models more complex than classical queueing network analysis. We present an approximate method to analyse open fork and join queueing networks with general service time distribution represented by Coxian distribution.

Some limit results on the queue length distribution for the model with two parallel queues with exponential service times, Poissonian arrivals and incoming jobs formed by two parallel tasks have been shown by Flatto and Hahn [9]. Brun and Fajolle [7] obtained the Laplace transform of the response time distribution for the same model, and an approximate solution has been proposed by Rao and Posner [16]. When the system consists of $k \geq 2$ homogeneous exponential processing units and incoming jobs are formed by k parallel tasks, Nelson and Tantawi [13] have presented approximate solutions for the mean job and task response time. Bounds on the average job response time for a system with general service time and inter-arrival time distributions have been proposed by Varma and Makowski [19]. A comparison between different parallel processing models in terms of mean response time was presented by Nelson, Tantawi and Towsley in [12]. A more general model with $k \geq 2$ heterogeneous servers and general arrival service time distribution was considered by Baccelli, Massey and Towsley [2] who provided bounds for the job mean response time, while Kim and Agrawala [10] obtained the transient and steady-state solution of the virtual waiting time. More complex systems, where processing units are connected in series and parallel, have been analysed by Baccelli and Makowski [1] by deriving bounds on response time.

Bounds on some performance indices of the fork and join queueing system have already been proposed in the literature. Balsamo e Donatiello [3] were the first to define this method for obtaining bounds on the mean number of jobs in a heterogeneous fork and join system with Poissonian arrivals and exponential distribution of service times. Similar methods were used by Balsamo and Mura in [4] and [5] to derive an upper-bound and lower-bound pair on the job response time distribution in heterogeneous and homogeneous fork and join systems, respectively. Very tight bounds have been obtained at a low polynomial computational complexity. Only exponential service time distributions were considered in all these studies.

In this paper, we propose an extension of this method to deal with the general case of Coxian service time distributions, which represent a useful means to approximate any distribution that has a rational Laplace transform. This new extension is used to obtain a bounded approximation of the moments of any order for the number of jobs in the fork and join system. The accuracy of the proposed method can be tuned by choosing the appropriate values for the approximation parameters.

We consider a fork and join queueing system with $k \geq 2$ heterogeneous processing units. We present an algorithm to derive an approximate solution of the open fork and join queueing networks with Poisson arrivals and Coxian service time distribution. Specifically, we derive two approximations of the joint queue length distribution of the fork and join network (i.e., the number of tasks in each queue) and closed form expressions for all the moments of this distribution. Moreover, we prove that the proposed method provides lower and upper bounds on the queue length moments. The method is based on the analysis of the Markov process underlying the fork and join queuing systems for which two approximate processes are defined. By choosing an appropriate state ordering we identify a regular process structure which allows us to apply a matrix-geometric technique. Numerical results for several system scenarios are reported in [6]. In any case we observed quite accurate approximation results with a low computational complexity.

The paper is organised as follows. Section 2 presents the fork and join system, Section 3 deals with the approximate models which are analysed in terms of moments of the number of jobs in the system in Section 4. These approximate solutions are proved to be bounds on the moments of the original fork and join system in Section 5.

2 The model

In this paper we consider the open queuing network model S, as shown in Figure 1, which is fed by a stream of jobs arriving according to a Poisson process of parameter λ. A job arriving at the system is immediately served by the fork node, which splits the job into k independent tasks. Each task is assigned to one of the k service centers of the system, where it queues with the other tasks already in the center.

Tasks are selected for the service according to the First Come First Served policy, and receive a service time which is a random variable with a Coxian distribution [8]. A task after completion of the service at a service center reaches the join node where it waits until all its siblings have completed their service. Eventually, the job is completed and leaves the system.

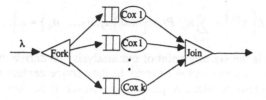

Figure 1: Open fork and join queuing network system S.

The task service times at the i-th service center, $1 \le i \le k$, are independent Coxian random variables with $\gamma_i \ge 1$ stages, as illustrated in Figure 2, where stage of the service j, $1 \le j \le \gamma_i$, is a negative exponential random variable with parameter $\mu_j^i > 0$.

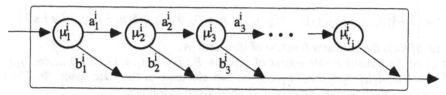

Figure 2: Coxian representation of service in service center i.

The service of the task is a random variable defined as the weighted sum of exponential stages and it includes at least the first stage up to at most the last stage. In service center i, at completion of service stage j, the task enters the new stage $j + 1$ with probability a_j^i, $1 \le j \le \gamma_i$, otherwise the service ends with probability $b_j^i = 1 - a_j^i$. After the last stage γ_i the task definitively leaves the service center, and hence we set $b_{\gamma_i}^i = 1$ and $a_{\gamma_i}^i = 0$. In order to guarantee the stability of the queuing system S and hence the existence of its steady-state behaviour, we suppose that the following condition is satisfied for each service center i, $1 \le i \le k$:

$$\sum_{j=1}^{\gamma_i} \frac{\lambda}{\mu_j^i} \prod_{h=1}^{j-1} a_h^i < 1,$$

that is we assume a constraint on the utilisation factor given by the left-hand side of this formula.

Each service center can be individually considered as an $M / C_k / 1$ node which has been analysed as reported in literature. Perros [15] obtained an exact analytic expression for the probability distribution of the number of customers in the service center. However, note that the fork and join synchronisation greatly complicates the analysis of the system. Specifically, this system does not show any product-form solution for the joint queue distribution of the number of tasks in the service centers. In this work, we propose a method to approximate this distribution, from which we derive a bounded approximation for the moments of the number of jobs in system S.

Let N denote the number of jobs in system S at random time. If n_i represents the number of tasks in the service center i, $1 \le i \le k$, then the following relationship holds $N = \max\{n_1, n_2, ..., n_k\}$. The m-th moment of the number of jobs N can be computed as follows:

$$E\left[N^m\right] = \sum_{n=0}^{\infty} n^m \, Prob\left[max\{n_1, n_2, ..., n_k\} = n\right], \quad m \geq 1 \qquad (2.1)$$

This formula is the starting point of our analysis. To derive the probability distribution of the maximum number of tasks in the service centers of the system, we define a continuous-time Markov process P, which describes the behaviour of system S.

Let (n_i, j_i) denote the state of service center i, $1 \leq i \leq k$, where n_i is the number of tasks in the service center, and j_i is the stage of the service of the task which is currently being served. We set $j_i = 0$ when $n_i = 0$. The state of the whole system at random time is represented by vector $((n_1, j_1), (n_2, j_2), ..., (n_k, j_k))$. The continuous-time discrete-space homogeneous Markov process has state space Φ defined as follows:

$$\Phi = \left\{\bar{n} = \left((n_1, j_1), (n_2, j_2), ..., (n_k, j_k)\right) \mid n_i \geq 0, \; 0 \leq j_i \leq \delta(n_i > 0)\gamma_i, \; 1 \leq i \leq k\right\}$$

where $\delta(A)$ is the indicator function of the event A.

Let Q be the transition rate matrix of process P, $\bar{n} = ((n_1, j_1), (n_2, j_2), ..., (n_k, j_k))$ and $\bar{m} = ((m_1, l_1), (m_2, l_2), ..., (m_k, l_k))$ be two elements of the state space Φ. Then the non-zero off-diagonal elements of Q are defined as follows:

$$Q = \left\|q_{\bar{n}, \bar{m}}\right\| = \begin{cases} \lambda & if \, m_i = n_i + 1, \; l_i = j_i + \delta(n_i = 0), \; 1 \leq i \leq k \quad (i) \\[2mm] a_h^r \mu_h^r & \begin{cases} if \, m_i = n_i, \; l_i = j_i, \; 1 \leq i \leq k, \; i \neq r, \\ m_r = n_r, \; j_r = h, \; l_r = h + 1 \end{cases} \quad (ii) \\[4mm] b_h^r \mu_h^r & \begin{cases} if \, m_i = n_i, \; l_i = j_i, \; 1 \leq i \leq k, \; i \neq r, \\ m_r = n_r - 1, \; j_r = h, \; l_r = 1 \cdot \delta(m_r > 0) \end{cases} \quad (iii) \end{cases} \qquad (2.2)$$

A transition of type (i) corresponds to a job arrival at the system. Both the two types of transitions (ii) and (iii) represent the completion of the service of a task in stage h of the Coxian service center r. In case (ii) the task enters the next stage of the service, and in case (iii) the task leaves the service center. Note that in cases (i) and (iii) when the service center is empty, the stage component of the state takes the value 0. The elements $q_{\bar{n}, \bar{n}}$ on the diagonal of Q are defined as the opposite of the sum of the off-diagonal row elements.

Let vector $\bar{\pi}$ denote the stationary state probabilities of Markov process P. It can be obtained as the solution of the linear system $\bar{\pi} \cdot Q = \bar{0}$, subject to the normalising constraint $\bar{\pi} \cdot \bar{e} = 1$, where $\bar{e}$ denotes the vector whose elements are all 1. Matrix Q is infinite, and to the best of our knowledge the exact evaluation of steady state probabilities $\bar{\pi}$ is still an open issue, except for the case of $k = 2$ service centers and exponential service times, that is for $\gamma_1 = \gamma_2 = 1$ stages of the Coxian services [13]. In the next section we propose a method for approximating $\bar{\pi}$ in the case of $k \geq 2$ service centers and $\gamma_i > 1$, $1 \leq i \leq k$ stages of the Coxian services. The approximate steady-state probabilities allows deriving the probability distribution of the number of jobs N, and hence its moments, according to formula (2.1).

3 The approximate models

In this section we propose two approximations of the steady-state probabilities $\bar{\pi}$, that lead to a bounded approximation of the moments of the number of jobs in fork and join system S. These approximations are obtained by two reductions of the state space Φ of the underlying Markov process P. So we define two new Markov processes for which we propose a particular state space ordering which allows us to identify a very regular structure of the processes, called a Quasi-Birth-and-Death (QBD) structure. This permits to efficiently derive the stationary state probabilities of the two processes by using the matrix-geometric technique proposed by Neuts [14].

3.1 The lower-bound process

Let us define a modified fork and join system S^-, obtained by system S with the constraint that all the queues except one have finite capacity. Without loss of generality, we assume that only the first service center has unlimited waiting room. The arriving tasks that find the queue full are lost. The new fork and join system reaches a steady-state condition because the utilisation of each service center in not greater than that of the original one of system S. Informally, the task loss leads to a shorter queue length of the modified system, hence it provides a lower-bound on the number of job in system S.

More precisely, we choose $k - 1$ non-negative integers $\beta_2, \beta_3, ..., \beta_k$ that represent the maximum number of tasks allowed in the service centers $2, 3, ..., k$, respectively. If a job arrives at the system when any of the service centers has reached its maximum capacity, then it is lost. The fork and join system S^- is described by a Markov process P^- whose state space Φ^- is a proper subset of state space Φ of process P, and is defined as follows:

$$\Phi^- = \left\{ \bar{n} = \big((n_1, j_1), (n_2, j_2), ..., (n_k, j_k) \big) \in \Phi \mid n_i \le \beta_i,\ i = 2, 3, ..., k \right\}$$

The transition rate matrix Q^- of process P^- is obtained as the submatrix of matrix Q of process P, restricted on subset Φ^- of Φ. Specifically, the off-diagonal elements of Q^- are given by formula (2.2) for $\bar{n}, \bar{m} \in \Phi^-$, and the diagonal elements are defined as the opposite of the sum of the off-diagonal row elements. Note that process P^- is a truncated process of P on the state space Φ^-.

The Markov process P^- is a QBD process. In order to prove this, we define the sets Φ_i^-, called levels, which are proved to form a partition of state space Φ^-. Subsets Φ_i^- are defined as follows:

$$\Phi_i^- = \left\{ \bar{n} \in \Phi^- \mid (n_1 = i,\ j_1 = 1 \cdot \delta(n_1 > 0))\ or\ (n_1 = i + 1,\ j_1 > 1) \right\}, \quad i \ge 0 \quad (3.1)$$

Theorem 3.1: Sets $\{ \Phi_i^-,\ i \ge 0 \}$ form a partition of the state space Φ^-.
The proof is given in [6].
Note that it can be easily proved that all the sets Φ_i^-, $i \ge 0$ have the same cardinality c^-, which is given by the following formula:

$$c^- = \gamma_1 \prod_{i=2}^{k} (\beta_i \gamma_i + 1) \quad (3.2)$$

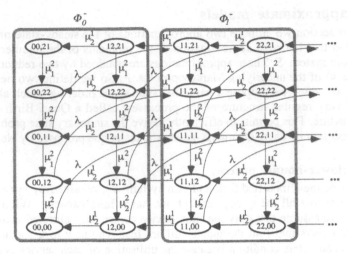

Figure 3: State transition diagram of process P^- **for** $k = 2$ **2-stages hypo-exponential service centers, and** $\beta_2 = 2$.

Figure 3 shows an example of the initial part of the state transition diagram of process P^- in the particular case of the fork join system S with $k = 2$ service centers. For the sake of simplicity we consider a system with 2-stage hypo-exponential service centers, which are a particular case of Coxian service centers with $\gamma_1 = \gamma_2 = 2$ and $a_1^1 = a_1^2 = 1$. We choose the threshold $\beta_2 = 2$ for the number of tasks that are admitted in the service center 2. Figure 3 shows the first two levels Φ_0^- and Φ_1^- defined by the partition given by formula (3.1).

Let us suppose that state space Φ^- is ordered for increasing level, so that the states which belong to Φ_i^- precede the states of Φ_{i+1}^-, $i \geq 0$ in the ordering. Moreover, we assume that the same state ordering is used within each level Φ_i^-, $i \geq 0$. For instance we can choose the lexicographic ordering within each set Φ_i^-. Then, the transition rate matrix Q^- can be rearranged in the block-tridiagonal form shown in Figure 4, according to the partition given by formula (3.1) and this state ordering. Figure 4 shows the non-zero block submatrices of Q^-, where A_0, A_1, A_2 and B are squared submatrices of order c^-, given by formula (3.2).

$$
Q^- = \begin{bmatrix}
B & A_0 & & & \\
A_2 & A_1 & A_0 & & \\
& A_2 & A_1 & A_0 & \\
& & \ddots & \ddots & \ddots
\end{bmatrix}
$$

Figure 4: Transition rate matrix of process P^-.

We observe that process P^- shows the QBD structure, because of the state partition and the particular state ordering of state space. Submatrix A_0 contains the transitions rates of type *(i)* given by formula (2.2), which correspond to job arrivals at the system. Such a transition represent the quasi-birth of the QBD process from one level to the next one in the ordering. Submatrix A_2 contains the transition rates of type *(ii)* and *(iii)* that occur when a task at the first service center completes the first stage of the Coxian service. These transitions represent the quasi-deaths of the QBD process from a level to the previous one in the ordering. All the other transitions are taken into account by the block submatrices B and A_1.

Let $\vec{\pi}^-$ denote the vector of stationary state probabilities of process P^-, and let $(\vec{\pi}_0^-, \vec{\pi}_1^-, \vec{\pi}_2^-, ...)$ be the partition of $\vec{\pi}^-$ induced by the state partition $\{\Phi_i^-, i \geq 0\}$, $i \geq 0$. Due to the QBD structure of process P^-, we can compute vectors $\vec{\pi}_i^-$, $i \geq 0$ by using the matrix-geometric technique [14] that we just summarise. The basic step of this method is the computation of matrix R^-, obtained as the solution to the following non-linear matrix equation:

$$(R^-)^2 A_2 + R^- A_1 + A_0 = 0 \tag{3.3}$$

Then, vector $\vec{\pi}_0^-$ of stationary state probabilities of level Φ_0^- is obtained by solving the following linear system:

$$\vec{\pi}_0^-\left(B + R^- A_2\right) = 0, \tag{3.4}$$

subject to the normalising condition $\vec{\pi}_0^-(I - R^-)^{-1}\vec{e} = 1$. Finally, steady-state probabilities $\vec{\pi}_i^-$ of level Φ_i^-, $i > 0$, are obtained by using the following formula:

$$\vec{\pi}_i^- = \vec{\pi}_i^- R^- = \vec{\pi}_0^-\left(R^-\right)^i \tag{3.5}$$

From the steady-state queue length probabilities of Markov process P^- one derives the moments of the number of job N^- in the system S^-, according to formula (2.1).

3.2 The upper-bound model

We shall now define a new modified model S^+ of fork and join system obtained by system S, with the constraint that the difference between each pair of queue lengths does not exceed a given threshold. We consider $k(k-1)$ non-negative integers $\beta_{i,j}$, $1 \leq i, j \leq k$, $i \neq j$, that represent the maximum imbalance between the number of tasks in each pair of service centers. If a task departure on service center i would cause the violation of the imbalance constraint $n_j - n_i \leq \beta_{i,j}$ with respect to some service center j, then the service center i becomes blocked until a service completion occurs in center j. Informally, the blocking of the service centers of the new system leads to an increase of the queue lengths with respect to the original system, and thus it provides a upper-bound on the number of jobs in system S. A stability condition of the new system S^+ is given in the following.

The fork and join system S^+ can be described by a Markov process P^+ whose state space Φ^+ is a proper subset of state space Φ of process P, as follows:

$$\Phi^+ = \left\{\vec{n} = ((n_1, j_1), (n_2, j_2), ..., (n_k, j_k)) \in \Phi \mid n_j - n_i \leq \beta_{i,j}, \ 1 \leq i, j \leq k, i \neq j\right\}$$

The transition rate matrix Q^+ is defined by formula (2.2) as for process P by considering $\vec{n}$, $\vec{m} \in \Phi^+$ and $\vec{n} \neq \vec{m}$.

Consider the following partition of state space Φ^+ into levels Φ_i^+, $i \geq 0$:

$$\Phi_i^+ = \left\{\vec{n} \in \Phi^+ \mid (\forall h \in H(\vec{n})\ n_h = i, j_h = \delta(i > 0))\right\}$$
$$\cup \left\{\vec{n} \in \Phi^+ \mid (\exists h \in H(\vec{n})\ n_h = i+1, j_h > 1)\right\} \tag{3.6}$$

where $H(\bar{n})$ is the set defined as $H(\bar{n}) = \{h \in \{1, 2, ..., k\} | n_h = min_{1 \le j \le k} n_j\}$

In other words, the i-level is formed by all these states for which the minimum number of tasks is exactly i, provided that all the service centers which have i tasks are in the first stage of the service, plus all these states for which the minimum number of tasks is exactly $i + 1$, provided that at least one among the service centers which have $i + 1$ tasks is not in the first stage of the service.

Theorem 3.2: Sets $\{\Phi_i^+, i \ge 0\}$ form a partition of the state space Φ^+.
The proof is given in [6].

It is easy to verify that all the levels Φ_i^+, $i \ge 0$ have the same cardinality, denoted by c^+. Indeed, we can define a bijective function $f: \Phi_i^+ \rightarrow \Phi_{i+1}^+$ as follows:

$$f((n_1, j_1), ..., (n_k, j_k)) = ((n_1 + 1, j_1 + \delta(j_1 = 0)), ..., (n_k + 1, j_k + \delta(j_k = 0))) \quad (3.7)$$

that maps each state of level Φ_i^+ into one and only one state of level Φ_{i+1}^+, $i \ge 0$.

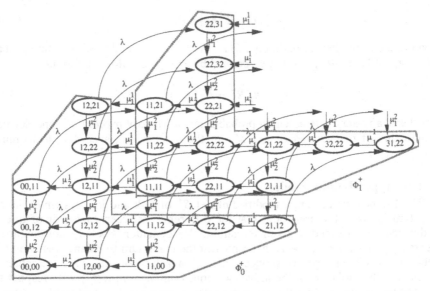

Figure 5: State transition diagram of process P^+ for $k = 2$ 2-stages hypo-exponential service centers, and $\beta_{12} = \beta_{21} = 1$.

We can prove the following upper-bound for the level cardinality:

$$c^+ \le \prod_{j=1}^{k} \gamma_i \left(\prod_{j=1}^{k} (\beta_i + 1) - \prod_{j=1}^{k} \beta_i \right) \quad (3.8)$$

Figure 5 shows an example of the state transition diagram of process P^+ for $k = 2$, $a_j^1 = a_j^2 = 1$, $\gamma_1 = \gamma_2 = 2$ and $\beta_{1,2} = \beta_{2,1} = 1$. Figure 5 also shows the levels Φ_0^+ and Φ_1^+ defined by formula (3.6).

By considering the state space Φ^+ ordered for increasing level, and by choosing the same ordering for the states within each level, the transition rate matrix Q^+ takes the block-tridiagonal form shown in Figure 4, as for the lower-bound model. Then, by using the matrix-geometric technique we compute matrix R^+ and the steady-state probabilities $\bar{\pi}_i^+$ of the level Φ_i^+, $i \ge 0$ by formulas (3.3)-(3.5). As proved by

Neuts [14], the condition $\lambda < \bar{\tau} A_2 \bar{e}$ guarantees the stability of process P^+ underlying the fork and join system S^+, where vector $\bar{\tau}$ is the solution to the following linear system:

$$\begin{cases} \bar{\tau}(A_0 + A_1 + A_2) = 0 \\ \bar{\tau}\bar{e} = 1 \end{cases}$$

The probability distribution $\bar{\pi}^+$ allows us to evaluate the moments of the number of jobs in system S^+.

4 Moments of the number of jobs in the bound models

In this section we derive closed form formulas for the moments of the number of jobs in the two modified systems S^- and S^+. These expressions are derived by formula (2.1) applied to the two models and by exploiting the recursive relationships that relate the steady state probabilities of the two QBD underlying processes.

4.1 Moments of the lower bound model

Let N^- denote the number of jobs in fork and join system S^-, and let $(\bar{n}_1^i, \bar{n}_2^i, ..., \bar{n}_{c^-}^i)$ be the set of states which belong to level Φ_i^-, $i \geq 0$. We define vector $\bar{x}_i^-$ as follows:

$$x_{i,j}^- = max\{n_{j,1}^i, n_{j,2}^i, ..., n_{j,k}^i\}, \quad 1 \leq j \leq c^- \tag{4.1}$$

that is component $x_{i,j}^-$ represents the number of jobs in the j-th state of the level Φ_i^-, $1 \leq j \leq c^-$. We rewrite formula (2.1) in terms of the partition induced by the state space partition, as follows:

$$E\left[\left(N^-\right)^m\right] = \sum_{n=0}^{\infty} n^m \, Prob\left[max\{n_1, n_2, ..., n_k\} = n\right] = \sum_{i=0}^{\infty} \bar{\pi}_i^- \cdot \left(\bar{x}_i^-\right)^m \tag{4.2}$$

where the m-th power of vector $\bar{x}_i^-$ is intended componentwise. Let β denote the maximum of the thresholds on the queue lengths $\beta_2, \beta_3, ..., \beta_k$. We observe that the number of jobs in each state of level Φ_i^-, $i \geq \beta$ is given by the number of tasks in the first service center, which is either i or $i + 1$ from the definition of levels given by formula (3.1). Without loss of generality we assume the lexicographic order of the states within each level. Let $\bar{y}$ be the vector of size c^- defined as $y_h = 0$ if $1 \leq h \leq c^-/\beta_1$, and $y_h = 0$ if $c^-/\beta_1 + 1 \leq h \leq c^-$. Then the relation $\bar{x}_i^- = i\bar{e} + \bar{y}$, $i \geq \beta$ holds.

Owing to this relation and from formula (3.5) we rewrite formula (4.2) as follows:

$$E\left[\left(N^-\right)^m\right] = \sum_{i=0}^{\beta-1} \bar{\pi}_i^- \left(\bar{x}_i^-\right)^m + \sum_{i=\beta}^{\infty} \bar{\pi}_i^- \left(i\bar{e} + \bar{y}\right)^m =$$

$$= \sum_{i=0}^{\beta-1} \bar{\pi}_i^- \left(\bar{x}_i^-\right)^m + \bar{\pi}_0^- \sum_{i=\beta}^{\infty} \left(R^-\right)^i \left(i\bar{e} + \bar{y}\right)^m \tag{4.3}$$

Due to the fact that vector $\bar{y}$ components are only 0s and 1s, the m-th power of vector $i\bar{e} + \bar{y}$ can be conveniently rewritten as follows:

$$(i\vec{e} + \vec{y})^m = i^m\vec{e} + \sum_{l=0}^{m-1}\binom{m}{l}i^l\vec{y}$$

and hence from formula (4.3) we obtain the following expression:

$$E\left[\left(N^-\right)^m\right] = \sum_{i=0}^{\beta-1}\vec{\pi}_i\left(\vec{x}_i\right)^m + \vec{\pi}_0^-\sum_{i=\beta}^{\infty}\left(R^-\right)^i i^m\vec{e} + \vec{\pi}_0^-\sum_{l=0}^{m-1}\binom{m}{l}\sum_{i=\beta}^{\infty}\left(R^-\right)^i i^l\vec{y} \quad (4.4)$$

The following theorem gives a closed from formula for this last expression.

Theorem 4.1: The m-th moment of the number of jobs in system S^+ is given by:

$$E\left[\left(N^-\right)^m\right] = \sum_{i=0}^{\beta-1}\vec{\pi}_i\left(\vec{x}_i^-\right)^m +$$

$$+\vec{\pi}_\beta^-\beta^m\left[\left(I - R^-\right)^{-1} + \sum_{h=1}^{m}\binom{m}{h}\beta^{-h}\sum_{r=1}^{h}\left\langle\begin{matrix}h\\r\end{matrix}\right\rangle\left(R^-\right)^r\left(I - R^-\right)^{-(h+1)}\right]\vec{e} +$$

$$+\vec{\pi}_\beta^-\sum_{l=0}^{m-1}\binom{m}{l}\beta^l\left[\left(I - R^-\right)^{-1} + \sum_{h=1}^{l}\binom{l}{h}\beta^{-h}\left(I - R^-\right)^{-(h+1)}\sum_{r=1}^{h}\left\langle\begin{matrix}h\\r\end{matrix}\right\rangle\left(R^-\right)^r\right]\vec{y}$$

where $\left\langle\begin{matrix}h\\r\end{matrix}\right\rangle$ is the Eulerian number defined by the following formula (see [11]):

$$\left\langle\begin{matrix}h\\r\end{matrix}\right\rangle = \sum_{j=0}^{r}(-1)^j(r-j)^h\binom{r+1}{j}, \quad h \geq 0, \, r \geq 0$$

The proof is given in [6].

We observe that the evaluation of this expression requires to compute the powers of matrices R^- and $I - R^-$ up to the m-th and the $(m + 1)$-th one, respectively.

4.2 Moments of the upper bound model

Let N^+ be the number of jobs in fork and join system S^+. By defining vector x_i^+, $i \geq 0$ as in formula (4.1) but for the states of level Φ_i^+ and by following the same steps as for the lower-bound model we obtain the following formula for the m-th moment of N^+:

$$E\left[\left(N^+\right)^m\right] = \sum_{i=0}^{\infty}\vec{\pi}_i^+\left(\vec{x}_i^+\right)^m = \vec{\pi}_0^+\sum_{i=0}^{\infty}\left(R^+\right)^i\left(\vec{x}_i^+\right)^m \quad (4.5)$$

We now observe that owing to the bijective function between levels defined by (3.7) the relationship $\vec{x}_i^+ = \vec{x}_0^+ + i\vec{e}$ holds for $i \geq 0$. This allows us to rewrite expression (4.5) as follows:

$$E\left[\left(N^+\right)^m\right] = \vec{\pi}_0^+\sum_{i=0}^{\infty}\left(R^+\right)^i\left(\vec{x}_0^+ + i\vec{e}\right)^m =$$

$$= \vec{\pi}_0^+\sum_{i=0}^{\infty}\left(R^+\right)^i i^m\vec{e} + \vec{\pi}_0^+\sum_{l=0}^{m-1}\binom{m}{l}\sum_{i=0}^{\infty}\left(R^+\right)^i i^l\vec{x}_0^{+m-l}$$

(4.6)

Theorem 4.2: The m-th moment of the number of jobs in system S^+ is given by:

$$E\left[\left(N^+\right)^m\right] = \bar{\pi}_0^+ \left[\left(I - R^+\right)^{-(m+1)} \sum_{r=1}^{m} \left\langle \binom{m}{r} \right\rangle \left(R^+\right)^r \bar{e} + \right.$$

$$\left. + \left(I - R^+\right)^{-1} \bar{x}_0^{+m} + \sum_{l=1}^{m-1} \binom{m}{l} \left(I - R^+\right)^{-(l+1)} \sum_{r=1}^{l} \left\langle \binom{l}{r} \right\rangle \left(R^+\right)^r \bar{x}_0^{+m-l} \right]$$

The proof is given in [6].

5 Proof of the bounds

In this section we formally prove that two process P^- and P^+ provide a lower-bound and an upper-bound on all the moments of the number of jobs N in the original fork and join system S, respectively. To prove the bounds we transform the continuous-time Markov processes in discrete-time processes by using the randomization technique, and then we apply the method proposed by Van Dijk in [17, 18].

Let us define the randomised process of P. Let Z denote the uniformised Markov one-step transition matrix obtained by the rate transition matrix Q of process P, defined as follows:

$$Z = \left\| z_{\bar{n},\bar{m}} \right\| = M^{-1} q_{\bar{n},\bar{m}} \quad \text{if } \bar{n} \neq \bar{m}, \quad \text{and} \quad 1 - \sum_{\bar{n} \neq \bar{m}} z_{\bar{n},\bar{m}} \quad \text{if } \bar{n} = \bar{m} \quad (5.1)$$

where M is given by:

$$M = \lambda + \sum_{i=1}^{k} \sum_{j=1}^{\gamma_i} \mu_j^i \quad (5.2)$$

Similarly, let Z^- and Z^+ denote the transition probability matrices of the randomised processes obtained by processes P^- and P^+, respectively. Z^- and Z^+ are given by definition (5.1) by considering matrices Q^- and Q^+, respectively. The discrete-time randomised processes have the same stationary state probability distribution of the original continuous-time Markov processes. For a given reward rate function $r(\cdot)$ let function $V^t(\cdot)$, $t \geq 0$ be defined as follows:

$$V^t(\bar{n}) = \sum_{k=0}^{t-1} M^{-1} \sum_{n} z_{\bar{n},\bar{m}}^k \ r(\bar{n}) = r(\bar{n}) M^{-1} + \sum_{n} z_{\bar{n},\bar{m}} \ V^{t-1}(\bar{n}) \quad (5.3)$$

Then by standard Tauberian theorems, the following limit is well defined and independent of the initial distribution $\mathcal{F}(\bar{n})$ at Φ:

$$G = \lim_{t \to \infty} \frac{M}{t} \sum_{n} \mathcal{F}(\bar{n}) V^t(\bar{n}) \quad (5.4)$$

The value G represents the expected average reward per unit of time of the original model when using the reward rate $r(\cdot)$. Similarly, let $V_-^t(\cdot)$ and $V_+^t(\cdot)$, $t \geq 0$ denote the functions defined by formula (5.3) with matrix Z^- and Z^+, respectively. Let G^- and G^+ be the limits given by formula (5.4) for functions $V_-^t(\cdot)$ and $V_+^t(\cdot)$, and some initial distribution at Φ^- and Φ^+. For the sake of simplicity we do not explicitly consider in the following the stage component of the state $\bar{n}$ of the system, so that if $\bar{e}_i$ denotes the k-dimensional vector whose components are all 0, except the i-th which is 1, we can write $\bar{n} + \bar{e}_i$ for the state equal to $\bar{n}$ except in the i-th component that is $n_i + 1$. Let us consider the following reward rate function:

$$r(\bar{n}) = \left(max\{n_1, n_2, ..., n_k\}\right)^m, \quad m \geq 1 \tag{5.5}$$

Hence the limit G defined in formula (5.4) is the m-th moment of the number of jobs in the system. Similarly, G^- and G^+ are the m-th moments of the number of jobs in system S^- and S^+, respectively. In order to prove the bounds we show that the relationship $G^- \leq G \leq G^+$ holds. To this aim we state the following lemma:

Lemma 5.1. The following property holds:

$$V^t(\bar{n} + \bar{e}_i) - V^t(\bar{n}) \geq 0 \tag{5.6}$$

for any $\bar{n} \in \Phi$, $1 \leq i \leq k$ and $t \geq 0$.
The proof is given in [6].

5.1 Proof of lower-bound

In this subsection we prove that system S^- provides a lower bound on the moments of the number of jobs in system S. The following lemma relates the two functions $V^t(\cdot)$ and $V^t_-(\cdot)$.

Lemma 5.2: For $\bar{n} \in \Phi^-$ and $t \geq 0$ the following relation holds: $(V^t - V^t_-)(\bar{n}) =$

$$= \sum_{j=0}^{t-1} \left(Z^-\right)^j \left[M^{-1}\lambda\delta(\exists i, 2 \leq i \leq k \mid n_i = \beta_i)\left(V^{t-j-1}(\bar{n} + \bar{e}) - V^{t-j-1}(\bar{n})\right)\right]$$

Proof: By using the second relation from (5.3) and the fact that Z^- remains restricted to Φ^- which is a subset of Φ, for arbitrary state $\bar{n} \in \Phi^-$ we can write:

$$\left[V^t - V^t_-\right](\bar{n}) = \left[Z V^{t-1} - Z^- V^{t-1}_-\right](\bar{n}) = (Z - Z^-) V^{t-1}(\bar{n}) +$$

$$+ Z^-(V^{t-1}_- - V^{t-1})(\bar{n}) = ... = \sum_{i=0}^{t-1}\left(Z^-\right)^i \left[\left(Z - Z^-\right)V^{t-i-1}\right](\bar{n}) \tag{5.7}$$

where the latter equality follows by iteration and the fact that $V^0(\bar{n}) = V^0_-(\bar{n}) = 0$. Furthermore, we can rewrite $(Z - Z^-)V^{t-i-1}(\bar{n})$ in terms of transitions which belongs to matrix Z and do not belong to matrix Z^-, as follows:

$$\left(Z - Z^-\right)V^{t-i-1}(\bar{n}) = M^{-1}\lambda\delta(\exists i, 2 \leq i \leq k \mid n_i = \beta_i)V^{t-i-1}(\bar{n} + \bar{e}) - \tag{5.8}$$

$$-M^{-1}\lambda\delta(\exists i, 2 \leq i \leq k \mid n_i = \beta_i)V^{t-i-1}(\bar{n}) \tag{5.9}$$

Expression (5.8) is related to the off-diagonal elements that belong to matrix Z and do not belong to matrix Z^-, and expression (5.9) represents the difference between the diagonal elements of the two matrices. Note that the condition in expressions (5.8) and (5.9) corresponds to the transition rates from the border states in Φ^- to state which belong to Φ and are not in Φ^-. Hence, by substituting this last equation in formula (5.7) we conclude the proof of the lemma. ◊

Theorem 5.2: The relationship $G^- \leq G$ holds.

Proof: By formula (5.4) we rewrite the difference $G - G^-$ as follows:

$$G - G^- = \lim_{t \to \infty} \frac{M}{t} \left\{ \sum_{\bar{n} \in \Phi} \pounds(\bar{n}) V^t(\bar{n}) - \sum_{\bar{n} \in \Phi^-} \pounds^-(\bar{n}) V_-^t(\bar{n}) \right\}$$

Since the value of this limit does not depend on the initial probability distributions we choose $\pounds(\bar{n}) = \pounds^-(\bar{n}) = \pi^-(\bar{n})$ thus obtaining

$$G - G^- = \lim_{t \to \infty} \frac{M}{t} \sum_{\bar{n} \in \Phi^-} \pi^-(\bar{n}) \left\{ V^t(\bar{n}) - V_-^t(\bar{n}) \right\} \tag{5.10}$$

By Lemma 5.2, we can rewrite the term $V^t(\bar{n}) - V_-^t(\bar{n})$ as a non-negative linear combination of terms $V^{t-i-1}(\bar{n} + \bar{e}) - V^{t-i-1}(\bar{n})$, $0 \le i \le t - 1$. By Lemma 5.1, and by observing that $\bar{e} = \sum_{i=1}^k \bar{e}_i$, one can easily derive that these terms are non-negative for each $\bar{n} \in \Phi^-$. This is sufficient to guarantee that $G - G^-$ given by formula (5.10) is non-negative, which concludes the proof of the theorem. ◊

5.2 Proof of upper-bound

Similarly as for the lower-bound model, we prove that system S^+ provides an upper-bound on the moments of the number of jobs in system S. The following Lemma 5.3 is analogous to Lemma 5.2, and relates the two functions $V^t(\cdot)$ and $V_+^t(\cdot)$.

Lemma 5.3: The following relationship holds for any $\bar{n} \in \Phi^+$ and $t \ge 0$.

$$\left[V_+^t - V^t \right](\bar{n}) = \sum_{h=0}^{t-1} \left(Z^+ \right)^h \sum_{i=1}^k M^{-1} \delta(n_i > 0) \sum_{j=1}^{\gamma_i} b_j^i \mu_j^i \delta(\bar{n} - \bar{e}_i \notin \Phi^+) \cdot$$
$$\cdot \left(V^{t-h-1}(\bar{n}) - V^{t-h-1}(\bar{n} - \bar{e}_i) \right)$$

Proof: By following the similar iterative steps of the proof of Lemma 5.2, we obtain the following relationship:

$$\left[V_+^t - V^t \right](\bar{n}) = \sum_{h=0}^{t-1} \left(Z^+ \right)^h \left[(Z^+ - Z) V^{t-h-1} \right](\bar{n}) \tag{5.11}$$

We rewrite the term $(Z^+ - Z) V^{t-h-1}(\bar{n})$ in terms of transitions which belong to matrix Z and do not belong to matrix Z^+, as follows: $(Z^+ - Z) V^{t-h-1}(\bar{n}) =$

$$= \sum_{i=1}^k \left[M^{-1} \delta(n_i > 0) \sum_{j=1}^{\gamma_i} b_j^i \mu_j^i \delta(\bar{n} - \bar{e}_i \notin \Phi^+) V^{t-h-1}(\bar{n}) \right] - \tag{5.12}$$

$$- \sum_{i=1}^k \left[M^{-1} \delta(n_i > 0) \sum_{j=1}^{\gamma_i} b_j^i \mu_j^i \delta(\bar{n} - \bar{e}_i \notin \Phi^+) V^{t-h-1}(\bar{n} - \bar{e}_i) \right] \tag{5.13}$$

Expression (5.12) corresponds to the diagonal elements that belong to matrix Z and do not belong to matrix Z^+, and (5.13) represents the difference between the off-diagonal elements of the two matrices. Hence, by substituting this last equation into formula (5.11) we conclude the proof of the lemma. ◊

Theorem 5.2: The relationship $G \leq G^+$ holds.

Proof: The proof follows a scheme similar to that of Theorem 5.1. In particular, by Lemma 5.3, we can rewrite the term $V_+^t(\vec{n}) - V^t(\vec{n})$ as a non-negative linear combination of terms $V^{t-h-1}(\vec{n}) - V^{t-h-1}(\vec{n} - \vec{e}_i)$, $0 \leq h \leq t - 1$. By Lemma 5.1, these terms are non-negative for each $\vec{n} \in \Phi^+$ and this guarantees that $G^+ - G \geq 0$ holds, which concludes the proof of the theorem. ◊

References

[1]   F. Baccelli and A.M. Makowski, "Queueing models for systems with synchronization constraints" Proceedings of the IEEE, Vol. 77,1989.

[2]   F. Baccelli, W.A. Massey and D. Towsley, "Acyclic fork-join queueing network" J. of ACM, Vol. 36, 1989.

[3]   S. Balsamo and L. Donatiello, "Approximate performance analysis of parallel processing systems" in "Decentralised Systems", M. Cosnard and C. Girault Ed., Elsevier Science, 1990, pp. 325-336.

[4]   S. Balsamo and I. Mura, "Approximate response time distribution in fork and join systems" in Proc. ACM Sigmetrics/Performance'95 Joint Conference, Ottawa, Ontario Canada, 1995.

[5]   S. Balsamo and I. Mura, "Synchronisation delay in hardware fault-tolerance techniques" in Proc. IEEE IPDS '96 Conf., Urbana-Champaign, Illinois USA, 1996.

[6]   S. Balsamo and I. Mura, "Bounds on queue length moments in Parallel Processing Systems with Coxian Services" University of Udine, Dept. of Math. and Comp. Sci., UDMI/04/97/RR, 1997.

[7]   M.A. Brun and G. Fajolle, "A distribution of the transaction processes in a simple fork and join system" in "Computer Performance and Reliability", P. J. Courtois, G. Iazeolla and O. J. Boxma Ed., Elsevier Science, North-Holland, 1988.

[8]   D.R. Cox, "A use of complex probabilities in the theory of stochastic process" Proc. Cambridge Philos. Soc., Vol. 51, pp. 313-319, 1955.

[9]   L. Flatto and S. Hahn, "Two parallel queues created by arrivals with two demands I" SIAM Journal of Applied Mathematics, Vol. 44, pp. 1041-1053, 1984.

[10] C. Kim and A.K. Agrawala, "Analysis of the Fork-Join queue" IEEE Transactions on Computers, Vol. 38, pp. 250-255, 1989.

[11] D.E. Knuth, "The art of computer programming" Addison-Wesley, 1973.

[12] R. Nelson, A. Tantawi and D. Towsley, "Performance analysis of parallel processing systems" IEEE Transactions of Software Engineering, Vol. 14, 1988.

[13] R. Nelson and A.N. Tantawi, "Approximate analysis of fork-join synchronisations in parallel queues" IEEE Transactions on Computers, Vol. 37, pp. 739-743, 1988.

[14] M. F. Neuts, "Matrix-geometric solutions in stochastic models" Johns Hopkins University Press, 1981.

[15] H.G. Perros, "On the M/C_k/1 queue" Performance Evaluation, Vol. 3, pp. 83-93, 1983.

[16] B.M. Rao and M.J.M. Posner, "Algorithmic approximation analysis of the split and match queue" Comm. Statis. Stochastic Models, Vol. 1, pp. 433-456, 1985.

[17] N. Van Dijk, "Truncation of Markov Chains with Applications to Queueing" Oper. Res., Vol. 39, 1991.

[18] N. Van Dijk, "Error Bound Analysis of Queueing Networks" in Tutorial of Performance'96, Lausanne, Switzerland, 1996.

[19] S. Varma and A.M. Makowski, "Interpolation approximation for symmetric fork-join queues" in Proc. Performance '93, Rome, 1993, pp. 245-273.

Springer
and the
environment

At Springer we firmly believe that an international science publisher has a special obligation to the environment, and our corporate policies consistently reflect this conviction.
We also expect our business partners – paper mills, printers, packaging manufacturers, etc. – to commit themselves to using materials and production processes that do not harm the environment. The paper in this book is made from low- or no-chlorine pulp and is acid free, in conformance with international standards for paper permanency.

 Springer

Lecture Notes in Computer Science

For information about Vols. 1–1169

please contact your bookseller or Springer-Verlag

Vol. 1208: S. Ben-David (Ed.), Computational Learning Theory. Proceedings, 1997. VIII, 331 pages. 1997. (Subseries LNAI).

Vol. 1209: L. Cavedon, A. Rao, W. Wobcke (Eds.), Intelligent Agent Systems. Proceedings, 1996. IX, 188 pages. 1997. (Subseries LNAI).

Vol. 1210: P. de Groote, J.R. Hindley (Eds.), Typed Lambda Calculi and Applications. Proceedings, 1997. VIII, 405 pages. 1997.

Vol. 1211: E. Keravnou, C. Garbay, R. Baud, J. Wyatt (Eds.), Artificial Intelligence in Medicine. Proceedings, 1997. XIII, 526 pages. 1997. (Subseries LNAI).

Vol. 1212: J. P. Bowen, M.G. Hinchey, D. Till (Eds.), ZUM '97: The Z Formal Specification Notation. Proceedings, 1997. X, 435 pages. 1997.

Vol. 1213: P. J. Angeline, R. G. Reynolds, J. R. McDonnell, R. Eberhart (Eds.), Evolutionary Programming VI. Proceedings, 1997. X, 457 pages. 1997.

Vol. 1214: M. Bidoit, M. Dauchet (Eds.), TAPSOFT '97: Theory and Practice of Software Development. Proceedings, 1997. XV, 884 pages. 1997.

Vol. 1215: J. M. L. M. Palma, J. Dongarra (Eds.), Vector and Parallel Processing – VECPAR'96. Proceedings, 1996. XI, 471 pages. 1997.

Vol. 1216: J. Dix, L. Moniz Pereira, T.C. Przymusinski (Eds.), Non-Monotonic Extensions of Logic Programming. Proceedings, 1996. XI, 224 pages. 1997. (Subseries LNAI).

Vol. 1217: E. Brinksma (Ed.), Tools and Algorithms for the Construction and Analysis of Systems. Proceedings, 1997. X, 433 pages. 1997.

Vol. 1218: G. Păun, A. Salomaa (Eds.), New Trends in Formal Languages. IX, 465 pages. 1997.

Vol. 1219: K. Rothermel, R. Popescu-Zeletin (Eds.), Mobile Agents. Proceedings, 1997. VIII, 223 pages. 1997.

Vol. 1220: P. Brezany, Input/Output Intensive Massively Parallel Computing. XIV, 288 pages. 1997.

Vol. 1221: G. Weiß (Ed.), Distributed Artificial Intelligence Meets Machine Learning. Proceedings, 1996. X, 294 pages. 1997. (Subseries LNAI).

Vol. 1222: J. Vitek, C. Tschudin (Eds.), Mobile Object Systems. Proceedings, 1996. X, 319 pages. 1997.

Vol. 1223: M. Pelillo, E.R. Hancock (Eds.), Energy Minimization Methods in Computer Vision and Pattern Recognition. Proceedings, 1997. XII, 549 pages. 1997.

Vol. 1224: M. van Someren, G. Widmer (Eds.), Machine Learning: ECML-97. Proceedings, 1997. XI, 361 pages. 1997. (Subseries LNAI).

Vol. 1225: B. Hertzberger, P. Sloot (Eds.), High-Performance Computing and Networking. Proceedings, 1997. XXI, 1066 pages. 1997.

Vol. 1226: B. Reusch (Ed.), Computational Intelligence. Proceedings, 1997. XIII, 609 pages. 1997.

Vol. 1227: D. Galmiche (Ed.), Automated Reasoning with Analytic Tableaux and Related Methods. Proceedings, 1997. XI, 373 pages. 1997. (Subseries LNAI).

Vol. 1228: S.-H. Nienhuys-Cheng, R. de Wolf, Foundations of Inductive Logic Programming. XVII, 404 pages. 1997. (Subseries LNAI).

Vol. 1230: J. Duncan, G. Gindi (Eds.), Information Processing in Medical Imaging. Proceedings, 1997. XVI, 557 pages. 1997.

Vol. 1231: M. Bertran, T. Rus (Eds.), Transformation-Based Reactive Systems Development. Proceedings, 1997. XI, 431 pages. 1997.

Vol. 1232: H. Comon (Ed.), Rewriting Techniques and Applications. Proceedings, 1997. XI, 339 pages. 1997.

Vol. 1233: W. Fumy (Ed.), Advances in Cryptology — EUROCRYPT '97. Proceedings, 1997. XI, 509 pages. 1997.

Vol 1234: S. Adian, A. Nerode (Eds.), Logical Foundations of Computer Science. Proceedings, 1997. IX, 431 pages. 1997.

Vol. 1235: R. Conradi (Ed.), Software Configuration Management. Proceedings, 1997. VIII, 234 pages. 1997.

Vol. 1238: A. Mullery, M. Besson, M. Campolargo, R. Gobbi, R. Reed (Eds.), Intelligence in Services and Networks: Technology for Cooperative Competition. Proceedings, 1997. XII, 480 pages. 1997.

Vol. 1240: J. Mira, R. Moreno-Díaz, J. Cabestany (Eds.), Biological and Artificial Computation: From Neuroscience to Technology. Proceedings, 1997. XXI, 1401 pages. 1997.

Vol. 1241: M. Akşit, S. Matsuoka (Eds.), ECOOP'97 – Object-Oriented Programming. Proceedings, 1997. XI, 531 pages. 1997.

Vol. 1242: S. Fdida, M. Morganti (Eds.), Multimedia Applications, Services and Techniques – ECMAST '97. Proceedings, 1997. XIV, 772 pages. 1997.

Vol. 1243: A. Mazurkiewicz, J. Winkowski (Eds.), CONCUR'97: Concurrency Theory. Proceedings, 1997. VIII, 421 pages. 1997.

Vol. 1244: D. M. Gabbay, R. Kruse, A. Nonnengart, H.J. Ohlbach (Eds.), Qualitative and Quantitative Practical Reasoning. Proceedings, 1997. X, 621 pages. 1997. (Subseries LNAI).

Vol. 1245: M. Calzarossa, R. Marie, B. Plateau, G. Rubino (Eds.), Computer Performance Evaluation. Proceedings, 1997. VIII, 231 pages. 1997.

Vol. 1246: S. Tucker Taft, R. A. Duff (Eds.), Ada 95 Reference Manual. XXII, 526 pages. 1997.

Vol. 1247: J. Barnes (Ed.), Ada 95 Rationale. XVI, 458 pages. 1997.

Vol. 1248: P. Azéma, G. Balbo (Eds.), Application and Theory of Petri Nets 1997. Proceedings, 1997. VIII, 467 pages. 1997.

Vol. 1249: W. McCune (Ed.), Automated Deduction – Cade-14. Proceedings, 1997. XIV, 462 pages. 1997.

Vol. 1250: A. Olivé, J.A. Pastor (Eds.), Advanced Information Systems Engineering. Proceedings, 1997. XI, 451 pages. 1997.

Vol. 1251: K. Hardy, J. Briggs (Eds.), Reliable Software Technologies – Ada-Europe '97. Proceedings, 1997. VIII, 293 pages. 1997.

Vol. 1253: G. Bilardi, A. Ferreira, R. Lüling, J. Rolim (Eds.), Solving Irregularly Structured Problems in Parallel. Proceedings, 1997. X, 287 pages. 1997.